Facilitating Empowerment

A handbook for facilitators, trainers and individuals

Christine Hogan

KOGAN
PAGE

DEDICATION

To my mum, Marjorie Hogan, whose courageous story appears in this book, and my father, Frank Hogan, who was my inspirational guide and mentor.

First published 2000

Kogan Page Limited
120 Pentonville Road
London
N1 9JN
UK

Stylus Publishing Inc.
22883 Quicksilver Drive
Sterling
VA 20166–2012
USA

British Library Cataloguing in Publication Data

A CIP record for this book is available from the British Library.

ISBN 0 7494 3297 7

Typeset by Saxon Graphics Ltd, Derby
Printed and bound in Great Britain by Biddles Ltd, Guildford and King's Lynn

Contents

About the author

Christine Hogan BSc (Hons), MEd, AIMM, is a Senior Lecturer in the School of Management, Curtin University of Technology in Perth, Western Australia. She is the Co-ordinator of Graduate Human Resource Development Programmes and teaches in the areas of Facilitation and Group Processes Skills, Conflict Resolution and Cross-cultural Communication.

Christine is also a professional facilitator. Her work focuses on introducing, developing and evaluating innovative teaching–learning processes in educational and business organizations. Her consultancy work in Perth and South-East Asia focuses on personal, organizational and community development.

In her spare time Christine paints on silk under the name of 'Isadora', after Isadora Duncan, the famous educational innovator and dancer.

Christine Hogan
School of Management
Curtin University
GPO Box U 1987
Perth
Western Australia 6001

Phone: 00–61–8-9266 7451
Fax: 00–61–8-9266 2378
E-mail: Hoganc@cbs.curtin.edu.au

Acknowledgements

It is very rare that a book or a project is the result of one individual's thought and/or work. This book is no exception.

To all my 'wisdom friends', who have journeyed with me in trying to find other and better alternative ways of thinking and doing things in order to try to create a better world. To Katrin and John Wilson, warm thanks for your thought-provoking sessions over coffee in your home, and to Katrin for your feedback on my jumbled thoughts. Also, I should like to thank Peter Frost, my 'spirit friend', for provoking me to 'do something' because I was frustrated with the way power is used and abused in organizations. My thanks to my adopted sisters, Gill Baxter and Carol Newton-Smith, for their lively, challenging feedback and conversations, support and love. To Thomas Daffern for the long discussions at ungodly hours and explorations into new territories of thought.

Thanks also to Steve Whiting for his mentoring on nonviolence and the Religious Society of Friends and to Rod Mitchell for his insight and contribution to the section 'Redefining who we are: gender issues'. Special thanks to my husband and best friend Steve for his unceasing patience, love and computer mentoring.

These exercises would not have evolved if I had not had so much useful, constructive feedback from participants, students and fellow facilitators. A big 'thank you' to you all for your fun, laughter, challenges, thoughts and support.

Last but not least, thanks to the many people at Kogan Page for their ideas and help through each stage of the publishing process: Philip Mudd, Henry Watson, Derek Atkins and Stella Wood.

Christine Hogan
February 2000

Introduction

The British moan about the weather, but nobody does anything about it. Power has always fascinated people. At present – as in the past – many authors are writing about 'power' and 'empowerment', but what is lacking are simple skills, tools and processes to enable human resource developers, managers, groups and individuals to change the way they think about and use power. 'Power' and 'empowerment' are recurrent themes permeating the whole change process. For empowerment to happen, however, there is often a need to establish how the vast array of powers that people may have, or may learn to use, lead to empowerment. There are needs for practical guidance, skills, processes and strategies.

The aim of this book is to meet this need. My aim is to demystify 'power' and challenge the narrow ways in which power has been described in the past. People use a variety of powers that have never been acknowledged in formal management literature. For example, sportsmen and sportswomen use positive self-talk and visualization processes – sometimes with remarkable results.

SCOPE OF THE BOOK

In this book I shall focus on a variety of empowerment exercises, including an 'Empowerment Cycle' that invites you to:

- discuss the changing nature of power and empowerment;
- recall past experiences;
- define an issue and turn it into a project;
- experiment with the enormous varieties of power available to be used on your project, using a power card sort that contains 60 power bases (see Appendix C);
- develop action plans having used power card sort exercises to experiment with the enormous varieties of available power bases.

The card pack takes power out of the theoretical and into the practical, or public, domain. This power pack challenges traditional management thought about power. Power is not just changing hands; it is being redefined. You are also encouraged to rename and/or add your own power bases.

It is easy to criticize previous definitions of power. John Stuart Mill, the British philosopher and economist who lived between 1806 and 1873, warns us that the ideas of every age will be regarded by future generations as absurd. Therefore I do not pretend to have the final definite answer to the power question. But what I *do* hope is that I have produced an insight into power that is easily understood by people from different cultures and social groups. I am providing a broader perspective and some new ways of looking at the development and utilization of wider power bases than have previously been considered.

Individual empowerment, or societal change, or both?

For me, empowerment is about 'choice' and the capacity to generate creative choices to help us solve problems and manage our lives (I will return to this definition in more detail in Chapter 1).

There are different approaches to empowerment emerging from the current literature. One school of thought focuses on working to change social structures and the distribution of power on a large scale. The other school of thought focuses more on individuals and groups and the ways in which they interact on an interpersonal or self-help level. The focus of this book is on the second approach whilst acknowledging broader structural, or even physical, constraints. After all, believing you have the power to leap tall buildings does not necessarily enable you to do so, no matter how much positive self-talk is used.

I have included discussion of the societal frameworks, which may influence the success or failure of efforts by individuals or groups to make changes in their organizations and/or their private lives. Indeed, highlighting some of the wider societal contexts may be particularly pertinent to your action plans. Some individuals and/or groups, especially in the development field, may find these exercises useful in identifying and managing sources of oppression and depowerment.

There will be times when all of us go through stages of feeling depowered. The question is, how can we manage this phenomenon? Empowerment in itself is not necessarily 'good'. It depends on how power is used.

VALUE STANCE

My value stance is that empowerment generally encourages discourse and that discourse is a valuable commodity. At the turn of the millennium, the speed and scope of social, cultural and technological change is greatly accelerated and leads at times to a lack of knowledge, understanding and ways of coping. This in turn may lead to:

- unquestioning following of instructions;
- regrettable actions that could be averted through more thorough deliberation;
- increased disparities of power and possible inequities.

At such times it is especially important to consider underlying values and objectives, and to query the basis of instructions. Such questioning is more likely to occur if people are both aware and empowered to do so.

Even increased communication is not necessarily 'good' in itself. It depends on what the communication is and what it is used for. Increased communication often (though not always) makes it easier to cope with change through tapping the resources and commitment of a wider range of people. Empowerment of people through greater awareness and enhancement of their own values, capabilities, resources and strategies can improve interpersonal communication, provided that the circumstances nurture these things to happen.

In some instances, conflict may increase and it is therefore necessary for management to build in 'provention' structures and processes for prevention and the management of constructive conflict. Conflict 'provention' means not only reducing the 'conditions that create an environment of conflict and the structural changes required to remove it, but more importantly, the promotion of conditions that create co-operative relationships' (Burton, 1990: 3).

Is it possible to empower someone else?

When discussing empowerment, questions inevitably arise such as:

- Who decides who should empower whom?
- Who empowers whom?
- Are so-called empowering processes actually being used to depower others?
- Is it possible to empower someone else?
- If it *is* possible to empower someone else:
  - when?

- where?
- why?
- how? and
- to what extent does that occur?
- Empowerment occurs with what resources, and to what effect?
- Who decides how much power others should be allowed?
- Who decides who decides?

These are structural questions. They can be asked of societies, organizations, communities, groups and individuals.

So, is it possible for a person to empower someone else? This is an interesting question. I used to think definitely 'No'. I now believe that, basically, empowerment is the responsibility of each of us as individuals; however, the extent of our empowerment can be facilitated by 'empowering people' and 'empowering structures'. Facilitators and/or managers can provide the environment, resources and processes for colleagues to take more initiative and power over what they do in their everyday lives. Organizations can provide the structures to enhance empowerment, but ultimately it is their choice; no one can force people to 'be empowered'. One important aspect of empowerment is that you take responsibility for your own life and development.

The responsibility for the empowerment process lies to a large extent (though not totally) with individuals and groups, to improve contributions to decision making or project management, or to oppose oppression. You need to be aware of the ethical uses of power. Although the skills and ideas in this book are intended to be used for individual and group empowerment, they could also be used to depower others or could be abused.

STRUCTURE AND CONTENT OF THE BOOK

This book is designed to be used either by individuals or by facilitators. In order to simplify messages for the reader, when I am making suggestions for workshop facilitators I will put these ideas in italics. Chapter 6 is aimed specifically at workshop facilitators.

Chapter 1 provides you with the theoretical background of the book: the changing meanings of 'power' and 'empowerment'; the rationale for enhancing empowerment; the causes of empowerment/depowerment; the ego defence mechanisms that participants may use for not making choices or empowering themselves.

Chapter 2 introduces the 'Empowerment Cycle', which is based on adult learning principles in that participants are invited to:

- discuss and 'mind map' (see below) past experiences of empowerment and/or depowerment;

- choose a problem and reframe it as a project or a future plan;
- identify the variety of power bases that are available;
- develop action plans.

With respect to the first bullet point above, 'mind mapping' is a tool that helps us to extract ideas from our brains and represent them in a graphical form. It stimulates creative thinking, summarizing and linking of ideas.

After the discussion on the Empowerment Cycle, a detailed elaboration of each power base is given in Chapter 3. Frequently, we cling to the power bases and strategies that we know well and with which we feel comfortable. As a result, we may limit our repertoire of appropriate responses. This chapter provides anecdotes and narrative about each power base to extend people's political awareness; it also provides you – either as an individual or as a human resource developer – with a useful resource of exercises and stories.

Chapter 4 provides you with a variety of other exercises on power, which may be used in a wide variety of workshop settings or follow-up sessions. Chapter 5 describes case studies in a variety of settings, from a marketing company to a non-profit-making organization and a group of senior citizens. Chapter 6 reflects on the whole empowerment process and feedback from participants.

Appendix A contains the cards that you may wish to photocopy and cut up to form your 'Personal Power Pack'. Individuals and organizations who have purchased this book are free to reproduce copies of the card pack for participants, so long as the source is cited.

Appendix B is directed at facilitators of workshops on empowerment, and it presents a sample one-day workshop designed around the 'empowerment cycle' for a group of up to 20 people within an organization who wish to explore how they can work in a more empowered way. This workshop design is not meant to be prescriptive and should be modified according to your facilitation style and the needs of your group. It ends with points for facilitators based on my own experiences with these exercises.

At the end of each chapter I have summarized the main points and left space for you to make your notes in a 'key point summary' as your learning and thoughts on the topics described within will be different from mine. I appreciate that there will be some areas of this book that are already familiar to you, but I hope that I bring a useful and interesting perspective to issues relating to empowerment.

Many different skills and strategies are required by individuals in the empowerment process. It is a lifelong journey; there are no quick tips and fixes. Wherever possible, therefore, I have given references to suitable texts in which authors describe how these skills may be developed further. I have also supported my ideas with stories from my own experiences and those of my friends and colleagues. I have used this strategy to try to bring concepts to life.

HOW TO GET THE MOST OUT OF THE BOOK

This book has been produced as a result of countless workshops on empowerment. Suggestions are given with the knowledge that all trainers and facilitators have different styles and ways of working with groups. Also, it is necessary to change structures of workshops based on the suggestions of group members and/or the needs of the group. There are wide margins for you to add your own notes and comments, so please use the book interactively and cover it with your thoughts.

WHY THIS BOOK WAS WRITTEN

Why did I write this book? It is the result of a conversation with my mentor, Peter Frost, at an Organizational Behaviour Teaching Conference in Singapore in 1991. I was criticizing the way that power is used and abused in organizations. In his quiet, thought-provoking way, Peter said, 'Well, why don't you do something about it... and present it at the next conference in Western Washington (USA) next June?' I went to my hotel room. June was only six months away. But after making up loads of excuses, I finally put pen to paper and produced a hand-written proposal for a workshop at the conference, which was ultimately accepted.

The whole workshop was developed initially on a mind map. I wanted to develop user-friendly exercises about power. Peter came to the workshop and subsequently used the exercises with managers and groups in Canada, South Africa and Iran. I have also used the exercises in Australia and the United Kingdom, with managers and their teams, teachers, migrant groups, Aboriginal groups and health workers. In Malaysia I used the exercises with Muslim businesswomen. In my university I use the cards with my postgraduate students, who come from a variety of different cultures and backgrounds. I used the exercises with Danish and Nepalese development workers in Kathmandu. What excites me is that the exercises are culturally transferable and adaptable to a wide variety of settings, either to use individually at home or in workshops.

The exercises in this book have been designed for and already used by:

- individuals;
- human resources developers, managers and consultants with teams and individuals;
- social and health workers and patients with long-term illness;
- teachers and educational change agents;
- multicultural groups working on issues of internalized racism.

Good luck! I hope you find the processes described helpful and stimulating. If you would like to contact me regarding aspects of this work please do!

1 Why are concepts of power and empowerment changing?

INTRODUCTION

The aim of this chapter is to give you further background information about changing concepts of 'power' and 'empowerment'. The results of depowering education systems and professions are described, as is the result of the Milgram experiment on the illusion of power. The reasons for acting in a depowered way are discussed so that you may identify ego defence strategies. The latter are normal responses; however, they should not prevent an individual from exploring alternative strategies. The sources of the power bases for the 'power card pack' are described.

THE POWER-SHIFT ERA

'Power' and 'empowerment' are concepts that are of interest to people throughout the world. Toffler (1991) calls this the 'power-shift era' – that is, a deep-level transformation of the nature of power. Recent events across the world reflect this and appear to interconnect through four levels of society (see Figure 1.1).

Individual level

On an individual level, people are more educated and better informed than ever before. Many are seeking ways of taking greater charge of their time and their lives. In Western countries, personal organizers, self-paced learning packages, how-to-do-it books (Jeffers, 1987; Brislin, 1991) and card packs are popular, useful and economical. Individuals are realizing that they may not be able to change the world but they can influence the spheres in

Figure 1.1 Empowerment changes impacting four levels of society

which they work, live and play. On environmental issues, individuals are using recycling bins and demanding non-polluting consumer goods.

In countries in the South (ie those previously described as the 'third world'), small-scale rural banks have been highly successful in helping 'the poorest of the poor' escape from the poverty trap through low-interest loans. Women skilled in traditional crafts are forming co-operatives to improve quality, diversify designs and market their products, thus taking control of the whole spectrum of their work.

Organizational level

On an organizational level, an awareness of personal power has led managers to rethink the way that they structure their companies. Hierarchies are being flattened; semi-autonomous work groups are stimulating initiative and enhancing the profitability and competitiveness of companies; and the roles and responsibilities of managers and workers are changing fundamentally (Block, 1990; Torbert, 1991; Vogt and Murrell, 1990). In many countries there are now moves towards individual contracts, enterprise bargaining and workplace agreements. These are being promoted to workers as being empowering strategies.

However, these structural changes need to be analysed with care because they are frequently designed to isolate individuals. Higher wages may be offered in a workplace agreement; however, this may be accompanied by the loss of occupational health and safety cover and sickness benefits, thus promoting less responsibility for management and indirectly higher costs and responsibility for workers. Whilst some people may initially gain financially, others may feel less empowered than before, when they knew where they stood.

> Power is changing hands, from dying hierarchies to living networks.
>
> (Ferguson, 1986: 234)

Community level

Since the development of speech, members of communities have co-operated for hunting, gathering and survival. Nowadays, communities are getting together formally to create power through combining and sharing concerns over common issues. Registered self-help groups are springing up all over the world to enable people to meet their own needs. Examples include neighbourhood watch schemes, learning centres, and childcare centres. Radio programmes have been established (eg 'grapevine' programmes) to help people with similar needs get linked together through phone-ins and discussions. E-mail and the Internet have now revolutionized communication for those who can afford, or gain access to, computers.

National and worldwide level

On the national and worldwide level, people-power movements can effect monumental changes. Events in communist countries in the last two decades, especially the removal of the Berlin Wall in 1989, and the people-power movement in the Philippines in 1999 all indicate a shift in the world order. Organizations led by Mother Theresa, Greenpeace, Sting and Bob Geldof indicate that people have the power to change the status quo.

WHY ENHANCE THE EMPOWERMENT OF ADULTS AND CHILDREN?

Empowerment is an issue because power and/or the lack of it pervades every aspect of our lives: our relationships in the home, at school, at college and at work.

Power to the people

The song 'Power to the People' by John Lennon raises an interesting issue. Power cannot come to the 'people' *en masse* until each of us takes the responsibility for our own empowerment. Lennon's lyrics contain phrases that may be useful motivators, but the empowerment process is more complex than his song implied.

The children's story

James Clavell describes (1983: 4) the ease with which children's minds are manipulated. The idea for the story came from a conversation with his six-year-old daughter, who came home from her first day at school and mindlessly recited the oath of allegiance to the United States and said:

> You owe me a dime. . . The teacher said everyone has to learn it and say it and then your dad or mum gives you a dime. . . How about another dime if I say it again?

Before parting with the reward, her father asked her what 'pledge' and 'allegiance' meant. She did not know. Clavell commented as a postscript:

> I realized how completely vulnerable my child's mind was – any mind, for that matter – under controlled circumstances. Questions like 'What's the use of "I pledge allegiance" without understanding?' Like why is it so easy to direct thought and implant others? Like what is freedom and why is it so hard to explain?

Teachers, parents, managers, lecturers and human resource developers all have legitimate power and authority. It is therefore important that we all consider the ethics of how we use or abuse that power and educate children from a young age about power.

THE LONG-TERM POLITICAL AND SOCIAL EFFECTS OF EMPOWERMENT

Empowerment of learners has political ramifications, as Freire (1972, 1974) described from his experiences in Brazil in the 1960s. It appears that there are contradictions in the educative process. For example, governments require that education systems develop the citizens of tomorrow, but there appears to be a clause written in small print indicating that government co-operation will only occur provided that these citizens conform to the government policies and social norms of the day.

No educational process is ever neutral

According to Freire (1972, 1974), education is designed to do one of two things. The first approach is to maintain the existing situation, ie the status quo, and the values and culture

Table 1.1 Comparison of the 'banking' and 'problem-posing' approach to learning

Banking Approach	Problem-posing Approach
Expert/teacher seen as possessing all essential knowledge/skills	Facilitator provides a frame-work for thinking, creative, active participants to consider common problems and find solutions
Learners regarded as 'empty vessels' needing to be filled with knowledge	Facilitator raises questions: why? how? who?
Expert/teacher talks and others listen passively, ie monologue and silence respectively	Participants are active, describing, analysing, suggesting, deciding, planning

of the dominant class, known as the 'banking' approach. The second method is to liberate people, helping them to become critical, free, active and responsible members of society – ie the 'problem-posing' approach.

In challenging the approach to learning, Freire compared the 'banking' and empowering or 'problem-posing' approach to learning (see Table 1.1). The problem-posing approach requires educators to let go of some of their 'position, legitimate and expert' power. For some, this is too threatening. Unfortunately, many institutions still keep to the 'banking' approach, which often depowers learners and also omits teaching learners how to learn (Downs, 1995), which then prevents them having learning autonomy for life.

The result of Freire's successful literacy programmes in Brazil was that peasants learnt to read and write and stand up against unjust landowners and money-lenders. The government forced Freire to leave, but the impact of his work lives on.

An important consideration that this example illustrates is who sets the limits of power and how much empowerment is desired and by whom? Who decides who decides? These questions must be answered by managers before embarking on programmes on empowerment. Refusal to do so may lead to confusion, distrust and disillusionment on the part of participants. It is important that power-holders are prepared to share power before the opportunity is offered. Once offered, any withdrawal will cause resentment.

The student riots of the late 1960s and 1970s had many outcomes regarding changes to old, established, tertiary-educational bureaucracies in the United Kingdom, France and the United States. However, in the author's experience at the University of London, the responses of academics varied: members of the 'old school' were averse to power sharing, while others welcomed students and their ideas and inputs to committees.

CASE STUDY: EMPOWERMENT AND THE UNEMPLOYED

Between 1978 and 1986, staff of the Technical and Further Education (TAFE) Division in Western Australia were asked to design courses for long-term unemployed people. Two types of courses evolved. One, entitled 'Foundation for Employment', focused on training participants in occupation-specific skills (eg. bartender courses). The other type, entitled 'Education Programmes for Unemployed Youth', focused on the development of long-term life skills and empowerment skills.

Lecturers interpreted the policies of this Participation and Equity Programme by encouraging students through the use of the Search Conference Process (Emery, 1976; Hogan, 1984, 1988) to participate in projects, set their own learning goals and develop strategies to achieve them. These strategies included contacting local councils, lobbying business people, and involving the wider community to take an interest in and responsibility for the needs and projects of the unemployed.

It was interesting to note that when unemployment declined in Australia in 1986, these empowerment programmes were the first to be axed (Hogan, 1988). The political maxim became 'Let's return to basics and the three Rs'. As governments appear to have to have 'new' projects to launch at the community, 'training' became the in-word and courses for unemployed were focused on specific jobs – even though frequently no job existed in those occupations.

The depowering professions

The medical, psychological, teaching and law professions, and others, have been described as the 'depowering professions' (Illich, 1977): through their expert and legitimate power in the community, consciously or unconsciously they depower their clients. In the medical example, the advent of new drugs and surgical techniques, and the ethical issues regarding the right to life and death, raise many questions. It is important that we are not depowered by the 'white coats' (or the 'mortar boards'), and that we take back the right to develop and make informed decisions regarding the development of our own minds and bodies. Even doctors have difficulty keeping up with and understanding all the new developments in their respective fields.

The ordinary populace, with less information, is at an even greater disadvantage; yet it is their bodies and lives that are the subject of discussion. It may not be realistic for everybody to be fully knowledgeable about every aspect of their existence, but where it matters, ideally enough understandable information can be made available for real choices to be made. We need to know how to question, find out more information about, and challenge established 'services' when necessary.

Having knowledge of the empowerment (and depowerment) processes ensures that we become the subjects of our own transformation and growth:

> There is no antidote to power but power, nor has there ever been. But there are ethical uses of power. In order to exercise justice against lawlessness, it is necessary to array lawful power. . . In order to defend individual freedom, it is necessary to enhance the power of individuals.
>
> (London, 1969: 80)

A colleague, Roger Allen, recently gave me two phrases – though neither of us knows where they come from:

> Power is what you take, not what you are given.
> It is easier to gain forgiveness than permission.

Whilst both make some sense and are both useful motivators, the issue of empowerment is inherently more complex than expressed by these epithets. An individual must have sufficient courage and self-esteem to be able to be proactive in the use of power. Like Lennon's song, this statement is a useful motivator, but it is simplistic. Some power is for 'taking'; however, a person who has legitimate or position power conferred on him/her automatically has potentially more power than a person without it. Thus the jailers in Greece during the rise of the Colonels were given – and used – extreme powers over their prisoners.

Self-development and the whole educative process requires an understanding of the factors that promote or mitigate against the learning process. People who are depowered may find it very difficult to learn and/or put into practice what they learn. They need encouragement and support.

THE ILLUSION OF POWER

We need to be educated to recognize our susceptibility in varying degrees to the 'illusion of power', as Milgram (1963) illustrates in his controversial research on obedience to authority. His 40 male subjects were from a variety of occupations in New Haven, Connecticut. The experiment was ostensibly designed to find out about the effects of punishment on learning. In reality, he was trying to establish just how far individuals would respond to legitimate power.

Upon arriving at the laboratory, each subject was introduced to a supposed co-subject, who in reality was working with Milgram. Both 'subjects' were asked to draw lots to

Table 1.2 Voltage levels where subjects break off their participation in the Milgram experiments (adapted from Vecchio *et al*, 1988)

Voltage level slight shock	Number of subjects stopping
15	0
30	0
45	0
60	0
Moderate shock	
75	0
90	0
105	0
120	0
Strong shock	
135	0
150	0
165	0
180	0
Very Strong Shock	
195	0
210	0
255	0
240	0
Intense Shock	
255	0
270	0
285	0
300*	5
Extreme Intensity Shock	
315	4
330	2
345	1
360	1
Danger: Severe Shock	
375	1
390	0
405	0
420	0
Danger XXX	
435	0
450	26

*At 300 volts, the learner no longer responded to the teacher

determine who would be the leader and who would be the learner. The lots were rigged so that the real subject always became the teacher. A man dressed in a white coat and addressed as 'doctor' instructed the subject to watch the learner and every time he made a mistake punish him by pressing a series of buttons that supposedly administered an electric shock. A series of 30 buttons supposedly went up to 450 volts, where the label stated 'Danger – Severe Shock – XXX'. The response to their instructions is given in Table 1.2.

Each time the supposed learner made a mistake, the 'doctor' instructed the subject to administer a shock. The learner was instructed to cry out with pain and at 150 volts yelled to stop the experiment saying his heart could not stand the strain. Most of the teachers became very upset, but the doctor merely instructed 'The experiment requires that we go on, you have no other choice, you must go on' (Milgram, 1963: 138).

Out of the 40 subjects, 26 (65 per cent) obeyed the doctor all the way to the button marked 'Danger XXX', ie enough current to kill the learner. Much controversy developed concerning the ethical aspects of this experiment as many of the subjects were severely emotionally disturbed when the experiment was explained to them.

The experiment indicated that an individual may be able to significantly influence or depower others merely because he or she is perceived to have power.

> Power is often in the 'eye of the beholder'.

THE CONCEPT OF POWER

'Power' means different things to different people. Therefore it is important to explore perceptions of power. One way in which this may be achieved is by inviting participants to draw and/or write their perceptions of power using symbols, signs, etc. A comparison will reveal that there are many different perceptions of the concept power.

Past definitions

In the past, power was regarded as a finite commodity to be fought for, protected and defended. Sun Tsu in the 5th century BC describes the use of power by army leaders. His book *The Art of War* is studied by managers today. An interesting point he made was:

> The best way to subdue an enemy is without the use of force.
>
> (Sun Tsu, cited by Heider, 1986: 35)

Early religious texts – the Hindu Mahabarata, the Christian Bible and the Islamic Koran – make numerous references to the power of light and darkness, and stories abound about people who developed 'special powers' for healing, leadership, etc.

Some understanding of the use of non-violent power was visible in Ancient Greece, as illustrated in the play entitled *Lysistrata*, written by Aristophanes in the 5th century BC. The story relates how women united in refusing to make love with their husbands as long as men insisted on going to war. The women 'won' and peace was restored. This strategy was suggested on Australian television before the outbreak of the Gulf War in 1991.

Frequently, management texts refer learners to the five power bases described by French and Raven (1959):

- *Legitimate power*: a person's ability to influence because of a position. The position may be gained through an appointment or promotion. It may give people authority provided that they are respected by the people under their control – ie people 'give' people power by acknowledging their 'right' to it. This power base may be used in legitimate or illegitimate ways – for example, a teacher may use power with children to enhance learning or to 'pick' continually on a few individuals. Legitimate power is socially conferred and can be redefined, withdrawn or even sometimes supplemented by coercive power – for example by the ruling generals in Myanmar.
- *Reward power*: deriving power from the ability to reward compliance through pay increase, promotion or recognition.
- *Coercive power*: power based on fear and the ability to punish through delegating undesirable work assignments, reprimands or dismissal. Coercive power may be legally organized or sanctioned. An interesting anti-war protest song in the 1960s highlighted the way opposing armies legitimized their killing as they all had 'God on their side'.
- *Expert power*: power held by individuals who gain it because of their high level of skills and/or knowledge, which gains them the respect of others.
- *Referent power*: power gained because of an attractive personality, charisma or charm.

These power bases have a number of important features:

- They all depend on the beliefs of others; that is, if followers do not believe that a person has these powers, these power bases lose their potency.
- Use of one may detract from use of another. For instance, use of coercive power may detract from the potency of charismatic power.
- They were developed at the end of the 1950s and are very narrow in scope.

My work has sought to gather together power bases as defined by people of different ages from different walks of life and cultures. These are described in depth in Chapter 3.

Power is not negative but its uses may be

Power has frequently been regarded as a negative force. This was partly due to the concept of power being linked to the behaviours and writing of Niccolo Machiavelli, an Italian philosopher and statesman (1469–1527). His name has become part of the English language, and to describe a person's behaviour as 'machiavellian' is highly insulting (unless, of course, that person actually values political treachery, the manipulation of others, and a pragmatic end-justifies-the-means approach).

It would appear that individuals have varying needs or perceived needs for power. McClelland (1984) describes the 'need for power' as a motivational force and distinguishes between the 'two faces of power', one being unsocial and concerned with exploitative dominance (including physical aggression) and the other being a more positive use of power associated with persuasion, influence and inspiration.

Power may give people greater choices – whether through use and access to resources, or choices of lifestyles etc. However, trainers need to beware of the 'you can do anything you want to' syndrome, which may ignore reality and give people false expectations (see Chapter 6). Also, there is the question of social responsibility. In a so-called civilized society, people who do exactly as they choose regardless of others are regarded as psychopaths!

Power is neither good nor bad; it depends on how and why it is used. It is an infinite force and resource that is constantly shifting or changing hands. Managers are frequently surprised by the synergy that results from sharing power with their team members. Indeed, a manager frequently increases his or her power by the increase in power of other associated persons. Power is not zero-sum in character.

The changing meaning of power is threatening to some of the current power holders, as Adair and Howl point out:

> Nobody talks about power. Those who have it spend a great deal of effort keeping it hidden. Those who don't, rarely risk raising the issue… Power is the ability to do what one chooses – the more power one has, the more options one has. Those without power are led to believe this is a personal failing; those with it come to consider it a sign of personal success.
>
> (1989: 20)

It is first necessary to define power. Originally it was seen as the ability to control others and/or their behaviour. Albert defines power as:

> The capability of human beings to organize or manipulate their environment (including other human beings, their thoughts, motivation, needs and desires, as well as their creations and artefacts) for human ends… it is a fact of existence.
>
> (1985: 12)

THE MEANING OF 'EMPOWERMENT'

The idea of empowerment is not new. Lao Tse, writing in China in the 6th century BC, said that a characteristic of great leaders is that when the task is done people will say 'we did it ourselves'(Lao Tse, cited by Waley, 1934: 101). And Samuel Smiles, a doctor living in Victorian England, started self-help programmes amongst the poor and wrote one of the first books on the subject in 1859.

Hopson and Scally define self empowerment as:

> a process by which one increasingly takes greater charge of oneself and one's life. By our definition it is not an end-state. One cannot become a 'self-empowered person'. It is a process of becoming in which one behaves in a more or less empowered way.
>
> (1981: 57)

This definition concentrates on the individual; Hamelink takes the empowerment theme more widely:

> a process in which people achieve the capacity to control decisions affecting their lives. Empowerment enables people to define themselves and to construct their own identities. Empowerment can be the outcome of an intentional strategy which is either initiated externally by empowering agents or solicited by disempowered people.
>
> (1994: 132–33)

The difference between the old definition of power and the new definitions of empowerment is that the latter imply interactions that increase power for all, not just for a few. Increased power also requires an increase in responsibility in the use of that power.

Part of the empowerment process is learning to recognize the activities by which you may lose the capacity to control decisions affecting your life and reduce your ability to define yourself and construct you own identity. For example, in the communication field, people have learnt to develop their own media using local TV and radio stations, newsletters and videos. People's networks have been set up using the public domains in cyberspace. In this context, Peacenet, founded in 1985, is one of the founding members of the Association for Progressive Communications, which connects people across the globe without respect to race, religion, gender or sexual orientation (Hamelink, 1994: 149).

Choosing where to focus your energies is empowered thinking

When I worked in a high school, I became very worked-up one day about a number of issues relating to school policy. At a staff meeting, the principal announced that he would round-robin the group and ask each staff member in turn for opinions. I anxiously awaited my turn and described my concerns. I listened to my colleagues and the general feeling was against one of the principal's strategies. I was aghast when he announced that, despite the negative reaction, he would go ahead.

After the staff meeting I turned to a colleague and dear friend and said in a frustrated tone 'Well, aren't you mad about that too?' With a sage-like grin, my friend replied 'Yes, I am annoyed. But I know I cannot change the man's outlook on every issue, and therefore I choose which battles I am going to fight. You can't take on everything. If you do, your energy will be dissipated and you won't be able to change anything.' The moral of this story is 'choose where you focus your energies so your energies are not dissipated'.

Empowerment is an ongoing process

Returning to the idea of individual empowerment, Rotter (1966), Seligman (1975) and Hopson and Scally (1981) point out that empowerment is not an end-state, but a process that all human beings experience. Throughout our lives we will behave in more or less empowered ways, depending on our level of self esteem and skill development, tempered by surrounding circumstances. Some people, as the authors above describe, have a greater tendency than others to be self-empowered.

Cultures vary in their tendency towards an internal control of events in comparison with an external control (or fatalism) as a result of events or catastrophes. For example, many people at the end of the Second World War felt pessimistic about the future because life appeared out of control. But this state did not last for ever as the rebuilding of Europe occurred.

Levels of empowerment can be monitored

Staples (1990) takes the idea of the empowerment process further by arguing that the process can be checked at particular points, ie that empowerment is a product as well as a process and that an individual can learn to monitor his/her progress through being critically conscious of how he/she takes power and what the end results are. (See Examples 3 and 4 in Chapter 4.)

DEPOWERMENT

A baby is born with 100 per cent positive self-esteem, a potential 'prince' or 'princess' (Berne, in Stewart and Joines, 1987). It is the centre of its own universe and it makes assertive and aggressive demands on parents. On the other hand, a child is almost totally vulnerable and, if neglected, would soon die.

What has happened to children who suffer lack of empowerment? At some stage in their development their self concept and esteem has been eroded by parents, siblings, their personal experiences, and societal circumstances. In other words, such children do not consciously allow themselves to be depowered; it is a subconscious process whereby they are depowered by the people around them and by their experiences. An extreme example would be individuals who suffer from anorexia or bulimia, and the associated extreme low levels of self-esteem, guilt and depowerment that they experience.

Therefore, parents, teachers and lecturers have a responsibility to teach individuals to identify the depowerment process and develop their empowerment skills. Adults have a dilemma in socializing children, for it may initially reduce the children's empowerment so that they cannot demand anything and everything, but it may also enhance other power bases. Boomer asserts that traditional teaching erodes a child's learning power:

> The infant learner is a powerhouse of private and public investigation. Infant apprentices use a continuing battery of 'Why?' and 'What's that?', experiments in play, imitations after demonstration, and a tenacity to get their own way as they power into the world.
>
> (1982: 2)

Parents are therefore confronted with a difficult dilemma. On the one hand they need to bring up children who have a sense of 'self' or 'spirit', who can 'stick up for themselves'. Indeed, many children are adept at the 'broken record' approach (repeatedly making nagging requests) to wear down the resolve of a parent. However, parents have to control and socialize children's behaviour so that their offspring can take part in the life of their community – but do it without breaking their spirit. Children therefore need to learn how to make their needs known in socially acceptable ways.

Some people develop behaviours of 'learned helplessness' through early conditioning, in which they perceive their actions as having little or no bearing on outcomes. The results are feelings of helplessness and associated depression. This learned helplessness may lead to overdependence on parents, friends, teachers or social workers. Seligman (1975, 1992) points to the need for structured experiences that enable individuals to achieve some sense of success as a result of their actions. The exercises in this book may be used in that context.

EMPOWERMENT IS ABOUT CHOICE

Before individuals can choose, they should identify the options and decide what they really want. Frequently, individuals do not have time or make the effort to determine what it is they really want. Fromm (1960) took this point more broadly and comments that an individual:

would be free to act according to his own will if he knew what he wanted, thought and felt. But he does not know. He conforms to anonymous authorities and adopts a self which is not his. The more he does this, the more powerless he feels, the more is he forced to conform. In spite of a veneer of optimism and initiative, modern man is overcome by a profound feeling of powerlessness which makes him gaze towards approaching catastrophes as though he were paralysed.

(1960: 255–56)

Learning to identify choices, Fromm (1960) calls it 'alternativism'. For individuals to realize that there is a choice, there has to be some awakening, so that individuals understand that:

There is always an alternative and we can choose. . . . None of the alternatives in some situations may be desirable, but it is the knowledge that there is *always* a choice that heralds the beginning of self-empowered thinking.

(Hopson and Scally, 1981: 57)

At that moment of realization, there is an awareness of an individual being a person separate from parents, teachers and employers. It is an awakening to the conditioning process, for example when for the first time a child stands up to his or her parents and sets a goal that is totally of his or her own making. This does not mean that there are no boundaries around our choices; we all have boundaries, but within them we still have choice. (See the section on the power of choice in Chapter 4.)

CASE STUDY: CONTEXTUAL FACTORS THAT INFLUENCE EMPOWERMENT

Reality is not always easy, as Wilson (1991) observed in Derby (a small isolated town in the north-west of Western Australia). Government 'change agents', who had been exhorting Aboriginal people saying 'you can become anything you like: doctors, lawyers, etc', were quickly put in their place by Aboriginal people, who elaborated on the stark reality of their situation.

It is important for you to think about the societal structures that might inhibit your progress no matter how empowered you may feel. Women, migrants, homosexuals, lesbians, disabled people, young people, Aboriginal people, unemployed and retired people are all examples of groups who are often treated inequitably by our society. Empowerment is about knowing about oneself, recognizing feelings, and setting and achieving goals, as well as understanding the societal subsystems in which we live. The contextual factors of the empowerment process are discussed again in Chapter 6.

Why people assume there is no choice

The Milgram experiments, described earlier, illustrate the need for understanding why people assume that there is no choice. Making a choice frequently requires positive self-esteem, decision-making skills, confidence and an acceptance of the responsibility for the outcomes (whether they are good or bad). Arnstein (1969) came to the same conclusions when analysing why citizens choose or decline from participation in decision making. Choosing not only requires taking responsibility but also means being held accountable for outcomes. Many people shun responsibility and accountability, especially in some cultures where making mistakes may incur severe embarrassment and 'loss of face' (Bond, 1986).

Ego defence mechanisms

Rosenberg (1969) identifies nine 'rationales' or ego defence mechanisms that people use consciously or unconsciously to obscure from themselves or others the possibility of choice by attributing the cause of action or non-action. It is not necessary to fight every 'battle'. In fact, Westerners tend to try to control aspects of their lives that at times are best just left. People from South-East Asia often have a far more centred sense of inner peace, gained by developing a tolerance and acceptance of some things that are totally beyond their control.

An important point here is 'not to blame the victim'. The poorest of the poor in Nepal may be stuck in the poverty trap caused by malnutrition and disease, ruthless landlords, extortionate interest rates, illiteracy, an inability to check on debt payments, landlessness, etc. The last thing they need is development workers insisting that they have 'choices' when structurally their alternatives may be severely limited unless the societal constraints are unfrozen to some degree. At times the decision 'not to act' may be a worthwhile one.

You may wish to go through each ego defence mechanism in turn and ask yourself which ones you use. (Do you giggle self-consciously?) However, please realize that you are not the only one who uses excuses; we all do at various times! The first stage is awareness; then you can decide later whether to act or not to act depending on the circumstances.

Deciding 'not to act' as a conscious decision may be the best way to deal with certain situations – for instance, requesting a raise in salary may not be the most appropriate strategy when a company is being restructured. An empowered decision may involve saying to yourself 'it is not appropriate to apply now. However, I'll make a note in my diary to remind myself in six months' time to review the situation and take action if circumstances are more favourable'.

There are 10 rationales, or ego defence mechanisms, that have been formulated. Rosenberg (1969) identified the first nine rationales and Albert (1985) added a tenth. They are:

1. *Denying that choice exists*: 'I did what I had to do. I had no alternative.'

2. *The actions of others*: 'I hit the student because he refused to answer my question.'
3. *External forces*: 'It was God's will/fate'; 'It was the will of Allah'; 'Things just happen'; 'ke garne' in Nepalese, which means 'what to do?'
4. *One's psychological history*: 'My parents taught me never to rock the boat.'
5. *People in authority*: 'I just followed orders and did what I was told.'
6. *Group pressure*: 'Everyone else went along, they made me do it.'
7. *Institutional policies, rules and regulations*: 'I don't like the fact that my tax money is used to kill people, but it's the law and I have to pay it.'
8. *Gender, social or age roles*: 'Children should be seen but not heard; who am I to question my elders?'
9. *Uncontrollable tendencies*: 'I'd like to do something, but I cannot change the way I am.'
10. *Cynical or despairing view*: 'It doesn't matter. Things won't change anyway.'

Community groups and development workers may wish to discuss the ideas of Sharp (1980), who in a discussion on the reasons why people are inhibited from *not* co-operating with users of power that oppress or exploit them, identifies seven blocks:

- habit;
- fear of sanctions;
- absence of self-confidence;
- feelings of moral obligation;
- self-interest;
- identification with the wielder of power;
- indifference.

A simple yet useful message to pin up at home has just 10 two-letter words:

If it is to be, it is up to me.

This is a simplistic message, but it is a useful self-motivator when things don't go as well as expected. I used it in the 1980s when working with long-term unemployed people, and it is very powerful.

CONCLUSION

The aim of this chapter was to elaborate on the changing meaning of power and empowerment. A wide variety of definitions of power and empowerment have been discussed. A rationale for empowerment has been described. The amount of depth you wish to go into may depend on your goals and those of your organization and/or community.

KEY POINT SUMMARY

Power is shifting on four levels:

1.   national and world;
2.   community;
3.   organizational; and
4.   individual.

Children as well as adults need to learn in an empowering problem-posing way.

The 'banking' approach to learning may depower learners.

Many professions depower clients, either consciously or unconsciously.

Empowerment has political and social ramifications.

Power is neither good nor bad; it is the objectives for which it is used that need scrutiny.

Empowerment is about identifying choices.

Choices are influenced by contextual factors.

Individuals make ego defence reasons for assuming there is no choice.

At times, the decision 'not to act' may be the most empowering choice at that time.

Your own points

2

The Empowerment Cycle and the power card sort

INTRODUCTION

The previous chapter was designed to 'set the scene', to get you thinking about the changes that are happening in the world. This chapter contains experiential activities surrounding the 'Empowerment Cycle' (and there are more exercises in Chapter 4).

According to adult learning theory (Knowles, 1980, 1984), adults are much more able to absorb new information when they can relate it to past experiences, especially when they are asked to recall 'empowering experiences' and 'depowering experiences'. It is often useful to do these exercises with a trusted friend so that you can both tell stories and be heard. To be properly listened to can be an empowering experience in itself. When experiences are discussed and compared, meaning and understanding deepen. The exercises are designed for you to open up your concepts of power; enable you to think about useful and non-useful 'power bases' and to decide which are most appropriate in specific situations. I shall encourage you to use a variety of power bases, to stretch your repertoire of behaviours.

The rest of the chapter explains the importance of prior preparation with, and involvement of, managers and participants in empowerment sessions. The meanings of 'participation' and 'empowerment readiness' are discussed. There is an overview of the 'Empowerment Cycle' in the context of a one-day workshop that incorporates the power card pack. You will find a list of the power cards in the next chapter and the cards themselves in Appendix C. You may reproduce as many copies of these as you like. Appendix A and B instructions contain the sample one-day workshop.

PREPARATION

Before you start, you will need to gather some plain paper and coloured felt pens for the mind-mapping exercises. Then you will need a photocopy of the power cards (see

Appendix A), a pair of scissors, and an envelope to store the cards in for later use. You will need a cleared table to work on or some floor space to spread out the cards.

THE EMPOWERMENT CYCLE

The empowerment process is a complex, long-term, stop-start process. It involves a number of stages that are not necessarily sequential; however, it helps participants to understand the process if they are shown the whole picture. The process is divided up into five stages as shown in Figure 2.1 below. Each stage will be described in turn.

Stage 1: Recall depowering and empowering experiences

The first exercise is designed to involve participants in recalling events that were both depowering (Figure 2.2) and empowering (Figure 2.3). These figures display typical mind maps developed by course participants who were asked to identify factors that depowered and empowered them under the headings:

- yourself;
- your cultural traditions from your country of origin and/or residence;
- other people;
- organizations and institutions;
- events;
- things, both material and spiritual.

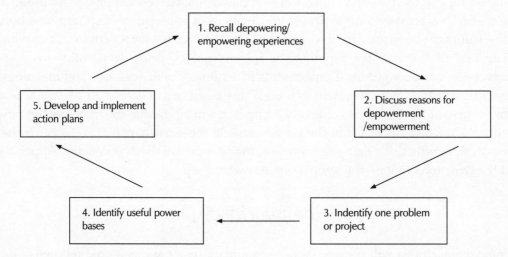

Figure 2.1 The Empowerment Cycle

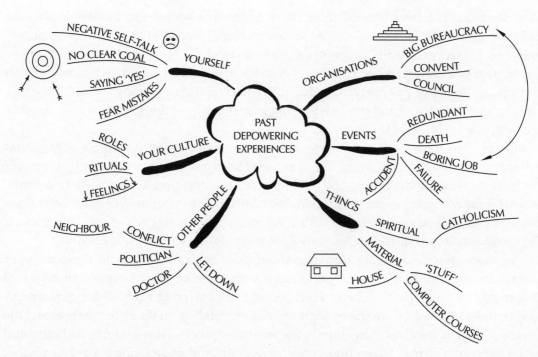

Figure 2.2 A sample mind map of past depowering experiences

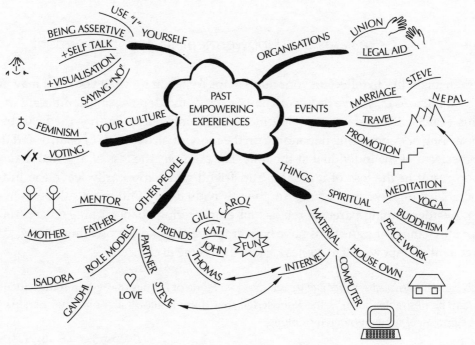

Figure 2.3 A sample mind map of past empowering experiences

Mind mapping is a right-brained thinking and visualization process developed by Tony Buzan in the UK (1974, 1993). In mind mapping, main ideas start from the centre on key branches. In Figures 2.2 and 2.3, some of these branches have been given for you – and you can see that you only need one or two words to know what they refer to. Then add smaller and smaller branches. Put everything down. There is no right or wrong way of doing this. Use plenty of colour and add symbols to bring your drawing to life. (Symbols also stimulate the right side of the brain.)

You can then draw lines and arrows around the outside, which indicate connections between ideas (see Figures 2.2 and 2.3). This use of lines has the advantage that you can see the linkages between the factors and issues in your life, and they also indicate how sometimes it is the way you perceive the world that contributes to your own empowerment and depowerment. If you are unfamiliar with mind mapping, you may wish to make lists under the above headings instead; but lists may limit you to linear, left-brained thinking.

This exercise will stimulate thinking about past experiences. If you compare your empowerment and depowerment mind maps with those of other people, you may find that an experience that is described by one person as empowering eg childbirth or marriage, may be perceived as depowering by someone else, depending on the circumstances and the person's frame of mind, or their stage in the transition process. It is useful to do both mind maps, although you may have a preference for one or the other. Drawing both gives you the whole picture.

Stage 2: Discuss reasons for depowerment and empowerment

You then might like to reflect on your mind maps. What do they tell you? You may find that some experiences may have been both empowering and depowering at different times.

This exercise illustrates that many factors are ambivalent, ie that they can be either empowering or depowering depending on the individual, the locus of control and the level of self-esteem of the individual at the time. For example, the loss of a parent may for one person result in the loss of a mentor and friend and temporarily leave the individual vulnerable to depowering factors. Another individual may find the death of an overpowering, overdemanding parent a release, an empowering chance to regain control of life. Major life changes or transitions have both empowering and depowering aspects.

Frequently, empowerment comes back to the theme of choice:

> *There is always an alternative and we can choose. . .* None of the alternatives in some situations may be desirable, but it is the knowledge that there is *always* a choice that heralds the beginning of self-empowered thinking.
>
> (Hopson and Scally, 1981: 57)

At this stage you may wish to think about the rationales and excuses you use to avoid making choices (see Chapter 1), and also about the external societal or organizational constraints (described in Chapters 1 and 6).

Stage 3: Choose one issue, problem or project to work on

The next stage of the process requires you to choose a problem or project on which to work. Again there is a choice. You may prefer to work alone, or with a friend on projects that you are working on in common. Or your friend could act as a questioning mentor to make you think about your project. What is important to emphasize at this stage is that you need to focus on just *one* open-ended problem.

You can use the power cards (see Appendix A) to think about many aspects of your project. We have a threefold nature that encompasses:

1. our physical being;
2. our spiritual being; and
3. our mental being.

With all three in balance, each of us has tremendous potential. They are interlinked, and so it is in some ways advisable to look into aspects of all three. This balance is wonderful – but also fragile. You can use the power cards to empower all or some of these three parts of yourself.

Taking a broader approach, there are four key types of power strategy for which you may use the power cards. Dunford (1992) identified the first three and I added the fourth. Of course there can also be combinations of the four shown below:

- to enhance power, ie to increase one's power source(s) – for example, to seek promotion or to develop your skills;
- to enact power, ie to take action using one's power source(s) – for example, to issue orders or to reward or punish;
- to challenge the power of another – for example, to challenge managerial prerogatives or to question the need for certain rules and regulations;
- to enhance the power of others – for example, to delegate and develop the skills of others.

If you want a team to pull together to change or create something, the team members can sort the cards together and then, according to the power base of each person, allocate roles and responsibilities.

The use of the power card pack is illustrated in Figure 2.4. However, it should be

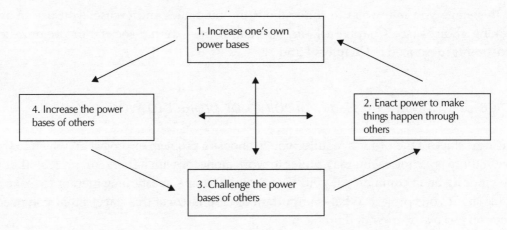

Figure 2.4 Four ways of using power cards

remembered that the card sort process is not appropriate for 'either/or' or closed questions with yes or no answers, such as 'Should I go for promotion or seek out another job?' or 'Should I take the new job?' But the process *is* suitable for the following types of questions:

- Individuals:
  - 'How can I go about writing and publishing a book?'
  - 'What do I need to do to make an informed career change?
  - 'What can I do about the interpersonal problems with Fred?'
  - 'How can I get more job satisfaction?'
  - 'How can I take charge of my life more?'

- Groups:
  - 'How can we get the whole organization behind the "x" change project?'
  - 'How can we bring more spirit and fun into our lives at the office?'
  - 'How can our group get Head Office to understand more about the problems in our region?'
  - 'How can our group of senior citizens take more of an active role in this organization?'

Stage 4: Identify potential power bases

The card sort exercise was developed to enhance your understanding of the large number of potential power sources available in a given situation. As mentioned in Chapter 1, I found the power bases described by French and Raven (1959) to be too limited in scope, namely:

- *Legitimate power*: a person's ability to influence because of a position.
- *Reward power*: deriving power from the ability to reward compliance through pay increase, promotion or recognition.
- *Coercive power*: power based on fear and the ability to punish through delegating undesirable work assignments, issuing reprimands or effecting dismissal.
- *Expert power*: power held by individuals who gain it because of their high level of skills and/or knowledge, which gains them the respect of others.
- *Referent power*: power gained because of an attractive personality, charisma or charm.

Believing as I do that living in the new millennium requires a new power paradigm and that everyone should be aware of every potential source of power, I searched for more power bases in the literature, and other power bases were added to the list – for example, the illusion of power using dress and symbols (Milgram, 1963).

In the 1970s, the advent of the Information Age led to the identification of the potential for people to gain possession or access to up-to-date 'information/data power' (Raven and Kruglanski, 1975). The important thing about information power, however, is to be able to ask the 'right' questions and analyse and use the results. Being swamped with too much information may be depowering! In the Middle Ages, information power rested with the monasteries. For most of the 20th century, information power was concentrated in universities. However, at the end of the century, information became so freely available via the Internet and home computers that organizations and even children without computers may be limited in their access to data.

Marilyn Ferguson (1986) described changes in the use of power in the 1980s as the 'Aquarian conspiracy', and entitled her book with this in mind. In a chapter on 'Right Power', she describes the new, more imaginative and rewarding sources of power needed for social transformation, eg the power of the individual as each of us is the 'difference in the world' (Ferguson, 1986: 241).

In the 1980s and the 1990s, other power bases were added to the literature, such as: positive self-talk power (Ellis and Harper, 1975); the power of questioning (Belbin, Downs and Perry, 1981; Downs and Perry, 1982, 1984) and the power of humour (Fry and Salameh, 1987).

'Power dressing' incorporates the 'power of illusion', and was much publicized, especially for women in the corporate world in the 1980s and 90s. However, it is not new, although the styles may have changed. Women in the corporate world were advised to dress more like men 'to be taken seriously'. Men, on the other hand, in Australia, where casual dress is more appropriate in the hot summers, are still in some organizations advised to wear ties and suits for the same reason. It is interesting that in historical times men dressed more like women for effect – for example, the long robes of the clergy and of kings. These and other power bases have been added to the power pack (see below).

Stage 5: Develop and implement action plans

Identification of power bases alone will not empower you unless you develop careful action plans for how you may use the power bases you have identified, as well as developing relevant time lines. This takes considerable concentration and determination. At a later date, you will then need to return to Stage 1 of the model and review and evaluate the experiences that have resulted from your action plans.

USING YOUR PERSONAL POWER PACK

Below is a list of the power cards, numbering 60 specific entries plus the opportunity for you to create your own. You will find the pack in Appendix C. If there are any that you do not understand, check out the explanations in Chapter 3.

Table 2.1 List of power bases and page numbers

Active listening	37	Letting go	88	Re-channelling energy	135
Body language	39	Love	89	Redefining who we are:	
Charisma	41	Media literacy	92	gender issues	137
Choices	44	Mediation	94	Reflection	141
Coercion	47	Meditation	95	Resources/resource	
Crisis	49	Men/maleness	96	exchange	143
Cross-cultural		Mind flexibility	99	Responsibility	144
communication	51	Money	103	Rewards	146
Delegation	53	Music/singing/		Saying 'No'	147
Experience	54	dancing	105	Senses	149
Expert knowledge and		Networking	106	Sexual attraction	151
skills	57	Passive resistance	109	Silence	153
Facilitation and group		Perseverance	111	Space; ambience	156
skills	59	Personal power	113	Spirituality	159
Feelings	63	Personal supporters	118	Stories and storytelling	163
Goal setting	68	Physical strength	120	Stress management	165
Humour/laughter	71	Physical well-being	122	Time management	168
Illusion	75	Position	123	Uncertainty	
Influencing powerful		Positive and constructive		management	170
people	77	feedback	125	Whole picture/gestalt	173
Information and its		Positive mind sets	127	Women/femaleness	175
retrieval	80	Problem solving and		Blank:	
Inspirational totems	82	decision making	131	Blank:	
Intuition	84	Public committal	133	Blank:	
Law	86	Questioning	134	Blank:	

Photocopy the cards in Appendix A and cut them up along the guide lines. You can then place all the cards together in one pile. Hold the pack of cards in one hand and turn over each card one at a time. You then need to consider each in turn in relation to your personal project. Note that it is useful if you have plenty of room to spread out the cards so that they can all be seen easily. Cards may only be discarded if they are already being used for your project or are totally irrelevant.

Action planning

Sorting the cards alone will not change your behaviour. You need to set action plans for each card. Transfer your chosen cards to the action planning sheet, also in Appendix A. Please note that not all the headings are applicable to each power card.

There is no limit to the number of cards that may be incorporated into a project. You will usually find that over a period of time you will invoke a large number.

Group/team strategies

If you want a team to pull together to change or create something together, members can sort the cards and then, according to the power base experience/skills of each person, allocate roles and responsibilities. Note that the division of labour here may be according to different criteria decided by the group. For example, a person who wishes to learn to use the power of influencing powerful people may wish to be partnered with an experienced person in this field so that he or she may learn by observation. Or the less experienced person may prefer to be coached and then receive feedback later. If a team is large, it is useful to divide it into groups even if those groups end up discussing the same project – an interesting aspect of this point is that, when the small groups unite to discuss ideas, they have often interpreted the power cards in different ways, so there is great scope for creative thought. (See particularly Case Study 3 in Chapter 5.)

EMPOWERMENT IN ORGANIZATIONS

Preparatory questions

Before human resource developers and managers decide to embark on an empowerment process within their organization, a number of questions should be addressed. Power needs to be directed towards goals and objectives. The cultural and ethical values of the organization need to be assessed. Power is neither good nor bad, but it is the way in which it is used or intended to be used that needs to be evaluated. To begin with:

- Who is being empowered?
- How and why are they being empowered?
- When will the change take place?
- In what context will the empowerment occur?
- With what likely intended (and unintended) results will the empowerment occur?

Once these issues are clearer, further useful questions include:

- To what levels of participation are managers willing to take the empowerment process?
- Is the organization ready for the empowerment process?
- What kind of workshop structure/s are most suitable?
- Should an outside facilitator be used or a team of internal and external facilitators?
- How can senior management be involved in the empowerment workshop without dominating proceedings?

Empowerment and participation

Empowerment in groups involves participation. In English the word 'participation' means different things to different people. One of the best models of the levels of participation I have found was developed by Sherry Arnstein (1969), a consultant in urban affairs in the United States who has worked with numerous government agencies and community groups there. As a result of her experience, she identifies eight levels of participation, which she defines as degrees of citizen power and depicts them as the rungs of a ladder, as shown in Table 2.2.

Table 2.2 Arnstein's Ladder of Participation

8. Citizen control
7. Delegated power
6. Partnership
5. Placation
4. Consultation
3. Informing
2. Therapy
1. Manipulation

Levels 1–2 she calls 'Non-participation'; Levels 3–5 she calls 'Degrees of tokenism'; and Levels 6–8 she calls 'Degrees of citizen power'. A brief description of each level is necessary here as attempts to create an empowered environment will need to include the upper levels – often, only the lower levels are used by management yet are still termed 'participation' and 'empowerment'. Although Arnstein writes about community use of power, I have cited organizational examples here.

1. *Manipulation*. At the manipulation level, citizens or members of private organizations merely serve to rubber-stamp the desires of advisory committees, who educate, persuade and advise the worker rather than the reverse.

2. *Therapy*. Managers allow workers to let off steam under the masquerade of 'participation'. Yet their anger or frustration is not heeded.

3. *Informing*. Arnstein maintains that information-giving is the first step towards legitimate participation, since workers at least become aware of some of their rights, responsibilities and options. As communication is only one-way, there is scope for misunderstandings. This one-way communication may be achieved through such channels as pamphlets, faxes, e-mail, etc.

4. *Consultation*. If consultation takes place, the communication should be *two-way* in that workers' ideas and opinions are solicited. Some managers go through the motions of 'consulting' but take very little notice of what has been said; as a result, distrust develops if no ideas are ever supported or implemented.

   Recently in a friend's organization, consultants employed by the managing director made a half-hour visit to his college. Based on that short visit they then made some radical changes. When my friend sent a memo pointing out the possible ramifications of such changes and the promise to consult, the managing director was reported to have thumped his desk and shouted, 'What do these people want? They were consulted!' It seems that the managing director used the 'token' levels to co-opt and manipulate others. The consultants collected data and views from the college staff; however, these were not reflected in the decision-making process and staff doing the job were not allowed any subsequent input.

   Another depowering tactic is where a facilitator appears to be consulting group members for their ideas, and these ideas may be acknowledged verbally but then discreetly omitted from the record of the discussion, ie ideas are eliminated and/or edited.

5. *Placation*. At the placation level, a hand-picked few 'worthy' workers are co-opted on to committees and begin to have some degree of influence – usually small – and the power-holders retain the right to judge the legitimacy of the advice. Arnstein refers to informing, consultation and placation as degrees of tokenism because the ground rules allow the have-nots to advise, but the power-holders retain the continuous right to decide.

6. *Partnership*. When partnership occurs, power is redistributed through negotiation between workers and power-holders. They agree to share planning and decision-making responsibilities through such structures as joint policy boards, planning committees and mechanisms for resolving impasses. Ground rules are established and only changed with mutual consent.

7. *Delegated power*. The level of delegated power occurs when workers achieve dominant decision-making authority over a particular plan or programme, usually as a result of negotiation.

8. *Citizen/worker control*. Finally, at this level workers are given full autonomy over an area and are put in charge of policy making and managerial aspects of a decision eg worker co-operative.

Arnstein's model is a useful tool for enabling people to understand more fully the concept of participation and to make them aware of the pitfalls of tokenism. Arnstein warned that token participation without the redistribution of power 'is an empty and frustrating process for the powerless' (1969: 176). It enables those with power to maintain the status quo because they can claim that people are consulted. She asserts in the same work that token participation was the level of participation in the majority of Community Action Programmes and Model City programmes in the United States.

With the above in mind, it may be prudent to find out at the outset of an organizational empowerment project exactly what senior management intends, so that participants can be told at any workshops what levels of participation are invited. If the levels of participation are made visible to workers, there is a basis for building trust. It is when there is a 'perceptual gap' of understanding between people that problems occur.

Arnstein's ladder can be applied to education, industry and community programmes that seek some form of participation. I frequently use this model with groups and immediately I get reactions like 'Now I understand why I got so annoyed. The manager was only consulting us, but we thought it was going to be a group decision'.

Empowerment readiness

An empowerment process involves change, which may be exasperating, painful and frustrating. The process also takes vast amounts of time and energy. Henkel *et al* (1993) designed an 'Empowerment Readiness Survey' consisting of 16 statements that address six dimensions of empowerment, which are as follows:

- *Communication*. How is information communicated? What is the tone behind the message? How much information is communicated?
- *Value of people*. Are people and their ideas valued? How is this shown? How do people respond to way-out ideas?

- *Ambiguity*. Is there tolerance for ambiguity? How do people respond to trial and error?
- *Concept of power*. How is power perceived? Is it shared? What level of power is being distributed? See Arnstein's model above. Is top management wanting 'citizen power', or merely consulting or even manipulating the workforce?
- *Information*. Are people willing to share what they know with others? Is there trust?
- *Learning*. Is the organization a learning organization, or is it 'business as usual'?

Henkel *et al* claim that the survey may be used in a number of ways: as an information-gathering tool before embarking on the empowerment change process; as part of a training programme on empowerment; by individuals, small groups or departments or the whole organization; etc.

They warn, however, that it should not be used either as a way of singling out individuals or for punitive purposes.

The survey has been used in organizations before they have entered into Total Quality Management processes and identifies three levels of empowerment readiness: not surprisingly 'ready', 'somewhat ready' and 'not ready'. The questionnaire for the survey may be found in the 1993 annual entitled *Developing Human Resources*, published by Pfeiffer and Co.

SETTING UP A WORKSHOP

As part of the process of dialogue in relation to an organizational empowerment exercise, workshops need to be held to obtain the views of relevant participants. Certain work must be done beforehand to ensure those workshops are valuable to the project.

A sound basis

As with any change or intervention process, prior preparation is most important. As an external consultant, I receive many requests for workshops on empowerment. I received one phone call from an HR manager, who said, 'We would like you to facilitate a workshop on empowerment. We've heard from others that it's so useful and fun.' My immediate response was 'Thank you, but tell me why your organization wants an empowerment workshop? Have upper management been consulted – after all this is an ongoing process?' As often happens, my questions were greeted with stunned silence. We chatted for a while and I suggested that the HR manager should get back to me after some more groundwork had been done. I didn't hear from that client again – and, knowing the organization concerned, I was not surprised, because their organizational culture was anything but empowering and I couldn't imagine that senior management would support any such initiative. They were just 'not ready'.

So my point here is for preliminary in-house work with senior management, because they must not only support and encourage moves towards a more empowered workforce but they must also support the initiative if times get rough. It is not a case of a one-off workshop; it requires a change in organizational culture. The underlying philosophy of empowerment and participation must be nurtured as:

> Once you teach an elephant to dance, you have to keep dancing until the elephant stops.
>
> (source unknown)

Preparing the participants

Another aspect of the preparation is communicating with participants, so that as far as possible they arrive at the workshop in a positive frame of mind and have time for thinking through problems and/or projects that they would like to address during the workshop.

Participation of management

There is considerable debate about the level of involvement and roles of senior management in workshops – ie should workers decide what they want and tell senior management (a reversal of previous modes), or should there be genuine co-operative discussion between workers and management?

In articulate groups, it is my belief that it is desirable to have senior mangers present throughout the workshop. However, in less empowered groups, senior managers may inhibit or dominate group discussion, and so it may be more productive to allow such groups to work together first and then invite managers in later. In one workshop I ran, a manager was present and sat tensely. When I asked for opening comments from those present, there was the initial thoughtful silence and then he jumped in with a response. Later he told me that he was trying to help me by 'getting the ball rolling', but unfortunately the opposite occurred and I had to use a great deal of encouragement to get others to talk. As a result of this incident, I always brief senior managers before a workshop and tactfully ask them not to dominate. I also use a number of 'equalizing processes' like card sorts to ensure the maximum possible levels of participation.

Physical preparation

This stage requires a lot of prior planning on your part. For group participation you will need flipchart paper, coloured felt pens and masking tape. For each individual participant you will need to provide a copy of the power cards, a pair of scissors and an envelope for storage of the cards for later use. You will need to set your room up for group discussion work and for individuals to later work on the cards alone, in pairs or in small groups, either on the floor or on tables.

CONCLUSION

The purpose of this chapter was to take you through the 'Empowerment Cycle'. However, it will come to life even more when you try it yourself. As with all experiential learning activities you have to do them, not just read about them.

My aim in this chapter was also to give facilitators an overview of the prior preparation required before embarking on empowerment workshops. Understanding by workers and management of the potential levels of participation, empowerment readiness and support of senior management was emphasized. An overview was presented of the processes and exercises described in this book.

The next chapter gives you a detailed explanation of each card in the power pack and exercises on some of the power bases. There are more exercises on empowerment in Chapter 4. If you want to see how other people have used the cards, look at the case studies in Chapter 5.

KEY POINT SUMMARY

The Empowerment Cycle consists of five stages:

- Recall depowering and empowering experiences.
- Discuss reasons for empowerment and depowerment.
- Choose one issue and turn it into a project.
- Use the power pack to identify potential power bases so as to help achieve that project.
- Develop action plans.

The first stage of recalling empowering and depowering experiences is based on Knowles' (1980, 1984) theory of adult learning, ie adults learn new concepts more easily when they can link them to previous experiences. Adults find it empowering to have their experiences honoured.

Mind mapping is more useful than list making as it enables you to make links and connections between ideas.

There are four ways you can use the card pack:

1. to increase your own personal power;
2. to exert power to get things done;
3. to challenge the power of others; and
4. to enhance the power of others.

Your own points

3

Explanations of each power base

INTRODUCTION

The aims of this chapter are to explain in detail each of the power cards and to provide you with a wide variety of activities to stimulate thinking. Your many life experiences will already have provided you with a great deal of knowledge about power. This chapter aims to stimulate your thinking further and as a result widen and deepen your understanding of power. Each power base is organized as follows:

- *Definition*. What is the power base exactly?
- *Rationale*. Why has it been included as a power base?
- *Stories*. These are to illustrate uses of the power base and to hook into and trigger recall of your experiences of that power base. Cases, and personal and traditional stories from different cultures are incorporated to enhance your understanding and potential uses (and also abuses) of each power base.
- *Activities*. You can use these as an individual or for facilitators in workshop situations.

There are 60 power bases in this pack (reproduced in Appendix C, and listed in simple terms in Table 3.1). There are also some blank cards for you to rename and/or add your own power bases.

Before you start to read this chapter in detail, it may help if you think about the following points:

- Human behaviour is very complex and as a result some power bases are overlapping – that is, not all the categories in them are always discrete.
- Use of one power base may incorporate, or have an impact on, the use of another. For example, use of coercive power may lead to the loss of charismatic power.

- Some power cards relate to you as an individual, whilst others involve how you relate to others.
- Some readers will have preferences for using the power bases that relate to their own internal world – for example, self-talk, prayer, etc – whilst others will prefer to use power bases that relate to others. It is useful to develop skills to enable you to work in both worlds, that is, your inner self and outer reality.
- The power bases are not of equal importance. Assessing which power base(s) to use is up to you, because it depends on how you perceive a situation; the potency of the power base(s) is situational.
- The length of description of each power base does not indicate its relative importance to other power bases.
- The effectiveness of the power bases may depend on your ease/skill in using a particular strategy, your personality and values. Therefore it may be useful to role-play or rehearse the use of certain power bases.
- Make sure you use a wide variety of power bases. Do not put all your eggs in one basket.
- Power may be unobtrusive. It is then potentially very powerful – for example, the media. It took many years before primary and secondary school teachers realized the need for children to be taught about the power that the media has in shaping values, thoughts and behaviour.
- The creation of new power bases on the blank cards is in itself empowering. You should not be constrained by my mindsets at the time of writing. By the time you read this in a published format, I will have added more categories.
- Some power bases are contradictory – for example, the Power of Perseverance and the Power of Letting Go. Unfortunately this is unavoidable. In most cases you will have to make decisions based on the information you have at the time.
- Whatever power base(s) you use will have consequences. These may be a mixture of positive, negative and interesting outcomes.
- Beware of the 'hyped' approach that some trainers use – for example, 'You can do anything you want to' when reality may not be so simple. Sellers of 'snake oil' and quick fixes ('I'm here to empower you') should be viewed with caution. There is a happy medium between encouragement, coercion and false promises.

Each time you try out an activity it is good to start with a positive mindset – for example, 'I'll give this a proper try and see what happens' rather than 'This looks odd, I'll just give it a quick try'.

Table 3.1 List of power cards

1. Active listening	21. Letting go	44. Redefining who we are: gender issues
2. Body language	22. Love	45. Reflection
3. Charisma	23. Media literacy	46. Resources/resource exchange
4. Choices	24. Mediation	
5. Coercion	25. Meditation	47. Responsibility
6. Crisis	26. Men/maleness	48. Rewards
7. Cross-cultural communication	27. Mind flexibility	49. Saying 'no'
	28. Money	50. Senses
8. Delegation	29. Music/singing/dancing	51. Sexual attraction
9. Experience	30. Networking	52. Silence
10. Expert knowledge and skills	31. Passive resistance	53. Space; ambience
	32. Perseverance	54. Spirituality
11. Facilitation and group skills	33. Personal power	55. Stories and storytelling
	34. Personal supporters	56. Stress management
12. Feelings	35. Physical strength	57. Time management
13. Goal setting	36. Physical well-being	58. Uncertainty management
14. Humour/laughter	37. Position	
15. Illusion	38. Positive and constructive feedback	59. Whole picture/gestalt
16. Influencing powerful people		60. Women/femaleness
	39. Positive mindsets	61. Blank:
17. Information and its retrieval	40. Problem solving and decision making	62. Blank:
	41. Public committal	63. Blank:
18. Inspirational totems	42. Questioning	64. Blank:
19. Intuition	43. Rechannelling energy	
20. Law		

1. ACTIVE LISTENING

Take the cotton wool out of your ears and put it in your mouth.

Definition

Active listening involves listening with your head and your heart; that is, you listen to the content of the message but also the feelings behind the message. The skills of active listening involve paying attention with empathy to the listener, as opposed to distracted, denying, cynical or 'ostrich' behaviour. New session leaders of Alcoholics Anonymous meetings are advised to '. . . take the cotton wool out of your ears and put it in your mouth'. It is good advice to all of us.

Active listening is a skill that can be learnt with practice. Here are some guidelines:

- *Listen and do not judge.* Try to keep an open mind and do not jump to conclusions.
- *Reflect the underlying feelings.* 'You must have felt upset'. 'I bet that made you feel really pleased/sad/mad'.
- *Ask for more information.* 'You mentioned your concerns about your work. Can you tell me more about what aspect of your work really bothers you?'
- *Paraphrase the content.* Use your own words, otherwise you may sound like a parrot. 'As I understand it you are fed up with. . . is that correct?' 'Ah, so your main point is. . .'. If you have misunderstood the message, the speaker will quickly correct you.
- *Work with the speaker's information.* Try to use only information that the person gives you voluntarily.
- *Let the person finish what he or she is saying.* A pause from the listener makes the speaker feel as if the listener is valuing and thinking carefully about what has been said.

Rationale: Why this power base was included

If you are a good listener, you can make the speaker feel he or she is the most important person in the world at that moment. It also enables you to pick up vital information regarding feelings as well as ideas. So this is a very useful power base. Active listening needs energy as we have to keep our wonderful minds and resulting leaping thoughts in order. In India they say that humans have 'drunken-monkey' brains.

Here is a story that is useful to bring home the importance of listening to the unheard:

The listening prince

An ancient Chinese king sent his eldest son to a great master to learn the arts of leadership required to be a king.

The master sent the Prince alone into the forest for one whole year. When he returned he was asked to describe all he heard. He replied, 'I heard the larks sing and the leaves rustle and the grass blow.'

The master sent him back to the forest to listen more carefully. The Prince was puzzled, but he returned to the forest and started to listen. At first he didn't hear anything new and time passed slowly.

Then one morning he started to hear new faint sound sensations. Joyfully, he returned to the Palace and said, 'Master when I really listened I started to hear the "unheard" – the sound of flowers opening, the sigh of grass receiving the early morning dew, the joy of nature awakening in the spring.'

The master was pleased and said, 'Now you have heard the "unheard" you are ready to become a king, for only when a ruler can listen to the people's hearts as well as to their minds is good leadership attained. To hear the unspoken, the uncommunicated feelings, the unexpressed joys and pains, is the quality of a truly great leader. The demise of kingdoms occurs when leaders only listen to superficial sounds and do not penetrate deeply into the peoples' true feelings and desires.'

Activity: individual practice

Write down the active listening skills on a card. Next time you are at work, or on the phone, try to observe yourself using (or abusing) these strategies.

Activity: group practice

In a workshop setting a facilitator can divide up the group into groups of three. Each person has a different role: a story teller, who tells a true story of an event in which his/her emotions were effected; an *active listener*, who uses the skills and appropriate body language noted above; and an *observer*, who silently notes down positive active listening behaviours and makes suggestions for improvement.

Timing: five minutes for story telling, and five minutes for positive and constructive feedback. The facilitator needs to remind the observer to give specific positive feedback and useful constructive feedback (see Power Card 38, Positive and constructive feedback).

2. BODY LANGUAGE

Non-verbal communication accounts for 65–93 per cent of what is communicated.
(Birdwhistell, 1970; Mehrabian, 1972 in Bartol *et al*, 1995)

Definition

Body language or non-verbal communication is the not-so-obvious part of communication. There are a number of such categories (Bartol *et al*, 1995):

- *kinaesthetic behaviour*; that is, gestures, smiles, stress, frowns, eye movements and posture;
- *proxemics*; that is, spatial distance between people;
- *paralanguage*; that is, tone and quality of voice, laughs and yawns;
- *object language*; that is, material things such as clothing, cosmetics, furniture.

Rationale

We cannot *not* communicate non-verbally and it conveys over half our entire message to others. Tone of voice, smile, stare, nod, sitting or standing often conveys more than the words we speak. Therefore we need to be aware of what messages we are communicating and also able to read the body language of others.

I saw a politician being attacked on TV for a recent action. Whilst answering, she spoke firmly but was smiling when she had nothing to smile or be happy about. When words and body language contradict, listeners get mixed messages and as a result tend to distrust the speaker. This incident shows how important it is to have knowledge and be aware of body language.

The power of the smile

In April 1992, I was privileged to attend a 'Mind Science' discussion between the Dalai Lama of Tibet and some psychologists and neurologists from the Perth community. The first thing that struck me about the Dalai Lama as he entered was his smile. Even his eyes smiled. He looked up and without saying a word seemed to be able to make eye and smile contact with the whole auditorium.

He turned to one of the panel guests on the stage, who looked physically tense and almost scornful. The Dalai Lama smiled and nodded. The other man glared. The Dalai Lama nodded and smiled again as if he was trying to reach the man and say 'It's all right. You know we are here to learn together'. The other man returned the nod, smiled slightly and relaxed – slightly. I wrote at the top of my page: 'The power of the smile'.

The Dalai Lama had not yet said a word but already his genuine smile was making contact with and putting hundreds of people at ease. Later, I read in one of his books, which said:

> I love smiles… For there are many kinds of smile, such as sarcastic, artificial or diplomatic smiles. Many smiles produce no feeling of satisfaction, and sometimes they can even create suspicion or fear, can't they? But a genuine smile really gives us a feeling of freshness and is I believe unique to human beings. If these are the smiles we want, then we ourselves must create the reason for them to appear.

(Tenzin Gyatso, the Dalai Lama, 1991: 13)

His genuine, sincere and affectionate smile and compassion surmounted the difficulties of cross-cultural communication and made a major impact on all who saw him.

Activity: video feedback

If you are a facilitator, borrow a video camera and ask the permission of a group to leave the video camera at the back of the room, focused on you. Watch the results at home. You will be surprised at the number of messages you are sending out inadvertently.

Activity: individual feedback

Talk to a trusted friend. Ask him or her to give you positive and constructive feedback on your body language. Remember to listen and not get defensive. (See Power Card 38, Positive and constructive feedback.)

3. CHARISMA

Some people just seem to be able to hold an audience spellbound.

Definition

The word 'charisma' is derived from the Greek word meaning 'gift'. The word was hardly used until a generation ago and now means different things to different people. It describes powers that cannot be logically explained, and this makes it all the more difficult to study. Charisma is both an innate quality and a range of skills and behaviours that can be learned, and some activities are presented below to help you do this. A charismatic person attracts others to them by some magnetism in their personality and presence. When they enter a room, others feel drawn to them. This is sometimes referred to as 'referent power'.

Rationale

Charismatic people make the people around them feel inspired, important and valued. They frequently describe a vision of a new goal or ways of doing things. Therefore charismatic people have most success during times of hardship or difficulty especially wars, recessions, for example, Nelson Mandela, Mother Theresa, Aung San Suu Kyi, Mahatma Gandhi, Martin Luther King and the Dalai Lama.

Charismatic leaders

The success of charismatic leadership is evident in many corporations: Bill Gates (Microsoft), Jan Carlzon (Scandinavian Airlines), Steve Jobs (ex-director of Apple Computers), Dick Smith (retired entrepreneur and adventurer), Anita Roddick (director of the Body Shop), Richard Branson (owner of Virgin Records/Airlines). Risk-taking entrepreneurs have learnt to be media personalities and assume the sparkle of film stars. Anita Roddick maintains the enthusiasm of her managers and staff at Body Shop all around the world by sending regular news videotapes of her travels and new environmentally friendly products. She has mastered the use of electronic media to keep her 'presence' or charisma alive and well in shops all over the world.

An important attribute ascribed to charismatic people by Brislin (1991) is the way that they give full attention to individuals. They listen with their whole being and show intense concentration on the subject matter at hand. They do not interrupt the speaker and even wait for a moment after the person has finished speaking as if to honour or ponder on what has just been said (see Power Card 1, Active listening).

Activity: charisma can be learnt

There are, however, contradictions, in that 'charisma' can be learnt! Politicians and media personalities are tutored in TV style and presence. John Heron, in his book, *Group Facilitation: Theories and models for practice* (1993), describes exercises in charismatic training. Here is one activity that you can use to develop your own presence and centring. It relates to four levels: presence, voice, language and purpose (see also Figure 3.1) and is as follows:

- *Level 1: Presence.* The grounding level is that of feeling 'the fullness of your presence'. This feeling may be very dependent on levels of self-esteem. If you are feeling very low and insecure, you may need to work harder to obtain this feeling. Use positive self-talk: 'I can and I will speak slowly and confidently'. Breathe deeply.
- *Level 2: Voice.* Allow your voice's timing, emotional tone, timbre, rhythm, inflection and emphasis, pauses and silences to arise out of Level 1. Remember that your voice is an integral part of your body.
- *Level 3: Language.* Let the timing and tone of voice and pattern of sound shape the choice of words, what you say, your ideas, judgements and opinions that you choose to put forward.

- *Level 4: Purpose.* Let your purpose, intentions and purposes in communicating be released by the cumulative impact of the previous levels.

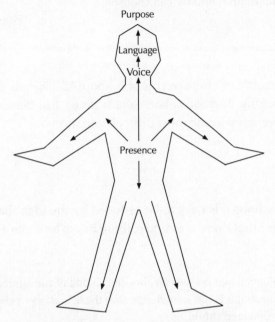

Figue 3.1 Developing charisma (adapted from Heron, 1993:42)

Activity: developing charisma

Separately or in pairs, take it in turn to do the following:

- Place your left hand on your abdomen and say 'I am present in my stomach' and occupy the whole of the lower part of your body. (Keep your left hand on your stomach throughout the rest of the exercise as this helps to remind you to stay centred.)
- Place your right hand on your chest and say 'I am present in my heart' whilst entering the thoracic space and integrating it with the lower part of your body.
- Place your hand on your larynx and say 'I am present in my voice' whilst entering your throat and linking it to the rest of your body.
- Place your hand on your forehead and say 'I am present in my head' whilst realigning your head next and spine with the larynx, chest and lower body.
- Finally, integrate the whole and say 'I am fully present'.

What did you notice in yourself and/or your partner as you did this exercise?

4. CHOICES

There is always an alternative, and we can choose.

(Hopson and Scally, 1981)

Definition

The essence of the meaning of empowerment is about 'choice', as described in Chapter 1. Choice is the act of making decisions about alternatives. But before choosing we need to generate *creative* choices, even in the most difficult situations.

Rationale

In disempowering situations it is easy to be seduced by the idea that there are no choices. For individuals to realize that there *is* a choice, there has to be some awakening so that there is understanding that:

> There is always an alternative and we can choose… None of the alternatives in some situations may be desirable, but it is the knowledge that there is *always* a choice that heralds the beginning of self-empowered thinking.

(Hopson and Scally, 1981: 57)

It is important that you think about and evaluate *all* options that are available to you before making a decision.

Activity: to identify the demands, constraints and choices in your job

Rosemary Stewart (1982) describes a simple framework that she developed to analyse work (be it inside or outside the home). The model has three categories and is applicable to any position. It can be used to think about the nature of a job and how each individual performs it. According to Stewart there are three areas in every job: demands, constraints and choices. See also Figure 3.2, below.

Demands

Demands are what a person in any job *must* do, for example:

- attend certain meetings;
- ensure that certain procedures like monthly reports are completed;
- see that a baby is kept clean, fed and healthy.

Constraints

Constraints are factors inside or outside the organization that limit what an individual may do, for example:

- resource (time, money, skills) limitations;
- technological limitations (old or slow computer or machinery);
- policy, legal and trade union constraints;
- attitudes of others to change;
- attitudes and expectations of others towards a job role;
- attitudes of clients and customers towards a job role;
- physical location and or climate;
- lack of confidence or self esteem;
- tight inflexible job description.

Choices

Choices involve what, how, where and when activities are done – for example:

- what to select and emphasize in certain aspects of a job;
- how to select some tasks and ignore others;
- whether to change an area of work;
- how to work as a change agent within the organization;
- how to develop personal expertise in some areas;
- whether to join certain committees;
- how a certain item of work should be done;
- whether to do the job yourself or delegate it;
- whether to devote a short or long time to the task;
- where and when the work is done;
- to work at home;
- to work into the night or over the weekend.

An example: Toni and Peta

The same job is frequently interpreted and performed in very different ways by two different people – for example, Toni and Peta (see Figure 3.2). The demands may be the same. Toni, having worked in a bureaucracy for many years, may perform the demands of

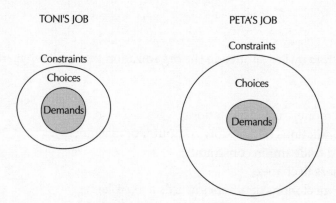

Figure 3.2 How Toni and Peta interpret and perform the same job

the job and may perceive the constraints as giving her very little choice or freedom for initiative. Peta, a new employee though given the same job description, may perform the demands of the job but also may take on many different projects and may also at times unknowingly break some of the formal and informal rules of the organization and get away with it.

Activity: demands, constraints and choices of your job

Take a sheet of paper and draw two concentric circles in similar fashion to those in Figure 3.2. Then add in the demands, constraints and choices of your job in the appropriate areas in and around the circles. You may have more choices than you realize; alternatively, if you only see constraints it may be necessary to challenge yourself on those constraints – for example, 'Are those barriers written in tablets of stone? What would happen if I changed that procedure?'

Activity: brainstorming to generate choices

Powerful people generate lots of alternatives. They always try to allow their minds to think of many ideas and strategies, including those that appear crazy. Brainstorming is a useful process that was first used by Alex Osborn in his advertising company in New York. The process is used to generate a large number of ideas (Rawlinson, 1981). Here are some suggestions on how to go about it. Remember the ground rules:

- the wilder the ideas the better;
- do not evaluate ideas;

- go for lots of ideas;
- build, or 'piggy back', on ideas;
- think of opposites.

Carefully state the issue. Frequently at this stage, people rush into brainstorming without really defining the problem. For example, you may be thinking about changing your job and wanting to brainstorm alternatives. You may wish to spend some time restating the problem: 'How many different jobs could I do?', 'In how many ways can I earn a living?', 'What do I want to spend most of my waking hours doing?'

See also the PMI process to evaluate choices in Chapter 6.

5. COERCION

Do it, or else…

Definition

Coercion is getting someone to comply with your wishes through threatening mental or physical punishment or inducing fear. Examples include threat or action to instigate dismissal, reprimands, demotion, undesirable work assignments, lack of choice on work and holiday rosters, suspension, transfer, salary cuts, or even dismissal. It can also include the threat of physical violence – to which I am strongly opposed.

Rationale

Coercion has to be used with great care. It is a very blunt tool and the user needs to be aware of the ramifications. Coercion often results in the recipients feeling very negative towards you and may even lead them to take revenge (or repeated non-compliance) at a later date (as parents often find to their cost with children).

I have included this power base because it is important to be aware of all power bases at your disposal. But you need also to be aware of its repercussions. Coercion may be necessary in some situations. For example, in an emergency a command like 'Leave me alone or I'll call the police!' may be necessary.

The power base of coercion is declining in strength for supervisors in some work places, where semi-autonomous work groups are being introduced and incentives and rewards are being developed and administered by team members as they become more self-regulating.

Revised Quaker views on coercion: when persuasion is not working

The Quaker movement in the United Kingdom has recently revised its approach to non-violence in order to incorporate a degree of coercion. This was explained to me by Steve Whiting of the 'Turning the Tide' programme. He and his colleagues train activists to use three levels of interaction:

1. *Communication.* 'We have a problem…'. (Think first what should the message be and to whom should it be communicated.)
2. *Persuasion.* 'Please do something to remove the problem…'. (Analyse who should be persuaded and what persuasion tactics should be used.)
3. *Coercion.* 'I will prevent you carrying on as normal until you solve this problem.' (Analyse what actions might be appropriate and effective.)

An interesting example of this definition of the term 'coercion' comes from the United Kingdom Quaker movement. Angie Zelter and three others scored a victory for the peace movement when a jury found them not guilty of causing and conspiring to cause criminal damage to a Hawk jet owned by the Ministry of Defence. The jury accepted Zelter's defence that she was preventing war crimes by disabling the jet, bound for export to Indonesia where they would be used for 'aiding and abetting murder in East Timor' in contravention of international law (Brown, 1999: 5).

Disadvantages of coercion

The ultimate in coercion is a threat to life and limb, physical force or even murder. Coercion is thus the least stable form of power. Its use may be dramatic, but compliance and success is often only temporary. There may be public compliance, but in private people may be complaining and/or sabotaging – for example, throwing a spanner in the works on an assembly line, or wildcat strikes, or some kind of computer sabotage may be being planned.

Coercion may be sanctioned, or 'legitimized', by the state. Martial law and capital punishment are two examples. In dictatorships, 'henchpeople' are often hired to carry out the orders of the power-holders, or sometimes the army or police are used. When used illegitimately, any physical attack can only be classified as assault (or worse).

Threats in class

In my second year of teaching, I was back in London doing some supply teaching. I hated it because there was no chance to develop a rapport with the students. I recall making one major mistake in relation to a third-year girl who had been repeatedly disruptive and rude in class.

I told her to stay behind and threatened that she would not go home until she apologized. A stand-off developed. I quickly realized that I had backed myself into a corner and sat wracking my brains for a face-saving way out. I knew I could not keep her for long. I made an excuse that I had an important meeting to attend and couldn't be bothered wasting my time with the likes of students like her whose only interest was to disrupt other people from learning. We both went home.

I felt rotten, especially as it wasn't my usual way of speaking to students. I was – and still am – ashamed that I let my anger get the better of me that day. It is interesting to reflect on how disruptive classroom behaviours can bring out the worst in both teachers and students. And, of course, in a supply situation you very often have neither briefing nor backing regarding the disciplinary procedures available to you.

Activity: reflection on how you feel when coerced

Think about a situation when you experienced being coerced into doing something. How did you react and feel? What did you do? Was the best outcome achieved? How could the situation have been handled differently?

6. CRISIS

> That which does not kill me makes me stronger.
>
> (Friedrich Nietzsche (1844–1900))

Definition

A crisis is a serious difficulty that requires an immediate response and maybe some action. It is a decisive moment or turning point, and sometimes a moment of difficulty and/or danger. It is usually something that is both important and urgent.

Rationale

The power of crisis has been included because this is when we are most open to new learning and change. Have you noticed how some people frequently stay in unhappy relationships and/or jobs because the alternative – that is, change – is seen as even more costly emotionally and economically? Sometimes a shift occurs when a bad situation improves

Crisis is

Danger and Opportunity

Figure 3.3 Chinese symbols for crisis

slightly and then reverts back, causing the desperation of renewed disappointment that sometimes prompts us into taking action. On occasions, we do not act until the pain of changing is seen as less than the pain of staying the same.

English and Chinese interpretation of 'crisis'

In the English language the term 'crisis' has totally negative connotations. The Chinese symbol in Figure 3.3 is very useful because it enables us all to appreciate that a 'crisis' may not be totally negative.

The Chinese see 'crisis' as offering two concepts (denoted by the two symbols in Figure 3.3), namely 'opportunity' and 'danger'. A crisis is like a two-sided coin. We can choose how to respond. For example, in 'danger' mode we might react: 'Oh this is awful, how could they make me redundant? This is the end of everything for me. I can't do anything about this'. But in 'opportunity' mode we might say: 'Well, this feels horrible. I cannot believe it. I'm angry and hurt. But, maybe there is a chance here to try out something different. I've always wanted to try xxx but I didn't want to give up my secure job because of my family commitments. Now maybe I could give it a try…'.

A crisis generates energy

In Japan, people talk about the 'last fart of the ferret', that is, if a ferret is cornered and thinks it is going to die, as a last attempt to scare off the enemy it will emit a terrible smell. A similar thing happens with humans: if really trapped, we can sometimes summon up superhuman powers to enable us to get out of a mess.

Crises may result from failures or mistakes. But failures and mistakes are rarely fatal, even though admittedly they can be devastating at the time and even though they tend to linger on in our minds. The surrounding events can be very powerful. Nevertheless, we should use what we learn from them to empower ourselves to react to even greater challenges. In practice, however, we rarely evaluate or learn from our successes but, rather, just repeat them.

Generating a crisis situation

If things are going wrong or things are too hard to handle, it is frequently better to cut your losses. For example, if you know a project is not going to work, it may be better to generate a crisis situation in order to get people to sit up and take notice.

In 1991, I tried to organize an expedition to China for management students. I advertised for students and we discussed the learning goals and the fact that they would have to raise funds and practise entrepreneurial and organizational skills to make it all happen. A group of twelve students met and were keen to go. Some seriously started to get to work; however, it quickly became evident that the others really had not taken the project seriously and were excusing their tardiness with, 'Oh, I'll just get a loan' or 'I've got some money coming from my Gran'.

Two fell by the wayside and then another couple dropped out. I was worried and held a meeting and confronted the remaining six with my concerns. I then said I would leave the room so that they could decide whether or not they were really serious about the goal without being influenced by my presence. Half an hour later they had made their decision: they didn't think they could get the money together in time. I then had to step in to debrief them after their disappointment and frustration. They still wanted to go ahead with an outdoor leadership day and we used this as a way of going through the 'mourning stage of a group'. Although I also was disappointed, I do not regret their decision to this day.

Activity: your reactions to crisis

Think back to a crisis in your life. What were the dangers and what were the opportunities? How would you deal with a similar crisis in the future differently?

7. CROSS-CULTURAL COMMUNICATION

What I said is not really what I meant.

Definition

Cross-cultural communication is the ability to understand and be understood by people of different cultures from your own. I am not referring here merely to foreign-language abilities, although obviously these are of importance. Mixing with people from a variety of cultures helps us to open up our minds and extend them. The power of learning about other cultures is that it helps us learn about our own.

Rationale

Brislin (1991) claimed that cross-cultural communication is an emerging major power base of the 21st century. Indeed, teachers, workers, managers and lecturers are faced every day with communicating with people from different cultures and backgrounds. The opportunities for cross-cultural encounters and *faux pas* regularly face us everyday when dealing with overseas workers, tourists, businesspeople, immigrants and refugees. Cultural translators have an enormous advantage in the multicultural societies of Australia, the United States and the United Kingdom.

Language is a code for expressing our ideas, but often it is inadequate to express the complexity of feelings and connotations of our ideas. Therefore in cross-cultural communication there is even more scope for misunderstandings. Gandhi was a powerful communicator because he was able to communicate with people of different cultures and subcultures across India. He had the power of translating profound Hindu philosophy into ordinary language, so that uneducated workers could understand. He could also communicate with the British Raj, and as such his power as a 'cultural translator' was great.

Activity: questioning behaviour

In order to make sense of many confusing stimuli in our environment, our brains quickly categorize, make decisions and jump to conclusions. We take the behavioural rules and ways of thinking for granted; they are almost invisible. It is only when someone breaches these codes of behaviour that we notice. One useful strategy to use in cross-cultural situations that are confusing is to ask questions. It sounds simple, but it works and enables us to understand other people's worldviews.

Watching films about other cultures and cross-cultural encounters is fun. I recommend the following: *Farewell My Concubine, Madam Sowztka, Mississippi Masala, The Wedding Banquet, Wild Swans, Iron and Silk, The Scent of Green Papaya, Traps, My Beautiful Launderette, A Tale of O, Blue eyes* and *A Class Divided*. See Chapter 5 on the use of films. There is also a wealth of books about diversity of culture.

There are now many courses for businesspeople on cross-cultural communication. If you are working in a cross-cultural environment or are going to work overseas, it is advisable to undergo some form of cross-cultural training. Some key authors to look out for in this field are Adler (1996), Brislin and Yoshida (1994), Cushner and Brislin (1995) and Hofstede (1980, 1991).

8. DELEGATION

I never do what I can delegate to someone else.

Definition

Delegation is the assignment of some work or duties to someone else. When you delegate, you also pass on some power to another person, who then has the necessary responsibility and authority to complete the task. Delegation is not abdication of responsibility. Although some responsibility and accountability are delegated, the delegator is still ultimately responsible and accountable.

Rationale

Delegation is increasing as a result of flattened hierarchies and restructuring. Job roles are changing radically at all levels. The resulting shifts of power and authority are causing many changes in job descriptions; people at lower levels are being given more authority and decision-making powers. This needs to be accompanied by skills training and empowerment courses.

Effective delegation

Here are some guidelines relating to effective delegation:

- Be clear and specific.
- Describe the reasons for the task and its importance.
- Give or negotiate realistic deadlines for completing a task.
- Pause to allow the listener to think of questions.
- Listen actively, checking for compliance or non-compliance.
- Be clear about the amount of responsibility you are delegating.
- Monitor if necessary.
- Do not always delegate to the same willing people: they will either be seen as favoured 'pets' or may later become overworked.

Barriers to effective delegation

There are some barriers to effective delegation. For example:

- *Some people are reluctant to let go of their power.* No person in any organization, whether it is a school, a home or a workplace, can do everything. This would be totally depowering. There is a story of the late Sir William McMahon, an Australian Treasurer and Prime Minister, who on taking the role of Treasurer instructed his secretary to send him all details on the department. The result was he was deluged with paper and interruptions and he quickly revoked his decision.
- *Some people are unwilling or unable to accept responsibility.* Supervision and/or training may be necessary.
- *People lack confidence and need moral support.*
- *Some organizations do not encourage risk-taking.* Performance appraisal systems may be geared to rewarding successes and 'safe' behaviour.

Delegation in the home

In our home, we delegate some of the housework because my husband and I work full time and we do not have time to do everything. Employing help in the home also helps to provide other people with a job. Some jobs – for example, decorating – we enjoy and do ourselves. Our leisure time is scarce and highly valued. Therefore it would be depowering to spend it doing things we do not enjoy.

Activity: delegating part of your duties

Next time you feel stressed, think about what you could delegate at home or at work. Do you need to have a family conference to discuss a reallocation of roles and responsibilities? Are there any jobs that you can just ignore?

9. EXPERIENCE

Experience is not what happens to you but what you make of what happens to you.
(Aldous Huxley, British novelist and essayist, 1894–1963)

One ounce of practice is worth tons of learning.

(Mahatma Gandhi)

Definition

Experience is the wisdom, skill or knowledge gained in our everyday lives by personal encounter, observation and reflection. Experience is a valuable teacher, all the more so because it is so democratic. We all have so many experiences every day, but do we have the skills to learn from them – and *do* we learn from them? There is a French expression which says 'Those who forget the past are condemned to repeat it'.

Rationale

A manager, who was a participant in one of my workshops, said one day: 'I have had 10 years of experience in this job'. Half-jokingly I replied: 'Is it 10 different years or one year repeated?' After the workshop, she came and spoke to me and said that what I had said was very meaningful for her as she was thinking of a career change because she felt stultified – and, yes, her job was repeating each year!

Kolb's Experiential Learning Model

Kolb (1984) developed an easy model, which is a useful tool to help us learn from experience. The model is illustrated in Figure 3.4 and comprises a four-stage cyclical process:

- *Experience*: having an experience;
- *Reflect*: reviewing and reflecting on the experience;
- *Generalize*: drawing conclusions from the experience;
- *Apply*: planning the next steps.

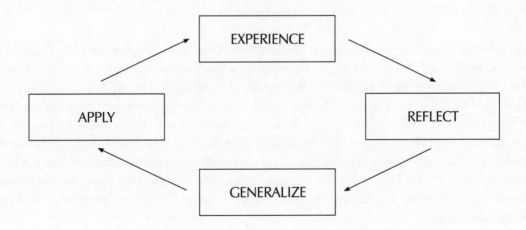

Figure 3.4 Experiential Learning Model (adapted from Kolb, 1984)

Kolb's model does not mean that we should get stuck in this cycle. In fact, it is more like an upward spiral, as next time we come to a similar experience we will be older (and hopefully wiser) and the people and the situation may be different. So we should learn from the past but not condemn ourselves to repeat it.

Also note that we do not necessarily go around the stages of this model sequentially. We miss stages – for example, we may jump from an experience to applying new learning without reflecting on it. However, this simple model helps us analyse our actions and see if we miss out any of the stages. The model is very easy to remember (and therefore apply at any time) by remembering the mnemonic 'ERGA' formed from the first letter of each stage.

I recall with great pleasure the elation I felt when listening to a first-year student after he facilitated a workshop with the class. He commented:

> My mind was working so fast that, while I was talking, all four stages were happening almost at once. In other words, I was talking to the group, reflecting at the same time on their reactions, drawing conclusions, and also modifying my voice, my eye contact and what I said as I went along.

This was a very profound response because here was a student who was analysing the working of his own mind, analysing and internalizing a model, and learning from experience in split seconds of time.

Experiential learning involves trial and error and enables you to modify your behaviour in different situations. It is a very personal way of learning. People may experience the same activity, but learn very different things from it.

My father

My father was a major mentor in my life. He taught me how to take calculated risks. He encouraged me when I would get to the edge of a risk and almost turn back. When I was attending the University of London, at the age of 21 I announced in my final year that I was thinking of buying a one-way ticket to India and would find my way home to London overland in my two-month summer holiday. My mother was horrified and immediately set to work to dissuade me. My father took a more thoughtful approach and admitted that at my age he would have loved such an experience. He said, 'Go and find out about all the different kinds of insurance policies. Find a respectable company that offers high medical cover and includes a clause that will pay for one parent to fly out to bring you home if you became seriously ill. If you do this you can go.'

This was the easiest part of the whole venture. I went and returned three months later weighing less than six stone in weight (having had severe dysentery), but I had had many experiences and learnt so much about foreign countries that are now inaccessible. I also developed a deep love for Asia that has continued throughout my life. When I returned, my father congratulated me and said 'You did it! No one can ever take that away from you. Well done!' Some years later I recognize that he was echoing the words of the German philosopher, Friedrich Nietzsche: 'What you have experienced, no power on earth can take from you'.

Activity: Applying the Kolb experiential learning cycle

Next time you have a significant experience, take a moment to go through the Kolb cycle. Keep a journal and note your thoughts.

10. EXPERT KNOWLEDGE AND SKILLS

It must be right. He's an expert.

Definition

An expert is a person with a high level of intelligence, skills or knowledge in a particular sphere, reinforced by publicity and honours by others, by research and by publications. Such a person may gain expert power.

Rationale

We can use the research and data produced by experts to support our arguments in meetings and projects. However, nowadays, who stays an expert for long? The information explosion has created problems even for people who specialize in one field. How can anyone keep totally up to date? Even with electronic data searches, the amount of reading is overwhelming. Nowadays 'expertness' is frequently difficult to maintain as knowledge and/or skills are changing so fast. My husband quickly found this out after finishing a computing degree: his knowledge and skills became quickly outdated.

As people move up the organizational ladder, they may gain position power but lose expert power and become less knowledgeable than their team members. This is why it is important to move decision making down the organization. Managers are frequently the least knowledgeable to make technical decisions because of a lack of specialist knowledge. Managers therefore at times have to change from the power of knowledge to the power of maintaining an overview of the whole situation (see Power Card 59, Whole picture).

In a brewery in Perth, Australia, brewing experts were recently asked to pass on their skills and knowledge down the line. Some of them resented this as they knew their expertise to be a source of power.

I met an interesting character in a country town in Australia who intrigued me. Outside his shop I saw a sign that said 'Ben Savage, Master Craftsman and Silversmith'. I was impressed and went inside and asked him how he had become a 'master craftsman'. He answered jovially, 'I had the sign painted'. He was an ex-dingo-hunter who had taken up silversmithing. Such proclamations, however, do not work unless the evidence backs up the claim. In fact, he was a highly skilled man and had won many prizes for his creations. So others were also giving him the title of 'master craftsman'.

Computing knowledge and power

Technocrats are people who wield great power through their expert knowledge and skills of computers, programming, the Internet, etc.

I recall when my husband got a new job in charge of the computing at his college, I asked him after his first day how the heads of department had reacted to him at his first meeting. Steve grinned and said 'They were very friendly. After all, they know that I control the computing software, labs and budget for their departments!' Computing knowledge certainly is powerful in today's organizations.

Here is a second example. Three years ago my sister Elizabeth, who lives in New Zealand, developed a very unusual illness called sympathetic reflex dystrophy. She was experiencing acute and chronic pain. I immediately tapped into the medical database at my university and accessed far more information than her doctor had about the disease. Then came the problem of how much to send to her, especially as some of it was so depressing. Here again it was the ability to interpret and use the data. Her doctor copied everything I sent her and the articles enabled her to ask informed questions using the language and data of the experts.

Professional organizations

Professional organizations are groups of people with similar jobs, skills or interests who join together to enhance their area of expertise and support their development and that of other members. If you are affiliated to an organization you can gain kudos, respect and (frequently) help and support from experts in your field.

For instance, when I became a teacher, before I set foot inside a classroom, my father insisted that I join the teachers' union in case there was an accident in the classroom. He pointed out that the teachers' union would automatically give me free legal advice and if necessary representation.

Membership of committees of professional organizations can also give credibility and status in the professional community. People who sit on the boards of these committees have the power of definition, that is, the thumbs up or down. They are 'gate-keepers' and 'legitimizers', in that they have the power to open doors and put their stamp of approval on new ideas.

In the present economic climate, governments are trying to suppress the use of collective bargaining in favour of individual contracts. This I believe can seriously erode the negotiating power of individual workers, especially migrants and women. But such people can contact professional organizations for expert advice or support.

Activity: reflection

What are you expert at? Think about how you relate to experts. Where can you get expert help or advice if you need it?

11. FACILITATION AND GROUP SKILLS

Enjoy the journey, that is, the process.

(Mahatma Gandhi)

Definitions

The word 'facilitation' means to make easy. Sometimes, there is confusion as the word 'facilitation' and its roots may be used as:

- a noun: a facilitator and facilitation;
- a verb: to facilitate;
- an adverb: behaving facilitively;
- an adjective: a facilitative individual or a facilitative group (namely one in which the majority of participants have facilitative mindsets and behaviours).

Facilitation concerns encouraging open dialogue amongst individuals with different perspectives so that diverse assumptions and options may be explored. This is in contrast to the current dualistic, win–lose, competitive, debating styles of discourse in Western societies.

A 'group' is two or more people who influence and interact with each other to achieve a common task. The roles of individuals may be different or at times overlapping. The terms 'group process' or 'group dynamics' refer to the ever-changing levels of physical and mental energy in a group over time. 'Process skills' also involve knowledge of individual and group processes, some of which have been described in this book – for example, brainstorming (see Power Card 4, Choices), visualization, comparison and evaluation processes like the PMI pluses, minuses and interesting points (Chapter 6).

Rationale

We live in an increasingly complex, ever changing environment. As a result, people have to join together in the workplace and communicate in groups to make plans and to solve problems. New job roles in facilitation have thereby evolved in the second half of the 20th century, and so a working knowledge of groups and their facilitation is a useful power base.

Group meetings

Group process skills and knowledge gives you an edge at meetings.

There are some people who operate by 'Robert's Rules of Order' (the formal meeting rules developed for the British Parliament in 1876), and Socratean-style debate as developed by the ancient Greeks has been seen as the 'norm' in the past for most formal meetings. In this mode, people argue for and against an idea. But in this win–lose battle, many good ideas are lost. The style of debate is guaranteed to favour the most loud, articulate and persistent individuals and the power-holders, since people tend to listen to them more and take their ideas more seriously.

From the 1970s onwards, however, more informal styles of conducting meetings have developed, some based on 'Interactive Meetings' procedures such as those developed by Doyle and Straus (1993). In these meetings, minutes are kept as 'wall minutes' in front of everyone. In this way, no ideas are lost and many ideas can be presented to people at once.

Activity: planning an agenda and being 'process aware'

Next time you plan a meeting agenda, why not try out the format described by Doyle and Straus (1993). The example plan given in Table 3.2 shows an outline for a safety campaign. Instead of one-word agenda items, phrase each as a question (this helps to communicate exactly what is required and stimulates prior thinking about issues). If people suggest items, put their names in brackets so that they are prepared to introduce the item. Work out the stages you need to go though. Often, all or some of the four stages shown are involved. A sample formulated agenda that has been developed on this basis is shown in Table 3.3.

Table 3.2 Stages of an agenda item

Content, that is, 'what?'	Process, that is, 'how?'	Time, that is, 'how long?'
Presentation of the issue	Presentation of information orally	9.00–9.05
Feedback on the issue	Round robin, for example, each person is asked to contribute in turn	9.05–9.10
Problem solving	Brainstorming or listing of ideas	9.10–9.30
Decision making	Voting or consensus formation, decision by manager etc	9.30–9.45

Introduce and discuss the purpose of the three headings in the Doyle and Straus model to colleagues. The 'chewing gum' analogy is useful to explain the concepts – that is, if someone is chewing a piece of gum: the *content* is the gum; the *process* is chewing; and the *time element* is how long the gum takes before it loses its flavour.

Table 3.3 A sample agenda

CONTENT	PROCESS	TIME
What do you want to achieve?	*How will you go about it?*	*How long will it take?*
What is the purpose of the safety campaign? (Mary)	Presentation of goals by Mary	9.00–9.05
What have other team members noticed about safety issues in the workplace?	Round robin	9.05–9.15
In how many different ways could safety measures be implemented?	Brainstorming of ideas	9.15–9.30
Which methods need to be implemented in the short term? In the long term?	Decision making	9.30–9.45

Decision making

I was lost for words (for once) when I visited one organization and a person said 'We are very democratic round here. We discuss everything and vote all the time'. Such statements merely indicate a lack of knowledge of the variety of decision-making processes available.

There are problems with voting, because it tends to lead to 'win–lose' decision making. It is fast, but frequently the 'losers' do not feel motivated to put their energies behind the motion that is passed. 'Straw-poll voting' (ie a show of hands that is not binding, but which is supposed to enable the chairperson to get a 'feel' for how people are thinking) tends to polarize thinking.

Activity: a meeting evaluation

At the end of a meeting you attend, try getting participants to evaluate how it went. Note that question 2 and 3 in the possible evaluation questionnaire shown in Figure 3.5 asks participants to make constructive suggestions for change and to take responsibility for their part in the success or failure of meetings.

Later, collate the information and feed it back to everyone at the next meeting.

Activity: ongoing learning about facilitation

Facilitation and group processes are huge bodies of learning. If you are interested in learning more, there are many references, but I would recommend finding a course in a local community centre, college or university near you. See also Heron (1989, 1993), Hogan (1999), Hunter *et al* (1992, 1995, 1998, 1999), Kiser (1998) and Tyson (1997).

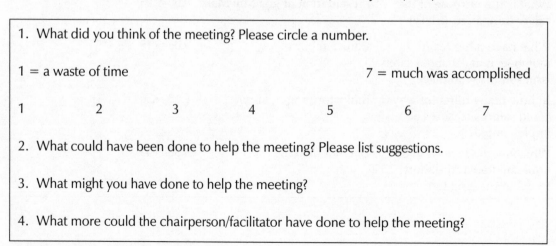

1. What did you think of the meeting? Please circle a number.

1 = a waste of time   7 = much was accomplished

1   2   3   4   5   6   7

2. What could have been done to help the meeting? Please list suggestions.

3. What might you have done to help the meeting?

4. What more could the chairperson/facilitator have done to help the meeting?

Figure 3.5 Meeting evaluation form

12. FEELINGS

The more fearful, the more nervous an athlete is, the better he performs.

(Muhammad Ali)

Definition

Feelings are physical and mental sensations. We cannot *not feel* unless we are dead.

Rationale

Feelings underlie everything we do. The power lies in how we identify, manage and harness our emotions productively, rather than suppress or deny them. Language invariably does not exactly convey how we feel at any one time.

Activity: becoming 'feeling literate'

Some people find it very hard to identify their feelings. In my experience this occurs more frequently – though not always – with men, partly due to their societal conditioning. Dick (1987: 23) suggests that it is useful to identify your feelings at many stages in your day; that is, it is not a simple linear process. Another way is to look at a list of feeling words and ask yourself to identify the feelings you are experiencing. Table 3.4 gives some words to consider when performing such an exercise.

Appropriate assertiveness

Assertiveness teaches us to use feelings to enhance communication using the following stages: 'When you...' (describe the behaviour of the other person) 'I feel...' (name feelings, for example anger, frustration, elation) 'because...' (give reasons). 'I want/would like...' (describe the desired behaviour).

Although this model is useful, it may sound very synthetic when you first try it out as a new skill. Therefore it is necessary to rehearse and/or practise. This assertion model is also based on Western values of openness and directness, and the 'receiver' of the message may feel accused of causing the feelings. People from non-Western cultures may find this approach too direct and rude. A discussion of different approaches to assertive behaviour is enlightening and useful for people of all cultures.

Table 3.4 Feeling vocabulary

Happy	Sad	Angry	Confused	Scared	Jealous	Weak	Strong	Loving	Physical
Calm	dissatisfied	annoyed	baffled	frightened	envious	deflated	able	affectionate	hungry
Amused	bad	cross	bewildered	anxious	insecure	feeble	active	warm	hot
blissful	depressed	disgruntled	chaotic	fearful	threatened	defenceless	assertive	caring	cold
alive	awful	hateful	harassed	apprehensive	dissatisfied	deficient	assured	empathetic	thirsty
bubbly	lonely	disguised	stunned	horrified	hurt	pathetic	bold	sympathetic	sexy
excited	burdened	enraged	unsure	terrified	revengeful	disabled	certain	ecstatic	shivery
delighted	dejected	exasperated	crazy	insecure	distrustful	emasculated	capable	friendly	ill
ecstatic	deflated	fed-up	dazed	jumpy	suspicious	exhausted	confident	pity	awful
cheerful	disappointed	frustrated	disorganized	worried	doubt	exposed	courageous	fondness	terrible
elated	disturbed	hostile	disoriented	nervous		vulnerable	determined	like	drunk
feel good	low	hot-tempered	distracted	panicky		frail	energetic	fancy	drugged
fine	hurt	indignant	distraught	petrified		fragile	forceful	passionate	itchy
glad	gloomy	infuriated	disturbed	shaky		gentle	firm	adoring	sweaty
great	dreary	irate	doubtful	shy		inferior	healthy	enchanted	wet
joyful	down	irritated	flustered	stunned		ill	independent	cherish	dry
loving	worthless	livid	lost	threatened		impotent	intense	tenderness	tired
marvellous	unwanted	mad	misunderstood	timid		insecure	positive	erotic	exhausted
peaceful	unloved	outraged	mixed up			passive	powerful	sexy	energetic
pleasant	unhappy	provoked	muddled			powerless	productive	desire	hurt
proud	upset	riled	nonplussed			lethargic	resistant		in pain
relieved	sorry	seething	perplexed			puny	secure		nauseous
satisfied	self-pitying	sore	puzzled			run-down	curious		relaxed
thrilled	embarrassed	stormy	surprised			sickly	desperate		tense
wonderful	grieved	uncontrollable	uncertain			unable	eager		restless
lovely	hopeless	aggressive	undecided			unfit	desirable		sensual
dismayed	miserable	bored	vague			useless			greedy
helpless	moody	cool	helpless			worn-out			
hopeless	negative	impatient	stupid			apathetic			
ashamed	painful	stubborn				guilty			
fed-up	terrible					listless			
deathly	sober								
	distressed								

(*Source: Hopson and Scally (1982) Lifeskills Teaching Programmes No 2, Lifeskills Associates, Leeds UK*)

The nonviolent communication model

Marshall Rosenberg (1999) developed a different model for what he calls 'nonviolent communication'. Rosenberg's main aim is for 'connectedness' and 'empathy' so that some sort of nonviolent dialogue will ensue. His model has four stages, and these can be invoked by both the sender and the receiver of a communication. The stages can be summarized as follows:

- *observation*: the receiver states what he/she actually observed the other person saying or doing;
- *feelings*: the receiver states how he/she feels about the action (eg pleased, irritated, frustrated);
- *needs*: the receiver states what needs connected to the feelings are not being met;
- *requests*: the receiver makes a request as a question rather than a command.

Here is an example of a trainer talking to a disgruntled participant: 'When I see you clicking your pen [observation], I feel discouraged and distracted [feelings] because I need to be able to think clearly to explain today's workshop to the group [needs]. Would you be willing to stop clicking your pen? [requests]'.

If both sender and receiver are trained in this method, some form of dialogue will usually ensue. However, a likely response from the disgruntled participant might be a grunt or negative outburst. The trainer might then respond: 'I notice from your sigh [observation] that you are feeling frustrated with being here [feelings]. Do you have a need to be somewhere else or for something else to be happening here? [needs]. Would you be willing to tell us about what is bothering you? [requests]'.

Managing fear

There are two kinds of fear: rational fear based on fact (for example, fear of fire is a useful protection against burns) and imaginative fear based on our thoughts or supposed intuition. Fear has an uncanny way of bringing forth exactly what we are afraid of. 'Fear is a coward', however, so that if you confront it, it will frequently lose its potency. Our imagination often conjures up far worse things than actually happen. Furthermore, familiarization with the frightening 'thing' can help to us to manage it or even make it go away.

The skill is to harness useful levels of adrenaline that are generated by fear. Adrenaline speeds up our thoughts and metabolism. It pumps through our bodies to make them ready for a 'fight' or 'flight' response to danger. Many people fear giving a speech in front of an audience more than death itself; however, management of that fear can heighten performance. Even experienced actors feel fear, but they learn to harness it. Susan Jeffers

(1987), in *Feel the Fear and Do It Anyway*, suggests learning to feel and manage fear rather than eliminate it.

Activity: reversing the fear

Frankl (1959) suggests that 'anticipatory anxiety' or fear may sometimes be overcome by 'paradoxical intention' – that is, a reversal of the fear. He describes a person with a deep fear of sleeplessness resulting in tensions at bedtime. Frankl suggests reversing the issue, so that a person fearful in this way should try to stay awake as long as possible.

Activity: catastrophizing

Another way to change your attitudes to your concerns or worries is to confront the underlying issues. This is sometimes called 'awfulization' or 'catastrophizing'. In this strategy you make a list of all the worst possible scenarios, and then work out what you would do if they happened. This helps you to work through issues and prepare mentally in case they occur. Often, these things *don't* happen; but if they do, you are more prepared.

Activity: handling hurt and criticism

It is useful to learn how to handle criticism gracefully. Ashley Brilliant drew a cartoon with a superb line of positive self-talk: 'I may not be perfect, but parts of me are excellent'.

We often get our egos caught up with feedback. We need to be able to listen to criticism of our personalities and/or skills and then decide whether or not we wish to adapt our behaviour as a result. One useful skill is to 'roll with the punch' rather than immediately getting defensive. If someone says 'Your work was awful', try asking for more information: 'You said my work was awful. Can you tell me which aspects you are talking about?'

Managing feelings in conflict situations

Keeping control over feelings can be useful when under time pressures or in arguments. People who remain cool even when attacked personally can give the appearance of being powerful and 'able to take it', especially if they acknowledge and empathize with the other person's anger. Also, the attackers often then appear to lose credibility. This does not mean that you should mask feelings that lead to contradictory body language. Controlled anger can be a very powerful tool. Uncontrolled anger, however, can lead to 'loss of face' and respect.

Activity: buying time

When you are angry and upset, it is often hard to think straight. A useful strategy is to 'buy time'. Try: 'Look, we're both clearly very concerned and upset about this issue. Why don't we think about it overnight and talk first thing tomorrow?'

Managing anger and negativity

The Dalai Lama is believed by Tibetan Buddhists to be the manifestation of Chenrezig, the Bodhizattva of Compassion. Despite being exiled from his homeland since 1959, he has endeavoured to wage a non-violent struggle for the liberation of Tibet. He maintains that:

> genuine compassion is based on a clear acceptance or recognition that others, like oneself, want happiness and have the right to overcome suffering. On that basis one develops some kind of concern about the welfare of others, irrespective of one's attitude to oneself. That is compassion.

> (Gyatso, 1995: 62–63)

The Dalai Lama, during his teachings in Perth in April 1992, discussed the basis of negative thoughts. He commented 'Negative thoughts do not hurt the person you are angry with, only you'. If thoughts develop into anger, we cannot be sure if the outcomes will be positive or negative. Because anger is blind, it eclipses part of our brain related to our rationality. So the energy of anger is always unreliable, and we need to look at the controlled energy of a compassionate attitude, reason and patience (Gyatso, 1992).

Activity: drawing anger

Anger is usually seen as a negative emotion. However, it is energy that motivates us to try to solve problems. Bilodeau (1992) and Kaplan (1994) have developed exercises on management of anger in conflict situations. Here is an example.

Find some coloured pens and draw your perception of anger. Put your drawing to one side. Now list times in your life when you were angry and when your anger energized you into some form of *positive* action. Take another sheet of paper and redraw anger. Are there any changes in your perception?

Kaplan made a study of the way people draw anger (1994). At the beginning of her workshops, she asks participants to draw anger. Many commonalties usually develop – for example, the use of strong red, orange and black colours, and angular figures and designs. At the end of her workshops she asks for a redrawing and invites discussion. Marked changes in the graphics occur as participants widen their perceptions of this emotion.

See also Power Card 40, Positive mindsets.

13. GOAL SETTING

Alice to Cheshire cat:	Could you please tell me where I should go from here?
Cat to Alice:	It all depends on where you want to get to
Alice:	It doesn't really matter
Cat (with great disdain):	Well in that case it doesn't matter which direction you go in, does it?

(Lewis Carroll, *Alice in Wonderland*)

Definition

Goals are dreams with deadlines – our aims and purpose in life. You cannot have goals without dreams. Goals are the targets or the end results of our ambitions. People, groups and organizations have goals. Goals give meaning and purpose to our lives. Friedrich Nietzsche commented: 'He who has a why to live can bear almost any how'.

Viktor Frankl (1959) refers to this quotation in his description of himself and other prisoners in a concentration camp in the Second World War. If fellow inmates became listless and lost the will to live, Frankl would try to find out what a person might live for. He himself was motivated to survive to rewrite the manuscript of his book that had been destroyed by the Nazis. Others chose to live for the day when they would see loved ones again, or resume their careers.

Rationale

The incident outlined in the *Alice in Wonderland* story above could be encapsulated into 'If you don't know where you are going, you may end up somewhere else'. Goals give us direction and meaning in life.

Drona and Arjun, from the Mahabharata

In the *Mahabharata*, the famous Indian epic story, there is an excerpt that illustrates the need for total concentration on a goal. It focuses on Drona, who in Ancient India was the teacher of royalty, a guru of martial arts, especially archery.

One day, Drona decided to give his apprentices a test in archery. He chose a fine tree in the distance and placed a wooden bird high in its branches. The first prince arrived and Drona asked him to draw back his bow and aim at the target and said, 'What do you see?' The prince replied, 'I see the forest and the trees.'

A second prince arrived and was asked the same question. 'What do you see?' asked Drona. The apprentice responded, 'I see a wooden bird in the branch of a tree.'

After some time Arjun arrived and was asked the same question. He paused, raised his bow very slowly, and fixed his view along the sight of the arrow. 'What do you see?' said Drona. 'I see the eye of the bird,' he replied. Drona smiled and said 'My son, you have truly achieved mastery. I am proud of you.'

Guidelines for goal setting

If empowerment is about taking charge of your life, then it follows that spending some time in setting goals will help you to expend your energies in the right direction. Here are some suggestions:

- Think about your values in life first, for these will underpin any goals you set.
- Try to describe and visualize your goals.
- Set stretching but realistic goals. For example, if you are writing a book and tell everyone you are writing a best-seller, and then only 2,000 copies are sold, you will appear to have failed. However, if you tell people you are writing your first book and hope to sell 2,000 copies, you will achieve your objective.
- If you have a particularly big goal, it may help if you divide it up into small, achievable steps.
- Pin up some sayings that appeal to you. For example, 'Take every day as it comes' is the advice given by many different organizations all over the world. 'Seize the day' was the catch phrase of the schoolmaster in *Dead Poet's Society*. Alcoholics Anonymous works on the principle that alcoholics can learn to say 'I won't have a drink today' and thereby achieve a small goal. 'Yesterday is history, tomorrow is a mystery, concentrate on today'. To try and give up alcohol for a lifetime is an overpowering goal for some people. At the beginning, alcoholics work on each minute, then each hour, and then each day.

Goal setting in career planning and lifestyle

Goal setting is not for everyone. Some people prefer a more relaxed view to life and like to 'take every day as it comes'. Indeed some would argue that excessive goal setting leads to continual striving and dissatisfaction. In time-management programmes, there is now more focus on identification of overall values and lifestyle concepts before focusing on goals and associated action plans. The following story illustrates this.

The millionaire and the boat

The story of 'The Millionaire and the Boat' (source unknown) can be used to lighten the seriousness of career-planning workshops and stimulate thinking about the value differences that underpin our career and life aspirations.

A millionaire had just arrived at a tropical island in his whale-sized white yacht. He walked along a jetty and met a local fisherman. They sat staring out to the turquoise sea talking. The fisherman described his simple, subsistence level existence and pointed proudly to a rather old and flaking boat moored in the harbour.

The millionaire was not impressed and said, 'If you take your boat out twice a day, instead of once, you could make a profit and gradually you could build up enough money to get a loan from the bank and then you could buy another boat then get another loan and then get a fleet. Then you will be able to be like me and go off for vacations on a yacht to an island like this.'

The puzzled fisherman looked at him, shook his head in bewilderment and replied, 'But I'm already here.'

Activity: maintaining balanced goals

The advert jingle 'A Mars a day helps you work, rest and play' is useful here. Three aspects of our lives need to be kept in balance. Use the information in Table 3.5 to identify your values, goals and tasks trying to ensure that you give equal balance in your work, family/social and relaxation/sleep lives. As you note down goals under each column be aware of any gaps.

Remember that you should be getting on average six to eight hours of sleep per night. Many workaholics regularly go into 'sleep deficit' but sleep deprivation is the first strategy

Table 3.5 Values, goals and tasks: achieving a balance

Work values	Family/social values	Relaxation/sleep values
Work goals	**Family/social goals**	**Relaxation/sleep goals**
Work tasks	**Family/social tasks**	**Relaxation/sleep tasks**

used to torture and disorientate people (Coren, 1997). If your work column is full, but there is little in the other two columns, spend time on developing them *and* appropriate action plans to make them happen. Tell your family and friends about these goals and elicit their help and support. People rarely lie on their death beds wishing they had spent more time at work. Plan some rewards or activities to celebrate the successful completion of your goals.

Problems of obsessive goal setting

James Thurber once said, 'Those who are hell-bent usually get where they're going'. However, there is a contradiction here. It must be remembered that obsessive, single-minded goal directed behaviour may mitigate against the accomplishment of other activities, may be selfish, may even hurt others, and may lead to uncompromising single-minded behaviour.

Some obsessive goal-setters forget to rest and celebrate achievements. As a result, they are on a constant treadmill and never seem satisfied.

Remember, too, that not all goals retain their validity over time. Viktor Frankl and the chief doctor in a concentration camp (described above) noticed a dramatic increase in the death rate beyond all previous records between Christmas 1944 and New Year 1945. There was no increased workload or disease, and the only explanation they could think of was that the majority of prisoners had been clinging to a belief that the war would end by Christmas 1944. As they lost hope and courage, their power of resistance decreased and many died.

See also Power Cards 4 (Choices) and 27 (Mind flexibility).

14. HUMOUR/LAUGHTER

A laugh a day keeps the doctor away.

Definition

Humour may be defined from two perspectives: the skill to make others laugh, and the ability to laugh at oneself and with (rather than at) others.

Rationale

Having a sense of humour and the ability to laugh at our problems helps us to keep life in perspective. Chimpanzees and gorillas laugh, but only after being physically tickled (so don't go around the zoo trying to tell them jokes). Our sense of humour was developed early on in our evolution. It is a vital part of our humanity.

When you laugh, all sorts of great things happen to your body and mind. It's like having an internal aerobic work-out. The study of laughter, or 'gelotology', by William Fry (1987) at the Stanford Medical School and others reveals that when you laugh:

- endorphins are released in your brain, which give you a high;
- your lungs get exercised as you take in more air;
- your heart rate is increased;
- any anger is defused;
- you burn off some kilojoules;
- your digestion improves;
- stress, anxiety and depression are lessened.

Five types of humour

There are five different types of humour based on our psychological needs. Each will be briefly described in turn, and I have added two more to the list.

- *Aggressive humour.* This may involve punitive 'put-downs' or insults to others or yourself and can be potentially depowering. However, for aggressive people it may be an antidote to violence, so that they may get their 'kicks' from this kind of verbal abuse. I heard of one manager who thought it was funny to say to someone, 'See me on Monday' (without adding the context) 'That will give him something to chew on over the weekend'. Some joke!
- *Sexual humour.* There are two kinds of sexual humour: disappointment and enjoyment. Sexual humour should be used very sparingly in groups in case it causes offence.
- *Intellectual humour.* This involves spurs, plays on words, puns, goon-type humour, and satire. In Australia, 'chiak' is used as good-humoured banter to send up people and situations.
- *Defence-mechanism humour.* Here you can make jokes at your own expense and send yourself or the situation up. On holiday, when we tend to get into really difficult situations, Steve and I tend to laugh and say 'This is us enjoying ourselves, ha ha… relaxing on holiday ha ha… We worked all year for this. We could be at home in a comfortable house, with our feet up with the cats…'.
- *Social/political humour.* This can be useful for bonding and team building in the workplace. It is best used when there are no victims, and so stay clear of racial jokes or jokes at the expense of other departments that could be a sign of 'group think'.

- *Sarcasm.* This is regarded as the lowest form of humour as it usually means getting laughter at someone else's expense. It can be very depowering.
- *Pythonesque humour.* 'Pythonesque' humour exaggerates and can be used to turn a serious moment into a funny, but nevertheless highly poignant, encounter. If someone is really verbally attacking you and you are aggressively protecting yourself, it is possible quickly to change tack and imitate John Cleese. For example, exaggerate and say, 'Oh… so it's all my fault! I'm a worthless beast, it's all my fault…'. This is a John Cleese type of Monty Python/Basil Fawlty answer. If you are lucky, the aggressor will see the funny side of things and start laughing; if not, you may need to try something else! Using humour is a risk: sometimes it may backfire, but it is a skill that can be learnt.

The ability to laugh

During my stay in Nepal, I observed that the Nepalese have an incredible capacity to laugh and smile, even under duress. One day, in a bus I observed our cramped conditions alongside chickens, sacks of potatoes, rice, etc. Every time the bus lurched violently through potholes, my fellow passengers laughed. In Australia, in the same conditions we may have laughed once and then we would usually have started to complain that it was about time the government repaired the road. The Nepalese appeared very stoical and light-hearted.

The propensity for laughter amongst the Nepalese sometimes causes cross-cultural misunderstandings. A Danish colleague in a workshop told how he had fallen over and hurt his leg and was so hurt because a passing Nepali had 'laughed his head off'. Meanwhile the Nepalese in the room were also laughing (and so soon were the Danish participants as the laughter was contagious). This led to instructive explanations: the Nepalese explained that they were reared by their parents to laugh at mishaps in life as a way of managing and coping with life's many problems.

The value of humour

Humour and emotional shifts in groups

John Heron (1989) talks about the use of 'emotional shifts' that can be used by facilitators to lift a group whose thinking is becoming too serious and bogged down. For example: 'Of course I talk through my head at times – some people say all of the time'. Laughter releases tension and uplifts the spirit.

'Joking about a situation involves a sense of self-detachment. Viktor Frankl (1959) describes his reaction and that of others to the strip-search on entering a concentration camp. Having been shaved, they were then told to shower. Immediately, Frankl realized that he had been stripped of all his past and his future. Some joking started: 'Well at least the water here is real'. They were clinging on to some sense of reality. They were not trying to demean their awful plight; however being united in some nervous giggles helped them from breaking down immediately.

Humour can be used as a form of 'political *aikido*' to defuse a potentially explosive situation. A joke in a tense meeting can defuse a hostile atmosphere and get people out of a tense, blocking mindset. For example: 'Well, well, aren't we doing well? We've been here only 15 minutes and already World War Three has broken out!' Telling a joke in a group is a risk, but it can be very powerful if it works. But you have to be careful that the intervention does not sound sarcastic.

Telling 'in' jokes about a funny, past, shared experience can heighten the sense of in-group identity (and also exclude others). It can be used to divert or deflate criticism. Mild humour at your own expense can give the impression that you are a person who can laugh at yourself, and it doesn't have the risk of offending others.

Humour and giving feedback

Humour is a powerful communication tool. It can be used to give some feedback and may enable you to trigger some insight in another person – even to bring home some unpalatable truths in a palatable way. I once lived in a flat with five other people. We had a whiteboard in the kitchen and communicated with each other (telling people to do their share of the household work etc) by writing humorous insults.

Humour to cover mistakes

Humour can also be a recovery tool. You can sometimes use it to get yourself out of an embarrassing situation. Public speakers regularly turn a mistake into a joke, and their audiences warm even more to them as a result. For example, if someone spots a spelling mistake in an overhead transparency, the speaker could reply, 'Ah so you are awake! Excellent! I put that there to see if you were paying attention'.

Activities to enhance humour in your life

Here are some suggestions to develop the power of humour:

● Try 'humour immersion': seek out humour that you enjoy; get some videos of comedy shows you like. Analyse the humour they use. Save some of the jokes to use with your friends. Work out what makes you laugh and learn to use that technique.

- Try it out, take a risk.
- Get playful/silly with other adults or with kids.
- Develop a sense of lightness. Learn to giggle; wear something funny.
- Stick up cartoons around your work area or on a mirror that you look in first thing in the morning.
- Collect jokes and keep them in a small notebook as an *aide mémoire*.
- Try a joke to defuse tension at a meeting.
- Try out your humour in lifts, hospital queues, at supermarket checkouts.

15. ILLUSION

You need serious hair.

(Line from the film *Working Girl*)

Definition

Illusion is the act of changing appearance, demeanour and statements in order to impress or deceive. For example, there are many symbols in our society that give the illusion of power: white coats, padded shoulders, power dressing, furnishings, and sitting behind a big desk in a large office with deep carpets and expensive decor.

Rationale

At times, there is a fine dividing line between illusion power and real power. You need to be able to distinguish between the two, and at times it is useful to know how to create the illusion of power for your own purposes.

The prime minister's trappings of office

Symbols of power create an illusion of power. In 1977, we returned to Kathmandu to find work. My husband used his newly acquired surveying skills on the Tribhuvan International Airport runway survey. I cycled round the valley furiously on a red bike, taking slides for teaching kits for social studies. We lived on Steve's local wages and had just enough to eat. One weekend, Steve's manager lent us one of the cars that had been leased from the Prime Minister by the project consortium. It was a fine car and had the Prime Minister's crest on the front.

We decided to drive up to the Chinese border. On approaching the checkpoints along the road, we were somewhat abashed and embarrassed as booms were quickly lifted and patrols jumped to attention and saluted as we passed. We have always enjoyed trekking and meeting local villagers. Our impoverished financial state meant that we stayed in Sherpa lodges, but we found it very difficult to hide the car and its illusion of wealth and power in little villages along the way. I am sure we were the subject of much village gossip for months afterwards.

Power and uniforms

A clinical nurse specialist in Human Resource Development recently told me about how nurses had depowered themselves from their former formidable military-style uniforms to the simple shifts that made them look like 'supermarket checkout chicks'.

When she was promoted, this nursing specialist was allowed to wear 'civvies'. She noticed immediately that, when she turned up for work in an expensive suit, high heels, etc, doctors and specialists smiled and spoke to her more frequently and in a more collegial fashion. Her network in the hospital changed immediately. When she went into work in her uniform, orderlies and nurses spoke to her more. She said 'If I want to get something done, I think about who I have to go to see and dress accordingly'.

The illusion of power, especially through dress and symbols of power such as a doctor's white coat, were illustrated by the Milgram (1963) experiments described in Chapter 2.

Bluff as an illusion

In the story of *Alice in Wonderland*, there is a scene where Alice encounters the wicked queen, who immediately points at Alice and shouts, 'Off with her head'. Alice in a very imperious tone quickly retorts, 'Nonsense!' and the queen shuts her gaping mouth and goes silent. There is power in bluff and bluster. For instance, 'We are conducting enquiries' is a frequent blocking comment made to stall outsiders trying to make complaints within bureaucracies.

Activity: dress codes

Observe the dress codes and furniture layout of others. What is your style? Remember empowerment: choosing to be yourself or adapting yourself when you choose. What do you want to convey to people through your style of dress etc? What do you choose to change in different circumstances – for example, for job interviews?

See also the power of the individual.

16. INFLUENCING POWERFUL PEOPLE

I've got friends in high places.

Definition

Powerful people may be influenced by being given information, and by being lobbied or persuaded to support a project or new idea.

The word 'lobbying' stems from the right of British citizens to walk into the lobby of the House of Commons and request to see their Member of Parliament (if the House is sitting).

Rationale

Some people feel intimidated by powerful people, while others feel it is unethical to lobby (see brown-nosing below). Like it or not, powerful people hold aspects of power that are useful to tap into. Powerful people cannot be ignored or left out of projects.

Consciously giving information to power-holders

I was once employed in Technical and Further Education to help initiate training courses for the unemployed in order to respond quickly to community demands. One mistake our team made was that at times we were so busy 'doing' work with unemployed people that we often forgot to promote our successes with the conservative administration at Head Office.

We changed this by inviting power-holders to morning coffee to meet co-ordinators, who told them about their successes and needs. We also hired a well-respected academic researcher to evaluate our team from the perspective of the community. The resulting document was used to support our case for further funding.

One community project officer who continually invited politicians and local dignitaries to meet and talk with the unemployed in her centre also impressed me. The visitors quickly came to understand the pressures on the young unemployed and not to categorize them all as 'spongers'. She also encouraged the youngsters to attend local council meetings, and Rotary and Rotoract clubs as a way of dispelling myths in the community. In this way, support was gained for local projects and the young unemployed became more empowered.

Some people feel it is wrong to lobby people of higher rank or status about their projects.

This is understandable. I was interested at a meeting recently when one person voiced concerns about lobbying. We were involved in developing a policy paper that would be presented at a major board meeting. Another participant answered by saying 'People frequently are flattered that you take the trouble to contact them before a meeting'.

It is interesting to question the morality of lobbying. The advantages are you may give individuals more information about your project. Remember, though, that it may also give them time to think about it and get their opposing views ready beforehand. So lobbying does not just benefit the lobbyist.

In Japan, creative ideas at meetings are almost frowned upon as they may embarrass important people. There it is an accepted practice to visit people individually beforehand to explain and lobby for support.

Political lobbying

Lobbying at high levels is a very complex process. As a result, some organizations actually employ professional, specialist lobbyists to push their cause at political levels. In getting powerful people on side, it is useful to think of the future: it is a mistake to depend on one or two champions since they may not always be around to offer support.

Lobbying can be very useful before meetings. It allows you to find out the objections of others and answer any qualms they may have before an open debate. They may help you rethink your proposal by pointing out some flaws before you go public with your ideas. If you need more skills in open debate at meetings, ask a friend to role-play the opposition, taking a devil's advocate role. This will help you to answer difficult questions from power-holders apparently 'on your feet'.

A senior nurse administrator told me about how she wanted to bring about change in her organization 'I did a force-field analysis of those for and against the change. I then compiled a list and went to see each person individually (ie both those for and against the change) until I had worn them all down'. It was a carefully calculated process.

Three approaches to get funding

The division of funding amongst departments in large organizations often leads to fights over resources, especially money. Here are three different ways to approach requests for funding:

- *The 'foot in the door' technique.* When I was at secondary school, the nuns required huge sums of money for major building campaigns. They first of all got parents involved in fund-raising projects; they then got the support of local politicians. They started the building project even though they did not have the full amount of capital, saying 'God will provide'. They later came back to the parents and the politicians to ask for more. Having identified themselves as patrons of the school, parents and politicians granted the next request in order to protect the first investment – in other words they backed their first decision, or else it may have made the first decision look foolish.

- *The 'Afghan' technique.* The opposite tactic to this is what I call the 'Afghan bargaining tactic' and is often used when asking for funding. In this approach, you request far more than you actually need, because you expect to be cut back. When travelling overland through Afghanistan in 1971 (before the Russian invasion), I was impressed by the proud Afghan people and their prowess at bargaining. I noticed with surprise many empty buildings in the middle of the desert. When I asked what they were, the local people informed me that they were hospitals. Before the Russian invasion, the United States and the USSR were vying to give aid in order to gain political influence in the country. The Afghans, expecting to be cut back, in true haggling style asked for far more hospital buildings than they needed (and nothing for staffing and running the institutions). The aid givers nevertheless complied.

- *The bottom line, truthful technique.* Recently my husband used a third tactic, namely open truth. He assertively put in a request for funding at work, writing to the senior administrators: 'This is the sum we need for this project, I am not exaggerating knowing that you will cut me back. This is the amount we need; any less and the project won't work'. In other words he was open about his 'bottom line'. The administrators only granted part of the money, and so my husband returned it saying he could not do the project properly. They then sent him the full amount. When using this tactic, it is important to carry out what you say; otherwise you could lose face if the other party doesn't back down. (It is worth noting that this doesn't always work the first time. My husband had carefully worked on developing and maintaining his reputation for being an open and straight administrator.)

The first two of the tactics above are contradictory and you need to think carefully about which is most appropriate to your situation. The foot-in-the-door tactic cannot be used too frequently and the second request should not follow the first too quickly.

The power of people who appear to have less power

Do not ignore people who appear to be of lower status than you in your workplace. When I started teaching, my father, a headmaster in an inner-city London school, gave me a piece of advice: 'Introduce yourself early on to the school caretaker and the cleaners. Get to know them and their roles. Never ever talk down to them. They know everything that's going on'.

His advice was very useful. School caretakers and cleaners who understand you and what you are trying to achieve will put up with mess and untidiness (my forte). They also tend to know more about what is going on behind the scenes than most!

The same is true in the case of (unelected) secretaries, advisers and press officers of politicians and other powerful people. Never underestimate the power of personal assistants who are often the 'gate-keepers' who can either block or open doors for you.

Activity: a support map

Draw a map of the people you know in your organization – both inside and outside your department – that you can contact for help or support. What do you notice? Are there any gaps inside and outside your department?

17. INFORMATION AND ITS RETRIEVAL

Knowledge is power.

Definition

Information and knowledge are things that are held to be true. The quote 'Knowledge is power' is a frequently used quotation, but it is simplistic. Knowledge is only power if:

- it is up to date and relevant;
- you know how to analyse, synthesize, react to and act upon it;
- you know how to find out whether and how the data has been manipulated or edited and/or presented from a particular viewpoint.

Rationale

Information and knowledge are fast becoming one of the most democratic forms of power (Toffler, 1991). Access to computer databases and the Internet gives us all almost limitless resources of data. However, there is a lot of skill required in analysing and identifying the quality and relevance of the data. This is a threat to those governments who wish to control thinking and/or keep things quiet – to control not just data but up-to-date data, relevant data, speed of retrieval and an ability to mix, match and cross-reference previously unrelated information.

Public and private information sources

Information gathering may be boring, but it is essential. There are two kinds of information:

- *Public information, both formal and informal.* In organizations, there are the formal power structures, as shown in diagrams of chains of command, and then there are the informal power structures, which do *not* necessarily relate to legitimate or position power or chains of command. It is always useful to get to know the people who know the real power-holders in the bureaucracy.
- *Private information.* This is frequently the latest and most up-to-date that you can obtain from your network or the notorious grapevine. In some organizations, people save this private information until it is politically useful.

Electronic databases

It is also useful to obtain electronic skills in information generation and retrieval: skills to do with general computing, electronic mail, databases, fax machines, etc. It is important not only to know how to access the data but also how the software is structured.

MeetingWorks is a software package used for electronic meetings held in synchronous time. Individuals can key in their own ideas, which are then scrambled with data from different terminals and displayed on a screen anonymously for discussion. At the end of a meeting, people cannot go into the database later and find out who said what. This is an important point that people need to know so that they can be open in their input of ideas.

Technocrats in organizations are now immensely powerful. The programmer who sets up an organization's information system may in fact be an 'electronic gatekeeper' who only allows a limited number of people in the organization access to certain categories of information.

Activity: data sources

Think about all the sources of data you access for your job. Are there any sources that you need to become *au fait* with? Are there any people who are gatekeepers of information that you need to get to know?

18. INSPIRATIONAL TOTEMS

I never go anywhere without my teddy bear.

(Steve, environmental scientist)

Definition

Inspirational totems, charms and amulets have been used by people of all civilizations since time immemorial. A totem is something with magical powers for the owner/wearer – for example, a precious stone, medallion or horseshoe. An amulet wards off danger and misfortune (eg the evil eye), whereas a talisman is believed to have some magical potency for the wearer to attract good luck and repel evil (Valiente, 1975).

Traditional charms like the *ankh* (which represents life and immortality) and the scarab (which represents resurrection and eternal life) originated in ancient Egypt. The swastika is even older and was used in prehistoric times by American Indians and Mexicans as well as Tibetans and Indians. The word 'swastika' comes from Sanskrit and means 'happiness' or 'well-being'. It is a shame that Hitler used this symbol for such evil purposes.

Rationale

Many people, from all walks of life, have charms or totems that give them support. Some regard the use of totems as idiosyncratic. Remember, however, 'Whatever makes you strong' as long as it does not hurt anyone.

There is a wide variety of uses of totems, which may serve different functions. For example:

- protecting self and others;
- extending the power of self or good luck;
- comforting oneself;
- healing;
- gaining power;
- 'scapegoating': releasing problems onto something exterior to oneself.

Holy water for protection

I remember when my father had first learnt to drive. He hired a car to take his mother on a day trip from London to the seaside. I remember that as kids we were very excited about the excursion. My grandmother was made comfortable in the passenger seat while we packed the last few items into the boot. My father jumped into the driver's seat – and then leapt out in horror feeling his very wet trousers. My grandmother (a devout Catholic) had sprinkled liberal amounts of 'holy water' on his seat so that we would have a safe journey! She was also wearing her St Christopher medal in a prominent place around her neck. Maybe she did not trust my father's driving!

Spiritual icons and relics

Religions and belief systems have a variety of icons and symbols: crucifix, scapula, relics, the Star of David. Some religions maintain totems from earlier times.

When I worked as a governess in Greece, I remember the evil eye medal pinned onto a new baby's pillow to provide protection from 'the evil eye', jealousy and the evil wishes of others. The family belonged to the Greek Orthodox religion, but the evil-eye custom related back far beyond the beginnings of Christianity. An icon is an image in the form of a painting or statue utilized in the Greek and Russian orthodox churches. They are not worshipped as such; however, possessing – or even just kissing – an icon, medal or relic gives believers comfort and a sense of power over their problems.

In Muslim communities a traditional amulet is the figure of a hand representing the Hand of Fatima, the daughter of Mohammed. However, it is believed that the symbol of the hand was used in pre-Islamic times to ward off the peril of the evil eye.

Activity: stress dolls and comfort

In Nicaragua, children are given tiny three-inch-high cloth dolls. They are encouraged to tell their problems to these dolls and put them under their pillows at night. When in trouble, 'hug your teddy' is not as silly as it may seem.

A lecturer friend of mine suggested that I should take my favourite teddy to bed after a particularly traumatic event at work. I must admit my husband was rather surprised; however, it was a very real comfort. Try it sometime!

Worry beads

Worry beads in Greece and the Middle-Eastern countries provide a legitimate role for restless hands. This has a rhythmic, calming centring effect. Being able to do something with ones hands is important especially if people feel anxious, nervous or embarrassed.

Worry beads are useful for people who are trying to give up smoking as it gives them something to do with their hands. In some cultures, beads may be used for meditation or prayer – for example, rosary beads.

Power animals

The American Indians assign to each person a 'power animal'. I rather liked this idea and chose as my animal a cat. This is rather useful, because in times of distress my cat can grow into a lion. I carry a small three-inch cat in my bag. Imagine my surprise during a workshop when an engineer, Steve Appleyard (quoted above) took out his power animal: a two-inch teddy bear. Many people in the room appeared shocked at first, but it really helped to open up the conversation regarding what things people used to help them through difficult situations.

Taking power by destroying symbols

It was interesting to watch the changes in the USSR and East Germany in the late 1980s and early 1990s. As communism was overthrown, it was the symbols of power that were quickly attacked and dismantled – the Berlin wall and the statues of Stalin in Moscow, for example. The same occurs in government departments every time there is a change of party. Names and logos get changed, at enormous expense to the taxpayer.

Activity: inspirational totems

Look around your home and those of your friends and ask them if they use any inspirational totems to help them through situations. You will be surprised at what you find out. Or, if you like the idea of totems, choose a power animal for yourself and, if you feel like it, buy yourself a small replica.

19. INTUITION

It is by logic that we prove. It is by intuition that we discover
(Jules Henri Poincaré, French philosopher and mathematician, 1854–1912)

Definition

Intuition is the immediate, unreasoned, sense or feeling that guides our decisions about people, places, incidents and things. So what is intuition? It is often referred to as identifying and listening to gut feelings. The word comes from the Latin *intueri*, meaning 'to look upon, to see within, to consider or contemplate'. A dictionary definition cited by Goldberg (1983) describes it as 'The act or faculty of knowing directly, without the use of a rational process'.

Rationale

Intuition is an untapped power and wisdom within us that is a legitimate help in many different circumstances (Goldberg, 1983). The Age of Reason in the 18th century, and the development of rationalism and empiricism, led to a belief that intuition was invalid. However, ancient and modern philosophers (Plato and Spinoza, Nietzsche and Bergson) all allude to a higher form of knowing. Psychologists such as Carl Jung, Abraham Maslow, Jerome Bruner and Malcolm Westcott all acknowledge the importance of intuition.

Intuition has many characteristics: it is non-sequential, serendipitous, inexplicable, non-linear, holistic, flash-like, often visual, often kinaesthetic. We often describe it as a 'gut feeling', 'I felt it in my bones', 'I felt a cold chill'. Intuition is part of rational thinking, but more than speeded-up rational thinking, it moves in leaps. It is unexpected and not automatic. It cannot be contrived or ordered. It has many facets. Intuition is one of many skills that differentiates human beings from computers. You may sense that a stranger is 'OK', or you may know intuitively not to trust him/her.

The operation of intuition

A gut feeling may tell us to take a new job or turn it down, to go on a journey or to cancel. Again, the skill is to separate wishful thinking and fear from intuition. Operative intuition is a very useful skill in business. It is often referred to as 'luck'. Some people say that 'availability' is a sixth sense – being in the right place at the right time.

Gender bias

Western society has allowed women to develop intuition more than men. But using intuition is a skill that can be developed. A person with low self-esteem may translate a mistrust or lack of confidence as intuition. Goldberg suggests that we need 'Not just more intuition, but better intuition' (1983: 28).

Activity: ways to use intuition

Goldberg suggests a number of ways to give direction to our intuition:

- determine the real problem;
- express it in writing by completing sentences such as:

  - 'What I know about the situation is…'
  - 'What I don't know is…'
  - 'The thing that bothers me is…'
  - 'Some of the things that might happen are…'
  - 'Other people think…'

Goldberg further suggests that as language is a rational linear process, it could be useful to involve other senses and thought patterns. For instance, you could:

- draw or paint the situation in colour, both realistically and as an abstract;
- play a representation of the situation on a musical instrument, or sing it;
- mime or dance it;
- create a symbol for it.

Goldberg warns not to force the process and recommends the motto of the Zen swordsmen: 'Expect nothing; be prepared for anything'.

Sometimes it is necessary to allow a period of rest, withdrawal or incubation. Meditation and/or sleep time is useful as the mind continues its work. Winston Churchill and Thomas Edison both slept comparatively little at night and took many 'cat naps' during the day.

How do we stop ourselves from being misled? Goldberg suggests keeping an intuitive journal to heighten our awareness and evaluation of intuitive sensations. It allows us to monitor which were successful intuitions and which were faulty, using the processes mentioned above.

20. LAW

The law is on my side.

Definition

The law is a compilation of rules that govern the behaviour of a community, state or country.

Rationale

Many countries now have labour laws to:

- protect the rights of individuals;
- ensure that they receive proper treatment in society;
- prevent age, racial, sex and disability discrimination;
- improve the position of women through affirmative action.

The power of the law is only usually invoked as a last resort after negotiation, mediation and other conflict-resolution processes have failed.

Advantages with invoking the legal system

Various forms of legislation have certainly improved the workplace and society, in general dramatically in Western Europe and the United States since the draconian times of the Industrial Revolution. Even the threat of invoking the legal system can nowadays be a power base in itself.

An offer I could refuse

Soon after I started work at a university, one of the more senior staff members, named Raymond, came to my room. It started off as a social call – 'How are you settling in?' – which I appreciated. Then the tack of the conversation changed: 'Um, Chris, you know you could do some consulting for us (he was co-owner of a successful company). There are a lot of advantages for you, like getting your typing done etc. However, if you continue to consult with Adventure World (the outdoor company I had worked with since 1983) I could not involve you with consulting work through my company'. I was completely taken aback. The ironic thing was that, for various reasons, I did not want to be associated with this person or his company.

After he left my office, I slumped down in my chair, shocked and angry at his threat. I had the added problem that I couldn't talk to anyone on the staff for advice. I rang the Legal Aid Department to find out my rights as regards fair trading. The Legal Aid lawyer told me the relevant pages and statutes to quote. His basic advice was 'You've got to bluff it out, really'. I worked out on paper three levels of reasoning with which to confront Raymond.

When Raymond returned, he visited me in my new and permanent office. When we had got over the pleasantries, I took the initiative. 'Raymond, I want you to withdraw your threat.' It was his turn to look shocked and he blustered that he had not threatened me. I went to stage two, appealing for the good of our future working relationship. He still did not respond so I went to stage three: 'According to page xx of the Fair Trading Act... etc.' Again he blustered and said he was not threatening me, but repeated his stipulation of where I consulted and with whom. I then got up very slowly... and silently... and walked to the door... I opened it and stood stock-still signalling from my own power base for him to go. (I could hardly believe it had gone this far.

I admit I had mentally rehearsed this move for use as a last resort but I had never done anything like it before.) He left. I sensed a feeling of finding my inner personal power, that I had rights, and that I was not going to be pushed around.

Problems with invoking the legal system

There are disadvantages to using the power of the law because:
- it is adversarial and often counters or prevents mediation;
- it frequently results in win–lose decisions;
- it is very time-consuming and stressful;
- it involves terminology that is often alien to most non-lawyers;
- it often requires the payment of high legal costs.

21. LETTING GO

Definition

Human beings have a wonderful capacity to become involved in relationships and with projects, places and things. But life is impermanent. We need to learn when to move on, but this is not always easy.

Rationale

Sometimes, persevering with something may be detrimental to health and well-being, and it may be necessary to 'let go'. The problem is to know *when* to let go. If a project or relationship is not working, there is the power of strategic retreat.

Letting go in Hong Kong

I have a tendency to persevere no matter what. When I was living in Hong Kong with my husband, I was crusading for what many others and I considered unjust employment practices. This resulted in a labour tribunal court case that lasted almost two years. Half-way through, my father suggested that I should 'let go'. I almost did; however, through persevering, my health and quality of life suffered deeply.

My tenacity was a trait that I had learnt through my convent schooling, but I had not learnt when to stop, and as a result I lost weight and became anorexic. I returned to Hong Kong 10 years later to lay that ghost.

The letting-go ritual

Letting go can be joyful. At other times it may involve mourning and loss. In order to let go of something, it is often necessary to have some form of 'ritual'.

When my sister left convent grammar school, she and her friends went down to Tower Bridge in London and ceremonially threw their school hats (which they had always hated) into the River Thames. I suppose they were trying to rid themselves of some of the school constraints that they rebelled against, and that they wanted to mark their passage into adulthood. Do you remember, too, the song 'I'm gonna wash that man right out of my hair' from the film *South Pacific*? The heroine, Mitzi Gaynor, sang as she ceremonially wiped her lover out of her life; the tangled relationship was being washed down the drain as she washed her hair.

See also Power Card 54, Spirituality.

Activity: implement letting-go rituals

Another way of doing this letting-go is to write down all the things that are annoying you and then tear up the paper into small pieces and throw them out. Or, in a safe place, set fire to the pieces of paper (away from smoke detectors; otherwise you could get very wet!).

You can develop your own rituals for letting go of some issue in your life. You can either involve others or do it alone. A friend of mine, whose husband had been killed, after deep grieving had her home redecorated and garden landscaped as a way of 'moving on' to the next stage of her life.

22. LOVE

Love conquers all.

(Geoffrey Chaucer, *The Canterbury Tales*)

Definition

Love is intense, unselfish attraction. I think all of us can recount stories of incredible hardship and problems being overcome through human love for other individuals. This love can take many forms: paternal, maternal, fraternal, sororal, platonic, homosexual or heterosexual.

Rationale

Love is a major energizing power source. We cannot develop or exist as human beings without it. It is one of the most beautiful and strong powers that human beings have – and it is limitless.

Love and animals

Love of animals can help alleviate illness, stress and old age. Sigmund Freud had a chow called Jo-fi; Robert Burns kept a pet ewe; and Samuel Johnson made a huge fuss of his cat Hodge. Such a relationship can be beneficial in both directions. When we stroke a dog or cat, our heart rate decreases – but so does that of the animal! Sometimes the mere presence of an animal in the room can do this. Also, a person who is looking after an animal feels valued and needed.

Pet therapy has been recognized as valid, and as a result pets have now been introduced into nursing homes, mental hospitals, rehabilitation centres and hospices. Love of an animal can also aid the healing process, especially where the mind is involved.

Lack of love

Celia Haddon (1985) describes a number of studies that show that people who have not married or who are not in long-term relationships are more likely to feel lonely and less satisfied with life, and to be more prone to fall ill.

If love is not obtainable by natural means, it can be obtained by joining self-help groups. The support gained enables people to find their own strength and power to cope. Four groups in particular are helpful: Alcoholics Anonymous (AA), Gamblers Anonymous, Overeaters Anonymous and Narcotics Anonymous. These groups have some things in common:

- All reject financial aid from outside the group. There is even a limit in how much a member can give.
- All steer clear of political affiliations and of controversy.
- All try to prevent the development of hierarchies.
- Each is independent, self-supporting and self-governing.

- People are allowed say what's on their mind.
- All groups exhibit listening with respect and honour without interruption.
- All use touch: people shake hands or put a hand on a shoulder
- All members are regarded as 'victims', but they are all required to take on the role of 'rescuer' in the Karpman triangle (described in Hollier, 1993, and shown here as Figure 3.6).

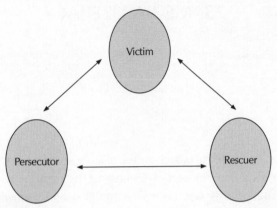

Figure 3.6 The Karpman Triangle

In the Karpman triangle, the three roles of victim, rescuer and persecutor are often rotated in families and in the workplace. For example a manager who is drinking too much takes on the victim role; a colleague may then start telling him off in a persecutor role; a secretary may start defending the drinker in a rescuer role.

The way to get out of this triangle is to:

- recognize the trap of the triangle;
- take on a more questioning and problem-solving approach;
- all try to help others and thereby increase their self-esteem.

Australia is one of the few countries that allow outsiders to visit AA meetings. What surprised me when I attended some as a visitor was the warmth of my welcome as a stranger and the willingness of members to talk and listen to one another.

In its extreme form, the power of love could be seen as passion or vocation for a cause. This is a driving force that empowers people to get things done. Frequently, the rewards go far beyond quick material success or monetary gratification, as is evidenced by the work of Greenpeace, helping and learning vocations, charities, and Mother Theresa.

Love itself can be abused, of course. Religious cults have cut individuals off from their families and then taken advantage of their new faith. The Reverend Jim Jones took advantage of the love of his followers at Jonestown, as did Reverend Moon (The Moonies),

Charles Manson (The family), Bhagwan Rajneesh (the Orange People) and Ron Hubbard (Scientology). These groups frequently require cadre-type isolation, where complete allegiance to the group is required in conjunction with rejection of outside influences such as family members and friends (see Power Card 3, Charisma.).

23. MEDIA LITERACY

The medium is the message.

(Marshall McLuhan)

Definition

A 'medium' in this context refers to a channel of communication – for example, talking, writing a memo, or sending a fax or e-mail. Choosing the right medium for your purpose is a powerful skill, as is interpreting what is being transmitted by various forms of media.

Rationale

Media literacy is an interesting power base because it was one of the last I added to the list. A friend pointed out the omission and I was rather embarrassed about it, especially as I used to teach Media Studies and had already shown my 'power base list' to numerous other people. It made me realize how important this power base is, because the power of media is such an implicit, unobtrusive force in our lives.

Recently, a colleague sent me a message. Normally, he scribbled notes in an informal way; however, this particular message was word-processed. I knew he thought it was important and he wanted me to sit up and take notice. The medium (ie a typed note) definitely was part of the message.

Media can appear remote, but they have the power of being intimate with us, invading our homes and influencing us to buy things we don't want, put our money into various savings accounts, make us miserable (or occasionally happy), vote for or support someone, and go to the fridge and eat certain products.

In the United States, TV evangelists have achieved immense popularity even though many have shown 'feet of clay'. When a person appears on television, he or she assumes a new status. As a result, nowadays it is important to be able to:

- analyse the meaning of images presented on TV so that we do not fall prey to always trying to be like the plastic people we see in front of us on the screen;

- know when and how to use a variety of media – and even how to prepare a quick press release that states a message in two sentences or thirty seconds (beware of problem of oversimplifying);
- understand the meaning of images produced through careful lighting, sound effects, camera angles, and image juxtaposition, so that we can interpret it rather than being influenced or manipulated by it;
- be able to send messages through TV or radio;
- use faxes and electronic mail.

Manufacturing images

Greenpeace activists carefully use the 'power of image' to arouse public opinion by utilizing images of small motorboats protecting whales against giant factory ships; demonstrating about French nuclear testing in the South Pacific; showing white seals being clubbed to death; or dropping anti-nuclear posters from the Golden Gate bridge in San Francisco.

These images are carefully planned and orchestrated. One of the most controversial was a photograph taken by David Bailey in 1984 for the anti-fur campaign. The photo depicted a female model trailing a fur coat behind her. As the fur dragged along the floor a wide trail of blood was left behind. The caption read 'It takes up to forty dumb animals to make a fur coat. But only one to wear it'.

The use of media by less powerful groups

Film, video, audiotape – and nowadays even the Internet – have been used by oppressed and/or less powerful groups to put their cases to politicians and the wider populace.

In Australia, Aboriginal groups have hired their own Aboriginal film crews to ensure that their story is properly taken to Parliament. Likewise, when leaders have visited Parliament, they have hired film crews so that meetings with politicians are recorded and taken back to show people in rural societies.

Activity: making media work for you

Think about all the media you use. Do you need to upgrade your skills? Do you need to upgrade your software – for example, installing e-mail filters that can save you time and energy by sorting your incoming electronic mail so that communications from different discussion groups can be filed together?

24. MEDIATION

Definition

The word 'mediation' comes from the Latin *mediare*, to be in the middle. It is a process whereby a third party acts as a go-between between two people in conflict. A mediator is similar to a facilitator, who helps two parties to problem solve and reach decisions that are mutually acceptable. Both parties have to be willing to shift their position and anxious to find a workable solution.

Rationale

There is an increasing use of mediation to solve disputes within families, organizations and communities. This is because mediation has been highly successful in many countries and is much cheaper and more empowering than the traditional methods used by the legal system. In mediation, both parties are part of the process and are involved in finding workable solutions to their issues, whereas when the legal system is invoked, dialogue is determined by lawyers and decisions by judges. Mediation works for a win–win solution; the legal system works for a win–lose solution.

Mediation requires that both parties are willing to try to solve their issues and are prepared to negotiate and 'shift' their positions. Mediation also requires the presence of a skilled mediator – or pair of mediators, usually one male and one female.

The advantages of mediation are therefore that:

- the process is aimed at achieving a win–win situation rather than one of win–lose, and as a result decisions are frequently adhered to in the long term;
- it does not involve alienating legal jargon;
- disputes are dealt with without a long delay;
- it is cheaper than litigation.

The disadvantages are:

- the actual mediation process takes time and energy and perseverance on the part of all participants and the facilitator;
- people only tend to seek mediation if they think they may lose through the legal system.

I heard recently that companies in India are starting to employ revered sadhus as mediators since these holy men are perceived as having great wisdom and are not politically aligned to any individuals in the workplace. Mediation is 'taking off' in the country as a cheaper, faster, more effective and 'healthier' method of dispute resolution.

Mediation skills can be learnt even at an early age. I have observed primary school children from Northern Ireland and Australia who have been taught to mediate playground disputes. It is a pity that in these countries the secondary-school system does not accommodate the continuation of such welcome responsibility and skills.

Activity: mediation practice

Next time there is an argument at home between your children or a disagreement between two staff members at work, try the following mediation steps if they are agreeable:

1. The mediator states the purpose of the session and roles of the mediator and participants.
2. The mediator states the ground rules: confidentiality, courtesy, and listening without interruption.
3. Party A makes a statement.
4. The mediator summarizes the statement: 'You said…', 'You stated that…'.
5. Party B makes a statement.
6. The mediator summarizes the statement: 'You said…', 'You stated that…'.
7. The mediator summarizes key issues and involves the parties in prioritizing the agenda of issues.
8. Issues are explored and clarified.
9. Caucus: if necessary, the mediator meets with each participant in turn in private for equal amounts of time. Information divulged during a caucus may be kept private.
10. The mediator facilitates solutions.
11. The mediator summarizes solutions, actions and time lines. For further reading see Beer, J E and Stief, E (1999).

25. MEDITATION

Definition

The term 'meditation' includes a wide variety of activities that have the common aim of stilling the mind. Usually our brains race with thousands of thoughts per minute. Meditation, on the other hand, relaxes the brain and reduces active thinking about the past, the present and the future. There are many different schools of meditation practice. However they all have three basic instructions:

- relax;
- focus on an object (for example, the breath, parts of the body in turn, a sound, a mantra, a colour, an image or even a pain in the body);
- let go of distractions, thoughts, sounds and sensations.

Rationale

Meditation is included as a power base because of the proven positive physiological changes that it induces. Breathing and pulse rates usually slow and oxygen consumption and body temperature decline. Meditation helps to combat stress and the ageing process. The effects of meditation are cumulative; they do not happen overnight. You need to practise for 10–20 minutes per day.

Activity: meditation practice

There are four main stages to meditation, as follows:

1. Find a sitting posture that enables you to develop physical stillness, stability and alertness. Sit either erect in a chair or cross-legged on the floor. It is important to be comfortable, but if you lie down you may go to sleep.
2. Develop deep, slow breathing to gain an even flow of air in and out of the body. As a result, the mind starts to calm.
3. Count each breath, for example, 1–1, 2–2, using the same numbers on the in and the out breath.
4. If you have stray thoughts, do not be concerned. Just let them go 'like clouds in the sky'. If you hear a strange noise, just name it 'Oh that's the air conditioner' and let it go from your consciousness.

There is a very useful book entitled *Creative Visualization* by Patrick Fanning (1998) that gives much valuable advice on the subject of meditation.

26. MEN/MALENESS

Be a man; boys don't cry.

Definition

The stereotypical characteristics of 'maleness' are linked to the ancient roles of hunter–killer, which required strength, virility, stamina and to some extent 'cold-bloodedness'. According to Leonard Shlain (1998), the different requirements of hunting – as opposed to gathering – meant that evolution equipped men and women differently. As a result, men and women have different perceptions of the world, of survival, of the meaning of commitment, and ultimately different ways of 'knowing' (Shlain, 1998).

Rationale

So why include this as a power base? It is here because both maleness and femaleness are stereotypes that are developed by societal and cultural conditioning. (We no longer have such firmly divided hunter–gatherer roles where physical strength was important.) The so-called characteristics of each gender are useful at different times. In all communities, men need the help of women and women need the help of men.

At times, it may be appropriate to redefine your life scripts. In order to thrive in today's society, you may have to change jobs frequently, manage changing relationships and move to different cultures; therefore to be able to redefine oneself is also important. This also relates to the ways in which homosexuals and lesbians have redefined their roles in society. See Power Card 44, Redefining who we are, and also the Power Card 60, Women/femaleness.

The impact of the warrior role

The traditional symbol of maleness is the phallus. The traditional roles of the warrior, seeker and hunter are of necessity currently being redefined because they are no longer appropriate in today's societies. The role of warrior was glorified in the role of soldier, which again is being reinvented. The male image of physical strength is being redefined as mental and emotional strength: 'brains not brawn'.

As the definitions here are in a state of flux, this power base is in some ways hard to describe. Although the roles mentioned above are necessary, they can result in behaviour that, if taken to extremes, may be perceived as negative – for example, aggressiveness and competitiveness.

Male norms and society

Men are empowered in gender relations in most societies. They were traditionally given power over the 'public arena' of life, while women were seen as having power over the 'private household'. Maleness and male stories have until the last part of this century been documented by historians and psychologists as the 'norm', while the female side of things has frequently been totally ignored.

Men have usually competed more than they have co-operated with others. Co-operation by men is more instrumental than intrinsic in value. Women are raised to co-operate (a necessary skill for child-rearing and nurturing) and to put others first without thought of reward; men, on the other hand, tend to think first before co-operating: 'What's in it for me?'

In privileged, private schools in the United Kingdom, the phrase 'the old boys' network' developed to describe a very powerful and useful networking system. Indeed, parents send their boys to these schools so that they will develop powerful networks to help them in their later careers. But the old boys' network requires the build-up and return of favours. It is rarely altruistic.

In Australia, the concept of 'mateship' is very strong, as European settlement was originally largely male dominated. This strong bonding has been a considerable advantage for males. When I first went to Australia in the 1970s, I was surprised at parties when I realized I was the only female in the kitchen with groups of men. The Australian women were talking together in another room. Whilst I thoroughly enjoy the company of both sexes, having been raised in England I found this cultural norm disconcerting. Like all norms this is slowly changing. The point I want to make here is that it is important not only for women to develop their own networks but it is also vital for men.

Two men saw two women in a café talking. The men were attracted to the women, and so they decided to approach them, saying 'Excuse us ladies, but are you alone?' Women together were in those days in Australia regarded as being incomplete – alone – and yet they were with each other. In my teen years I recall not valuing female company, such that the conditioning I received by society was that if I was not out with a male I wasn't really complete. I now value interesting company, whether male or female.

Stereotypes of men's work and women's work

The anthropologist Margaret Mead noted in her observations in Samoa that there were villages in which men fish and women weave, and those in which women fish and men weave, but in either type of village, the work done by men was valued more highly than the work done by women. We need to eliminate stereotypes of men's work and women's work. In our Western society, this attitude still prevails in places, as the following anecdote shows. We need to work to eliminate this unfair view of the world.

Down the mine

One problem is the way jobs are categorized into women's work or men's work. Even more so is the way in which so-called women's work is undervalued and downgraded.

The mine sites in the north of Australia used to be staffed predominantly by men. With advances in technology and power-assisted techniques, women have been employed over the past ten years in areas such as driving the huge haulpak earth-moving machinery. I heard an interesting anecdote some years after the mines became staffed predominantly by women:

> One day, a machine was parked up and needed to be moved. The foreman called over to one of the men: 'Hey, move that haulpak over there'. The worker turned around and said 'Not me mate, that's women's work'.

Activity: *the power of gender equity*

We have to work together as human begins to overcome conditioning, gender stereotypes and the resulting hurts. So I have chosen another power card to represent this: see number 44, Redefining who we are.

27. MIND FLEXIBILITY

The seed of mystery lies in muddy waters
How can I perceive this mystery?
Water becomes still through stillness.
How can I become still?
By flowing with the stream.

(Lao Tzu)

Definition

Our minds are our seats of consciousness, where memory, thoughts and feelings are perceived. Current wisdom states that we do not use even a quarter of the capacity of our brains, but that we can exercise our brains like a muscle to develop greater flexibility and powers of thought.

Rationale

There is a Chinese story about the trees in winter with branches weighed down by snow. The trees with rigid branches had limbs that broke off; while those whose branches bend under the weight of snow survive. Inflexible people with rigid minds in times of change may experience more difficulties than those who 'go with the flow'.

Mindsets in history: 'strategic retreat'

Consider the story of Napoleon's single-minded and obsessive goal of capturing Moscow. Despite the oncoming treacherous Russian winter, Napoleon pursued his goal apparently without considering consequences or alternatives. Kutuzov, the leader of the Russian army, was, in contrast, flexible. He commanded his army to fall back and as a result lengthened Napoleon's supply lines. Meanwhile, the French army began to be affected by the fearful cold and lack of food as the retreating Russians adopted a 'scorched earth' policy. Napoleon interpreted advance as success, whereas Kutuzov was more flexible and took into account the wider picture. It was interesting that Hitler repeated Napoleon's mistake.

The old Chinese man and the horse

There is an ancient Chinese story of an old man who had a horse that ran away. All his friends come around to commiserate, but the old man said 'I'm not worried about it, you never know what will happen'. A few days later, the horse returned leading a whole herd of wild horses behind it. Everyone congratulated the old man on his good fortune. The old man just smiled and said 'You never know what happens' and didn't make a big deal out of it.

His only son then set about taming the wild horses and fell off and was crippled. Everyone called around to bring sympathies. The old man said 'You never know what will happen'.

Some time later, government troops passed through the village, enlisting all the young men to fight in a war. Most marched off eagerly, but the old man's son was passed over because of his injuries. None of the young men returned.

Activity: reframing mindsets

Older participants sometimes depower or excuse themselves from doing something new by invoking the saying 'You can't teach an old dog new tricks'. This is an incredibly depowering excuse. A way of gently confronting is to say 'Oh really? Consider all the new things you have already learnt in your lifetime. Can you give me some examples?' An empowered person might change the phrase to 'You can teach an old dog new tricks, if the dog is willing'.

The ability to reframe mindsets is an important skill. Frequently, we limit our choices because of mindsets that we have adopted from our parents, from life scripts, from society, from the media, etc. Mindsets can nevertheless be powerful in helping and determining our lives. For example, consider the resulting implications of the following life scripts:

- 'Girls don't do that. They should always be ladylike.'
- 'Men don't cry.'
- 'Old age means poor health and limited activity.'
- 'Sheltered accommodation for old people is the beginning of the end.'
- 'Exile from my country is the end for me.'

Consider changing the above to:

- 'Girls – and boys – can try anything.'
- 'Real men – and women – show their feelings.'
- 'I'm going to grow old disgracefully and have a whale of a time.'
- 'Sheltered accommodation is the beginning of a new life free from the responsibilities of maintenance and from the problems of loneliness.'
- 'Freedom in exile' is the motto of the Tibetan people.

Activity: comparing perceptions

In pairs, face one another. Ask person A to describe the world as he or she sees it (eg window, wall, person B, etc). Ask person B to describe the world that he or she sees. Now ask person A to state his or her views on a major topic. Ask person B to try to walk in person A's shoes. Get person B to summarize the worldview of person A. Is there any shift in understanding?

'Groupthink'

Sometimes groups become 'stuck' and narrow in their way of thinking, leading to characteristics that Irving Janis (1972) calls 'groupthink' and that contain a variety of symptoms, which will be described here in turn.

- *Invulnerability.* A group may feel overconfident, believing that they are bound to win, or are so necessary that they cannot lose, or no one would dare to cut their funding. 'The Titanic will never sink' is a good example.
- *Rationalization.* Victims of groupthink frequently ignore warnings and rationalize their way of thinking. For example, Admiral Kimmel's group maintained that the Japanese would not dare to attack Pearl Harbor right up to 7 December 1941.

- *Morality.* Group members frequently start to believe that their group is right and just, as was demonstrated by the use of napalm bombs by US troops on civilians and large areas of farmland in South Vietnam. 'If we don't stop the Reds in South Vietnam, tomorrow they will be in Hawaii and next week they will be in San Francisco.'
- *Stereotyping.* When group members start to slip into groupthink, they begin to make rash generalizations about members of other groups – for example, 'The others are stupid and won't listen to reason'. Before the Bay of Pigs invasion fiasco in 1962, President Kennedy's advisers completely underestimated Fidel Castro's air force and army capabilities.
- *Pressure for conformity.* If someone disagrees frequently, they are pressured by people saying 'Don't rock the boat'.
- *Self-censorship.* If individuals disagree, they frequently learn to stay quiet rather than 'blow the whistle'.
- *Illusion of unanimity.* There can be an air of assumed consensus. Silence is assumed to be synonymous with agreement. People all superficially pretend to agree.
- *Mind-guards.* Certain people edit the information reaching the group members.

Activity: prevention of groupthink

Janis (1972) suggests that the imaginative use of outsiders can encourage rethinking and reframing of problems to prevent groupthink. I have heard of groups of high-school students who have been brought into the corporate environment for a day to be part of 'think tanks' for creative problem-solving.

Here are some suggestions that Janis made that you could adopt to help groups you belong to guard against 'groupthink':

- Appoint a group member as a devil's advocate to raise negative aspects of the group's plans.
- Invite in outsiders to enter into discussions, and listen to them.
- Take all warning signals seriously and examine them.
- Change your meeting venues regularly.
- Meet occasionally without the leader present (because, frequently, that person is listened to the most).

Activity: looking for groupthink

Think of a group to which you belong. Are there any symptoms of groupthink in its operation? If yes, what could you do? Pick any of the above suggestions and apply them to a group with whom you work.

28. MONEY

Money can't buy you love.

(The Beatles, 'Can't Buy Me Love')

Definition

According to the Beatles: 'Money can't buy you love', but some say it can help you to be miserable in comfort. Money is also one of the most versatile and transmutable power resources, for it can buy fun, time, expertise, loyalty and status. It can be used as a reward. Money is used to support the campaigns of politicians and immediately wins the giver favours, information and influence.

Wealth has taken many different forms through the ages (Toffler, 1991: 61):

- *First Wave*: salt, tobacco, coral, cotton cloth, copper, land, animals, gold, cowrie shells;
- *Second Wave*: paper money, the first known use of which was in China in 1024;
- *Third Wave*: paper superseded by plastic and electronic credit cards and smart cards. These are changing the way we use money. However, an empowered person realizes that the interest charges on this 'easy money' is the most expensive form of loan.

Rationale

Money is one of the most versatile, transmutable power resources; it can buy time, expertise, loyalty, and status. It can be used as a reward. Money is used to support the campaigns of politicians and immediately wins the giver favours, information and influence.

I was surprised in Nepal to see one festival where money safes were adorned with flowers and a statue of Laxmi, the goddess of wealth. I had had the misconception that people there were less money-conscious than people in the West. Money, in fact, has currency everywhere.

Take the case of Julie, a friend of mine, who had a child who was so ill with an ear infection that she called her doctor out – but was told that he was only available on Wednesdays to non-private patients. She commented: 'I was so scared my daughter would go deaf that I had no alternative but to take her to a private specialist, but not to that one. I didn't care what it cost'. She was lucky she had the monetary resources to give her the choice.

The Thatcher trend for privatization in the United Kingdom was on the grounds of giving people 'choice'. Unfortunately, frequently the choice was only available to those with the money to buy them that choice.

Money is not the only form of wealth

Power over the use and investment of money, rather than just having money, is important. Whilst wealth has been measured in these terms, there are other definitions that are rarely seen in statistics produced in the West. Examples include human relationships, support and comfort; the ability to laugh at life with one's friends, a healthy lifestyle, and satisfying 'work'.

I have observed these attributes in my travels in developing countries, but rarely see such criteria used in statistics evaluating an economy. In 1999, I was delighted to read that the King of Bhutan, a small kingdom in the Himalayas, talked in terms of measuring 'Gross National Happiness' as opposed to mere economic measurements of a country's wealth.

Money talks

Money certainly does talk, and people who have it or give it away often gain in influence. I was intrigued by the regulation of Alcoholics Anonymous whereby the organization constantly refuses to take money from non-members. AA members love to tell the story of how a gift of money from John Rockefeller Jr was politely rejected. Members of the AA believe that it must be self-supporting from its own membership, so that they retain the power on how it is run.

But even the biggest budget at some stage runs out. Money is a finite resource. Therefore this power base needs to be managed with care.

Activity: managing money

What incomes do you have? What outgoings do you have? If you are not sure, do you need to learn how to use a simple accounting package for your home accounts? How can you simplify your money management?

29. MUSIC/SINGING/DANCING

Whistle a happy tune and you won't feel afraid.

(From *The King and I*)

Definition

In the musical *The King and I*, Anna, the newly arrived schoolteacher from England, on disembarking in Bangkok instructs her son to 'whistle a happy tune' to take away their fear. Different people define and use music, singing and dancing in different ways. It's largely a matter of taste.

Rationale

When we listen to music, sing or dance, our bodies relax. Those activities induce different mind states. Some months ago, my husband commented that when he was in the garden he saw me dancing up and down in my art studio. I laughed and indeed I was dancing to music in order to get myself loosened up and in the frame of mind for painting!

The whirling dervishes of Turkey have used swirling dancing to induce states of hypnosis and meditation for centuries. Isadora Duncan, the US dancer, described the power of dance thus: 'If I could tell you what it meant, there would be no point in dancing it'.

In Chapter 1, I described the way in which I used the song 'Power to the people' and an imitation percussion band to start a workshop about empowerment. I frequently use music in classrooms to fill silence to make people feel more comfortable when they walk into a room full of strangers. I use it during group work to stimulate discussion – after all, if no one can hear the group next door it gives a feeling of privacy and intimacy. I use music to calm people or myself after work.

Gregorian chant music has recently become extremely popular for relaxation. Chanting has a similar impact on the brain as meditation.

Words often fail to express exactly what we intend. There is a Quaker expression 'The word divideth' since words fail to accurately express what we mean. Music, singing and dancing unites us as human beings as methods to convey meaning; to exalt life and death; to express joy and sadness.

Activity: the music in your life

Is there enough music, singing and dancing in your life? If not, what are you going to do about it?

30. NETWORKING

No one is an island

(adapted from John Donne)

Definition

A network is usually composed of your contacts beyond your immediate close friends. Apart from 'the old-boy network', the term 'network' has in recent decades been applied almost wholly in electronics. However, nowadays it is much more used to refer to social or business groups, as well as the electronic linkages occurring through intranets and the Internet.

Networking is the art of discovering patterns in the world and making useful connections for ourselves and for others (Smith and Wagner, 1983).

Rationale

Networking is a leaderless process for empowering people and their lives. It is not a one-way process; it is about being useful to others as much as others being useful to you.

Networks give people:

- access to informal information, for example, about promotional aspects or new careers;
- special favours, discounts, etc;
- information about ways around 'the system';
- data about who is who and who is really the 'power behind the throne';
- emotional support and love;
- access to skills you do not have;
- support through lobbying on committees;
- physical and emotional support – for example, babysitting, caring, minding a sick relative;
- power, by being a source of information and contacts for others and giving you access to up-to-date (though not always accurate) grapevine information.

Our networks act as a safety net in today's society. They gives us a sense of 'connectedness' as opposed to the modern malaise of anomie (a term resurrected from the Greek by the French sociologist Emile Durkheim, and literally meaning 'without law'). Anomie occurs as a result of the despairing loneliness and deeply sensed isolation and/or alienation experienced by individuals who have lost contact with their traditional moorings or community (eg some young street people). Networks are empowering because individuals are at the centre of your network; and there is no one in charge of your network.

Activity: rules for networking

The process of networking is a bit like being an explorer or a sleuth. It also enables us to weave new options into our safety nets. Smith and Wagner (1983) maintain that there are rules to successful networking. Evaluate yourself against these criteria:

- *Be useful*. Keep useful phone numbers, references, and locations to pass on to others. Make sure these are easily accessible and/or filed; otherwise you will find retrieval of information too time-consuming. I keep my contacts in a database now, with key attributes, so I can print out lists of specific people – for example, facilitators in Australia, or former overseas students.
- *Do not take over other people's quests or feel that you have to take care of everyone*. Let other people be useful to *you*. Networking is not a one-way process. One of the best ways of being useful to yourself and others is to let them be useful to you as well. If you do not, you place an awful burden of debt on them. Reciprocity in some cultures is very important. Helping others does build up a bank of people to whom you can say 'you owe me one'. In some cultures this is very important. It means that in times of need you can call on others for help – a useful form of insurance. However, it can get out of hand, and there is a need to remember the Chinese expression 'obligation is a curse'.
- *Don't be boring*. Don't show off by offering too many contacts. A couple of good contacts are better than 40. Too much information may overburden some people. Do not overwork a contact with too many requests.
- *Listen*. Active listening is important when asking for information and listening to the requests of others. It is important not to make hasty judgements or to tell people what they should or shouldn't do.
- *Ask questions*. Clarifying and probing questions enable you to find out exactly what sort of contacts people want. Sometimes this helps the seeker to become clearer about what is needed. It also saves them getting rejected by a contact who cannot provide what is sought. If you are seeking information, it helps if you ask assertive questions. You should never be afraid to ask – after all, the worst thing that a person might say is 'I'm sorry I can't give you that information' or 'I don't know'. However, this is easier said than done, and many inexperienced networkers are shy and need to be encouraged. In these cases, I always try to give them contacts who I know will treat them with consideration and kindness.
- *Don't make assumptions*. Successful networkers assume that most things are interconnected in some way. They are not afraid to try even obscure contacts. Smith and Wagner

talk about 'playing the wild card' and state that that is what sets human beings apart from computers in the information-retrieval game.

Managing a network: computerized databases

The only way I can keep up with a wide variety of people is to send out a computerized Christmas letter. I used to hate the idea of a mass-produced Christmas message, but I have noticed in recent years that this has become an accepted form of correspondence. I now look forward annually to receiving a variety of news from across the globe and have in some ways kept in closer touch with distant friends through this medium. I've also noticed that people are now sending fewer cards and more computer letters to save trees. Indeed, Christmas letters are now arriving by e-mail.

The giant bulletin board: the Internet and e-mail

The Internet is the most significant development in networking this century. It has democratized and revolutionized the capacity of people all over the world to communicate with one another quickly and cheaply.

Types of network

Facilitator networks

In Perth I belong to a 'Facilitator's Network', which is very informal in structure. There are about a dozen of us. We meet on the first Monday of the month either in our workplaces or homes in rotation at around 4.00 pm. When we first started meeting, we spent time trying to work out what we wanted and then soon settled into a structure of individuals taking responsibility to facilitate a session in an area of interest. It now gives opportunities to sound each other out on new ideas, to ask for feedback on things that have 'gone wrong', and to try out new processes and analyse them.

Self-help networks

The state of Western Australia where I live has a population of 1.5 million people. When I rang up the WISH (Western Institute of Self Help), I was astounded to hear that there are over 700 self-help groups in Western Australia alone. If you cannot find a support group to meet your needs, why not start your own?

Networks joining together

The joining together of various networks can be useful, since greater numbers have greater political clout. Gandhi called this the 'grouping of unities'. Before Indian independence, many different groups united against the British. Unfortunately, once independence was achieved, fighting between these groups immediately broke out. When there is an outside threat, there is frequently inside cohesion; remove the threat and inner tensions re-emerge.

Greenpeace is the world's largest environmental organization. It was founded less than 30 years ago in 1971 by two Americans and a Canadian. It now boasts more than 4 million subscribers and 24 member nations, and its policy of nonviolent direct action remains as controversial as ever. Their actions are not 'spur of the moment' events but carefully planned, strategic, non-violent confrontations.

Overseas networks welcome others

Quakers have a method for linking groups in different countries. The 'home' group issues a traveller with a 'travelling minute', which acts as an introduction to the new group. In the United States, members of The Religious Society of Friends can travel very cheaply using this system, because it introduces members to each other and they give each other cheap or free accommodation.

31. PASSIVE RESISTANCE

No one can make me do it.

Definition

Passive resistance involves withholding psychological or economic support. In simple terms it is a reluctance to show compliance, or disguised or open non-compliance.

Rationale

Passive resistance is extremely powerful. Even children learn at an early age how useful are phrases such as 'You can't *make* me do it' (much to the chagrin of their parents). Likewise, resistance movements have used 'passive resistance'; Gandhi, for instance, used it to unite Indians in taking on one of the biggest empires of all time: the British Empire. Gandhi's own hunger strike was immensely powerful.

Nevertheless, the path of passive resistance can be a dangerous one because it is generally an all-or-nothing approach – as evidenced by the suffragettes who were forcibly fed and the Irish hunger strikers who died. Another strategy is 'sit-ins', which were used very effectively by demonstrating university students at the end of the 1960s in Europe and the United States. Once again, however, there is a risk in the way in which police or army personnel deal with demonstrators.

Passive resistance is closely linked to the Personal power base (see Power Card 33).

Some examples of passive resistance

Some understanding of the use of non-violent, passive resistance power was visible in Ancient Greece, as illustrated in the play by Aristophanes entitled *Lysistrata*, written in the 5th century BC. The story relates how women united in refusing to make love with their husbands as long as men insisted on going to war. The women 'won' their point. This strategy was mentioned on Australian television before the outbreak of the Gulf War in 1991.

Similarly, in Andrah Pradesh in India the women were fed up with their husbands drinking *arak* on pay day. The men left little pay for the family food, and they also came home drunk and were often violent. The women got together and tied onto a donkey backwards any spouse who came home drunk. The donkey was then made to walk through the village. As a result of the embarrassment, there was a change in the habits of males. Later, the shopkeepers agreed not to sell liquor on pay day.

Electronic media, including Star TV, are helping people across the world learn about passive-resistance techniques. The Chinese student demonstrators in Tiananmen Square in Beijing were so successful that their demonstration eclipsed all other new items in that period. Similar passive techniques were used in the struggle for democracy in Nepal in 1990–91. Writers demonstrated on the streets seated with black scarves tied around their mouths, forcefully illustrating the lack of freedom of speech.

In organizations, some people are often, but not always, at the bottom of the hierarchy and labelled 'less powerful'. However, they have tremendous power for non-compliance and quiet passive resistance, which is why it is so important to involve people thoroughly in the change process. Passive resistance may be public and/or private.

Aung San Suu Kyi

Aung San Suu Kyi, the former leader of Myanmar's National League for Democracy party, exemplifies the power of the individual. In 1990 she led the party to a landslide victory despite being locked up during the whole campaign. She was imprisoned in her home in Rangoon between 1990 and 1995 (and in 2000 her movements are still greatly restricted).

However, she has still managed to hold on to her personal power. On a visit to Myanmar in 1993, I heard that the ruling generals were afraid of her because she was practising meditation and believed she had special powers.

In one of her essays (1991), she wrote 'It is not power that corrupts but fear. Fear of losing power corrupts those who wield it and fear of the scourge of power corrupts those who are subject to it' (p 26). People with high degrees of personal power are able to share power in the form of co-operative power.

Suu has courageously followed the Gandhian path of passive resistance and non-violence in her fight for human rights. Her presence in Myanmar is similar to the Quaker peaceful form of protest called 'bearing witness', a kind of passive resistance that is achieved by going to an undesirable activity and registering opposition by one's presence there. This is also the basis of the work of Greenpeace members. Suu's name means 'a bright collection of strange victories' and she is certainly living up to her name, as evidenced by her courageous stand for democracy.

Activity: observing passive resistance

Watch children around you and observe how much passive resistance they use. Watch people at work who pretend to comply with directives but quietly resist. How often do *you* 'dig your heels in' and resist? What happens?

32. PERSEVERANCE

If at first you don't succeed, try, try, try again.

Definition

Perseverance is about not letting go but instead using your will-power to put prolonged, patient effort into something. It's bit like a dog tugging on a cloth shaking its head in a determined fashion.

Rationale

Despite the foregoing analogy, perseverance is not 'bloody-mindedness' or 'not letting go', because you need to know when to stop if keeping going becomes detrimental to your health and well-being. Gamblers often do not know when to stop. (See also Power Card 21, Letting go.)

Yet persistence is often the art of success. Many successful people use the law of probability, for example, in applying for funding grants; successful people do not just submit one proposal but many, knowing that they have about a 1 in 10 chance of being successful. Rejections do not discourage them and they never 'put all their eggs in one basket'.

Perseverance is also a feature of a number of the world religions.

Two examples of perseverance

At a school in Western Australia in which I taught, I asked where the usual tuck-shop lady was. 'Oh, she's in Hawaii,' was the reply. Chatting to her deputy, I found out that our friendly lady behind the counter was always entering quizzes and competitions and as a result had an incredibly high success rate. She played on the law of averages that eventually she would win something: 'You win some and you lose some'.

On a major scale, setbacks may strengthen perseverance. In July 1985, the *Rainbow Warrior*, a boat belonging to Greenpeace, was being used to demonstrate against French nuclear tests in the Pacific. While in dock in New Zealand, it was sunk and one member was killed by an explosion caused by a bomb planted, it appears, by French agents. This action increased the resolve and perseverance of Greenpeace members, who used the slogan 'you can't sink a rainbow'. Immediately a new boat, MV *Greenpeace*, was sent to the area, and later the *Vega*:

> As for Greenpeace, the tragic death of Pereira and the loss of the *Warrior* seemed to underline the seriousness of its endeavours and to heighten its sense of purpose. Far from being deterred or defeated, Greenpeace was, in the next few years, to spread its name, influence and activities across a wider landscape than ever before.
> (Brown and May, 1989: 125)

The same perseverance is necessary nowadays with job applications. I knew a teacher who wanted to break out into industry. She sent off 300 letters and made numerous 'cold calls' to organizations. Out of all of these, she only got one acceptance, but that was all that was needed. Once she had her 'foot in the door' of industry, the next move was easier.

'Broken record' assertiveness

There is a useful technique that is taught in assertiveness training called the 'broken record' approach. To use this strategy, all you have to do is to mimic a record whose needle has got stuck: you keep repeating your statement, request, question etc. Eventually others often (though not always) give in merely because they want to get you off their backs. Here are the stages to follow:

1. Persist.
2. Stick to the point.
3. Stay calm, and take a deep breath.
4. Say what you want, be specific and repeat: 'I understand what you think, but this is very important to me'.
5. Try to find a workable compromise: 'I realize this is important to you, but I'm not interested in....'.

These strategies have to be used skilfully; otherwise they may be counterproductive. You need to know when to stop if you want to preserve a long-term relationship.

The politics of persistence, champions and Post-its

Good ideas do not necessarily get taken on merely because they are good. Ideas need champions and a work environment where new ideas are not just thrown away.

There is a story about the 3M company, where an employee walked around for five years with some glue he had invented that did not stick properly. Many people laughed at him, but he always took the glue with him to meetings. Eventually someone noticed that singers in a choir had problems with their book markers falling out of their hymn books. What was needed was semi-permanent markers: the idea of 'Post-its' was born, making a fortune for the company.

33. PERSONAL POWER

Each of us makes all the difference in the world.

(Ferguson, 1982)

Isn't that quote wonderful? The concept of personal power recognizes that we are all able to influence even the small zone around us in some way. In 1977, The Nobel Peace Prize was awarded jointly to the Peace People in Northern Ireland and Amnesty International. In both areas it was individuals who made the difference – for example, in the case of Amnesty International, by writing monthly letters to leaders who endorse torturing and imprisonment without trial.

Definition

Personal power comes from within. It is difficult to define, but people who exude personal power are noticeable because they appear to have an inner strength and confidence.

Rationale

Knowing yourself, your character and accepting yourself warts and all enhances self-worth and confidence. People with personal power tend to have a positive outlook on life and regard problems as challenges. They are proactive, assertive, problem solvers, rather than taking the victim role.

When asked 'What is the meaning of life?' Gandhi replied 'The meaning of life is to know oneself, but you cannot do this unless you identify yourself with all that lives. The sum total of that life is god'. Earlier, I mentioned that empowerment involved knowing oneself: knowing one's values, beliefs, feelings, needs (the things you must have to survive) and wants (the desired things not vital for survival).

It is important that we continue getting to know ourselves throughout our lives, especially as we grow and change through the stages of childhood, adolescence, adulthood, middle age and old age. We change in many ways. The child we once were is not the same person as the older person we are now, even though we may think we are the same.

Activity: consider the personal power of others

Think about people you know who have personal power. What are their attributes? They may include: energy and enthusiasm, clear goals and/or meaning in life, charisma, an ability to cope, persuasiveness, confident body language, ability to manage self and others, ability to manage rather than suppress emotions. In transactional analysis terms, these people think, 'I'm OK you're OK'.

Think, too, of people you know who have little personal power. Their characteristics may include: lack of assertiveness, compliance, non-acknowledgement of skills and attributes, emotions that swing out of control, fearful or beaten body language. In transactional analysis terms, these people think, 'I'm not OK, you're OK'.

People with personal power feel (most of the time) as if they are in control of their lives; people with little personal power often think like 'victims'.

Being yourself and being different

There is the power of being different. I was delighted by a quotation in *The Social Climbers* by Chris Darwin (grandson of the famous Charles) and John Amy (1991). Chris Darwin had been inspired by the advice given to him at the age of 13 by his grandmother: 'Chris, if you cannot be first, be peculiar'. He certainly achieved this by organizing a group of non-climbers to climb Mt Huascaran in the Peruvian Andes to partake in the highest dinner party in the world at 6,800 metres, and as a result he created a 'visual joke' and gained a mention in the Guinness Book of Records.

If participants in workshops talk about changing themselves, they need to first be clear whether, what, and why they really want to do this. I have met many people who prefer not to comply with some of the rules or mores of society – for example, men who like to wear an earring or pony tail and who do this from choice, preferring to hold on to their own mode of self-expression even if it may mean it takes longer to gain acceptance and credibility in some circles. In my own case, I dress in a variety of different colours and ethnic clothing, somewhat different to the norm for a School of Management. This can have advantages and disadvantages. On the one hand, people notice my colours and, as a result, they notice me. On the other hand, people who are conservative may prejudge me and not take me seriously, and so I have to win them over. I sometimes *choose* to adapt my style of dress a little in formal situations – in empowering language, not that 'I *have* to change' but that 'I *choose* to change'. There is a difference.

Activity: self-talk

The exercise I want you to consider here is adapted from Hollier *et al* (1993) and involves changing our driving 'self-talk' messages from 'I should' to 'I choose'. It implies that you are doing something from your own authority rather than rebelling or submitting. There is an example in Table 3.6. Follow the same procedure with something that applies to your circumstances.

Table 3.6 Changing self-talk

SHOULD	CHOOSE
(Demands you impose on yourself)	**Identify the outside pressures**
	Change the perspective
	Decide what to do
I should review the safety procedures at work. This is part of my job role and our company needs to comply with new legislation.	I know I need to be professional and review procedures.
	I choose to do this because it will be more efficient in the long term.
	I'll arrange a meeting to get everyone behind the project.

Remember that there are three stages in the 'choose' section: identify the outside pressure; change the perspective; and decide what to do.

How Yu Gong moved the mountain

An old poor farmer lived in a very mountainous area in China. He realized that if there were fields in place of the mountain he would have enough food to feed his whole family. So he started alone with a bucket and spade. His neighbours made fun of him, saying it was impossible to move the mountain, but Yu Gong persevered and said it *was* possible but it would just take time, and that after many generations the mountain would be removed and his family would be able to live with plenty to eat. Of course, eventually the mountain was removed.

Further comments

As a result of this kind of story in their history and culture, the Chinese have always been able to take a longer-term perspective on change than many Western countries. My father, on the other hand, always promised that he would remove the steep hill in our street that we had to climb to get to mass at St Joseph's church every Sunday – but of course he never succeeded. As a small child, who had infinite faith in my father, I believed he could do it. Unfortunately, or rather, fortunately, he never got around to it.

Alcoholics Anonymous works with 'the power of one', in that each individual member of AA carries the message to the next person without any hope of financial reward:

> I am responsible when anyone, anywhere, reaches out for help, I want the hand of AA always to be there. And for that I am responsible.
>
> (AA brochure, *Is AA for you?*)

Activity: finding meaning in our lives

Bookshops today abound with self-help books that are there to help us learn about ourselves. In one such volume with impressive content, Wayne Muller (1996) poses four very simple, but thought-provoking questions to help us find meaning in our lives. Try answering his questions for yourself:

Table 3.7 Finding meaning in our lives (from Muller, 1996)

QUESTION	YOUR RESPONSE
Who am I?	
What do I love?	
How shall I live, knowing I will die?	
What is my gift to the family of the earth?	

Co-option and placation

Of course, resisting peer pressure can be very hard. Being an individual who stands out from the crowd can be difficult. Committees now invite individual representatives to join the decision-making process. This appears to be a very honourable part of the democratic process; however, it is very difficult for a token black person or token disabled person to persuade a whole group if the members of that group are unwilling to see things from that person's point of view.

Allowing leaders of minority groups to participate in the decision-making process could be a way of placating them (see Arnstein's (1969) model in Chapter 2). However, if these leaders are treated well and are actively involved in the political process, even if they do not gain all that they have worked for, they are more likely to go along with the ultimate decisions. This reasoning has been documented by Tyler and McGraw (1986).

The reasons appear to be that leaders frequently:

- join the status-quo group;
- feel satisfied with the procedures;
- become weary with the long, tortuous debates and lose interest after they feel that their issue has been heard;
- become aware of the wider issues and see their problems in perspective.

When I was studying at The University of London in the 1970s, academics dealt with student unrest by inviting student representatives onto committees. Academic meetings are not lively, and frequently students lost motivation, especially with assignment and exam pressures.

34. PERSONAL SUPPORTERS

I couldn't have done it without my friends.

Definition

There is a variety of relationships open to us: close friends, mentors, peers in the same situation, study buddies, partners, emotional supporters, cheerleaders. These people are sometimes non-judgmental listeners; at other times, they can be 'critical friends'.

Rationale

McClelland's (1984) work on motivation highlights the learnt need for affiliation: we all need some form of love. (See Power Card 22, Love.)

Mentoring

The mentoring process has been used in a variety of cultures throughout history. In the Middle Ages, the guilds started the apprenticeship system whereby young people learnt skills from a master craftsman. Older healers frequently mentored young people so that information about healing herbs would not be lost.

In more recent years, the word 'mentoring' has been taken up by the business world. Frequently, older executives take on aspiring managers who remind them of themselves when they were young. Unfortunately, as a large majority of senior executives are male, it is young *men* whom they adopt to teach the tricks of the trade. These young people are then given access to networks, close supervision and constructive feedback, guidance and inside knowledge.

Unfortunately, mentors sometimes try to create clones of themselves so as to ensure that when they retire the organization will be run in the same way as before. The relationship also involves a top-down approach, with an imbalance of power between mentor and mentee (see the subsection on wisdom affairs below).

Sponsors

Organizations who seek to empower people to give up a habit or addiction, such as Weightwatchers or Alcoholics Anonymous, use 'sponsors' to give private emotional support for members.

Study buddies

Research at my university highlighted the loneliness of some first-year and mature students. As a result, I asked everyone in my classes to find a 'study buddy' or partner. It is intended that the roles and responsibilities of a study buddy are renegotiated at the beginning of each semester, but basically they consist of:

- cheering up your partner if he/she gets depressed;
- motivating your partner if he/she gets lazy;
- keeping your buddy up to date with lecture notes if he/she is ill;
- letting the lecturer know if a buddy is ill;
- sharing reading resources, articles and photocopies with buddies;
- acting as a 'critical friend', and challenging and building on one another's ideas.

Some students were sceptical at first. However, we soon found that giving people at the beginning of courses 'permission' to approach and work with one another produces results. I also use this technique on 2–5-day training workshops.

Role models

Role models are useful too – the risk takers who have gone out there and already shown us that it can be done. They might show us a new way of doing things, or how to confront the system, or show us a change process that works. One such is Sally Morgan, a Western Australian Aboriginal woman, who through her art and writing showed her people how to be proud of their heritage.

Be careful not to look at role models through rose-coloured spectacles; they are only human. Ensure you maintain your sense of self and your own identity. Remember that you have choices.

Wisdom affairs

Thomas Daffern, Director of the Green University in the UK is currently researching historical and current thinkers in terms of 'wisdom affairs'. These affairs are not necessarily of a sexual nature, but what they *do* involve is deeply fulfilling partnerships where there is a passionate pursuit of wisdom, truth and meaning as opposed to mere knowledge. There are examples from history, religion, mythology, art and science – for example: Buddha and Ananda; Sydney and Beatrice Webb (Fabian Society); Marx and Engels; Plato and Socrates;

Mohammed and Khadija (his wife); August Rodin and Camille Claudel; Simone de Beauvoir and Jean-Paul Sartre.

Activity: wisdom affairs

Consider your own set of relationships. Do you have any wisdom affairs? What are the implicit and explicit ground rules that you have developed together? How can you pursue wisdom and truth in a meaningful way?

Activity: plotting your network

Fill in the circle diagram shown in Figure 3.7. Note the people you are closest to in the inner circle of relationships. Include the roles of each.

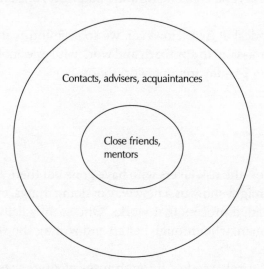

Contacts, advisers, acquaintances

Close friends, mentors

Figure 3.7 Your circle of relationships

35. PHYSICAL STRENGTH

My! What big muscles you've got.

Definition

You have many choices regarding physical strength: to develop your own physical strength through exercise; to involve others who have physical strength in your project; or to use mechanical means to provide the physical strength needed.

Physical strength is not as necessary as in the past. The power of human muscle can be a very useful asset. Among the reasons why people join gyms these days is to improve strength, muscle power, health and morale.

According to Toffler (1991: 34) from the days of the earliest hunters clubbing to death an animal, 'violence has been used to create wealth'; hunting and gathering, agriculture and industry have incorporated force and violence. The history of most labour movements in most countries has a record of blood and terror at some time in their development. This characteristic has not disappeared; it has merely changed its form, being less obvious because it is constrained by laws. Money has taken over as the main form of reward and punishment.

Rationale

Taken to its extreme, physical strength may be used for violent purposes. Surely the march of civilization is showing us that the use of violence should be avoided at all costs: it is just too expensive in terms of injury, human lives, the environment, and the long-term costs of reconciliation, as evidenced by the 1999 war in Kosovo.

So this power base has been included to show its importance and the need for us to learn *different* ways of resolving conflict. See Power Card 24, Mediation, and 43, Rechannelling energy.

The downside of physical strength

Muscle power helps you move, build or knock down physical objects. To use physical strength – or the threat of it – to overcome others is an abuse of this power. An adult may slap a child, but overuse of this method of control is role modelling that physical violence is an accepted way of dealing with things. Domestic violence in its extreme form appears to beget violence in succeeding generations.

People often look to the quantity of power that can be used; however, it is the *quality*, according to Toffler (1991), that is important. Violence, punishment and coercion are low-quality forms of power. They may result in temporary acquiescence, but in the longer term they produce resistance, revenge and retribution. Only a fool would believe that the Gulf War 'solved' the problems in Kuwait and the surrounding region. Since 1991 there has been much controversy about the use of 'institutionalized violence' by the military in the Gulf War and by police in many countries of the world (for example, South Korea and Bosnia).

The advantage that men used to have over women by generally having more physical strength is now diminished to some extent by the advent of computerized machines and technology. It is in employers' interests to enhance and maintain their workers' health.

Lifting and associated back injuries are issues that have been to some extent controlled by mechanized lifting devices.

36. PHYSICAL WELL-BEING

Physical well-being means knowing about your body and caring for it in a holistic way. Nowadays in Western society it is more important to have physical well-being than physical strength.

Rationale

Well-being is an important factor in staying empowered, since sickness saps mental as well as physical and spiritual health. Good diet and regular exercise help to control stress.

Activity: how balanced is your lifestyle?

Check on the balance of your lifestyle. Below is a list of seven items. Tick the ones that apply to you:

1. I don't smoke.
2. I exercise three times per week.
3. I sleep six to eight hours per night.
4. I have a moderate alcohol intake of no more than two glasses per day.
5. I eat three balanced meals each day without snacks
6. I eat breakfast every day.
7. I weigh within 5 lbs of the average weight for my height.

Add up the number of ticks. According to research by Belloc and Breslow (1972), if you are a woman and score six or seven points you are likely to live 7 to 10 years longer than the average for your age group. If you are a man and you score six or seven points, you will live 12 to 15 years longer. Lower scores have concomitantly lesser effects, and a very low score would indicate a shorter than average lifespan. Are there any changes you need to make to your lifestyle, before it's too late?

Activity: exercise at work

You can perform useful exercise at work, even if you are in a sedentary job. The exercises also form useful energizers, especially after lunch. Examples are:

- Rotate shoulders gently forwards and then backwards; lift them one at a time up and down.
- Gently move your head from left to right (do not rotate it) five times; then gently move your head forward and backwards.
- If you find it hard to remember to do the exercises, buy a computer package such as Gym Break, which you can set to interrupt you at the computer every hour. The package contains a variety of simple exercises you can do at your desk.

37. POSITION

'You can't argue with the boss.'
'Why not?'

Definition

Position power comes from the formal recognition given to a person by a recognized organization or legitimate authority. It is sometimes called 'legitimate' power.

Position power:

- is situational – for example, a manager may be in control at work, but at the golf club a worker may be in charge of the manager;
- depends on the beliefs of followers – if a person does not have credibility, no matter how much position power he/she may have, it may lose its potency;
- is not what it used to be, because being in a position of legitimate power used to automatically invoke respect but nowadays this is not automatic – children more readily question their parents and teachers, soldiers question the orders of their leaders, and workers question their supervisors and managers. Even patients are learning to question their doctors.

Rationale

There are times when the basis of legitimate power may itself need to be questioned. The person in the highest legitimate position need not necessarily be the most powerful. In the British TV comedy series *Yes Minister*, Sir Humphrey, the Permanent Secretary, was able to influence the decisions and behaviour of his hierarchical superior, the Prime Minister.

Furthermore, sometimes people are promoted to positions beyond their capabilities (called 'the Peter Principle'), and in these circumstances, too, position power may need to be re-evaluated.

The position power of educators and developers

For the first 1,500 years of the Christian era, many priests regarded themselves as gate-keepers, enabling or barring people's entrance to heaven and acting as intermediaries to God. As they were some of the few who could read and write, they were the guardians of books and learning. The Renaissance led to a strong demand for printed material. The advent of the printing press led to a new paradigm, where information and education started to be promulgated for the many.

The advent of the computer has had an even greater impact on the position of the educators. Teachers, lecturers and universities are no longer the 'keys to wisdom' through which a learner must learn. Computer-based distance learning and literature searches have enabled students to reach higher levels of learning without ever setting foot in a university. As Freire (1972, 1974) and Long (1990) point out, the power of educators and developers is changing to that of facilitators, supervisors, guides and *provocateurs*. Teachers have lost their traditional status in Western communities. In contrast, in South-East Asia, the traditional teacher-centred paradigms still exist, which is why learner-centred learning is alien to many Asian students who come to Australia to study.

Too much red tape?

In a university where I used to work, a Head of the School of Education came into my office one day and smiled and said 'So many things seem to be happening in here. You are lucky to work in the school you are in' (I was co-ordinating a Graduate Programme in Career Studies). I asked why she perceived that the School of Education could not be creative? Her comment was that there was 'too much red tape'. Yet we worked in the same institution and she had far more position/legitimate power than I had at that time. This was an interesting instance of a person giving away her position and personal power.

Activity: assess your position power

What position power do you have at work, at home or in the community? How do you use or abuse it? How do you share your power and delegate? (See also Power Card 8, Delegation.)

38. POSITIVE AND CONSTRUCTIVE FEEDBACK

'Well done, that was terrific! I especially liked. . .'

Definition

'Feedback' is a relatively new term in the social sciences. It comes from electronics and cybernetics experiments, but in behavioural terms it means 'a way of learning more about ourselves and the effect our behaviour has on others' (Hopson and Scally, 1982: 153).

It is important that people learn to both give and receive positive and constructive feedback. In my experience, in Western society, people are more likely to accept and absorb negative feedback if it is given skilfully and as constructive suggestions for improvement.

Rationale

The skills of giving and receiving positive and constructive feedback do not necessarily develop naturally. Indeed, there are many poor role models.

Positive feedback and praise

Perhaps the most useful, but little-used, type of feedback is praise. Yes, that's right: a simple pat on the back for a job well done, describing to the individual concerned exactly what it was that you liked. Praise can be incredibly powerful, not only as motivator, but it also does wonders for a person's self-esteem, which as I mentioned earlier is a very important factor in empowerment. Recognition given in front of others can be very powerful too.

These methods work within the home, at work and with our friends. (But be careful not to overdo it with some individuals, as it may evoke jealousy in others.)

The 'PIP' process involves giving **P**ositive feedback first followed by **I**mprovement suggestions and concluding with a **P**ositive, as shown in Figure 3.8.

Remember, too, that most people fear 'losing face' in front of others, especially their peers. Choose an appropriate time and place if even constructive criticism is necessary. Turn negative feedback into suggestions for improvement – for example, 'It will help you stay on task if you read the project guidelines more carefully next time. You could use a highlighter pen to emphasize key points' is better than 'You obviously didn't read the project guidelines properly as you were off the point'.

The notes below on giving and receiving feedback are adapted from Hopson and Scally (1982: 153–59).

Figure 3.8 The PIP process

Giving feedback

The following are useful approaches to bear in mind when giving feedback:

- *Be sincere.* It is better to stay silent than to be insincere.
- *Be clear about what you want to say in advance.* Mentally rehearse if necessary.
- *Be specific.* 'I liked the way Mary stepped in to help Jo…' is better than comments like 'It was OK' or even 'You do good work'.
- *Be selective.* Choose the most important issues first (especially if there are a lot of negatives).
- *Think about the type of person to whom you are going to give feedback.* This may influence how and what you say.
- *Offer rather than impose constructive feedback.* Ask 'Would you like some suggestions on improvements?'
- *Focus on behaviour rather than the person.* 'Joan, I think you need to be more aware of the clock because you left Mary with little time to sum up' is better than 'Joan, you were really selfish as you used up all the time'.
- *Refer to behaviour that can be changed.* 'It would help me if you looked me in the eyes when you asked me a question'. (Remember that eye contact varies from culture to culture.)
- *Avoid putting the person down or making superior-sounding judgements.* So avoid saying something like, 'You were crazy to do that when it was obvious to me that…'
- *Offer alternatives.* 'Perhaps next time you could do xxx…'.
- *Be descriptive rather than evaluative.* 'I noticed lots of examples of teamwork in the way you shared responsibility in the workshop and shared time equally' is better than 'The teamwork was good'.
- *Own the feedback.* Use 'I', not 'we' or 'you'. For example, 'In my opinion…' is better than 'We thought it was…' or 'You are…'.
- *Describe behaviours and feelings.* So: 'When you… I felt… I would have preferred you to…'.
- *Leave the recipient with a choice.* Feedback that implies 'Do it my way' may be rejected. However, there may be some feedback for which there is *no* choice – for example, 'Referencing is mandatory in academia; otherwise you will be penalized for plagiarism'.
- *End positively.* For instance: 'Finally, I must say that I enjoyed your workshop/presentation because…'.

Receiving feedback

In similar fashion, there are some guiding principles for when you are on the receiving end of feedback:

- *Listen to the feedback rather than immediately rejecting or arguing with it.* Let people finish. Keep your ego defence mechanisms in check.
- *Make sure you understand what is being said.* Ask clarifying questions – for example, 'So what you're saying is… Am I right?'
- *Check the feedback with others rather than relying on only one source.* 'Did everyone have problems hearing me, or was it just the people at the back?'
- *Ask for the feedback you want, but don't get.* 'I felt my voice shaking, did you notice it?' Or 'Can you tell me more about…'
- *Say 'Thank you'.* Thank your colleagues for their praise or advice.
- *Decide what you will do as a result of the feedback.* 'I choose to change…' or 'I choose *not* to change…'.

Activity: putting ideas into practice

Read the suggestions above. Prepare what you want to say in advance for a genuine feedback session. Start and end with positives. Think about how many times you praise your pets and how many times you praise your family members.

39. POSITIVE MINDSETS

I'll try anything once.
A bumble bee flies because it doesn't know it can't.

Definition

A person with a positive mindset will see a glass half-filled with water and say, 'Terrific, that glass is 50 per cent full'. A person with a negative outlook, however, will see the same glass and say, 'Oh dear, that glass is half-empty'.

Rationale

Conventional wisdom shows how much a positive mindset can influence our health and success in our ventures.

Positive self-talk

Mohammed Ali, the world champion boxer, was clever at boosting his self-confidence (and at the same time diminishing that of his opponents) by constantly repeating 'I'm the greatest'. Self-acceptance and self-love are very powerful. Self-promotion too can be powerful, so long as it is not overdone.

Some people find it very difficult to enter a room full of strangers. One lady told me how she copes. 'Oh, I just say to myself: "There are no strangers here, only friends I haven't met yet." If I say "hello" to one person, that makes two people who are feeling less apprehensive.'

A positive move

When my father-in-law died, my mother-in-law was faced with the prospect of living in, and maintaining, a bungalow on the outskirts of a small village in Yorkshire. She surprised us with her elation when a flat became vacant in sheltered accommodation in the village. The old people's home also invited her in for a number of coffee mornings so that she could meet people and see if she liked the organization. This helped her prepare mentally for the move, and when she moved in she was greeted by familiar faces rather than by strangers. She also had the room redecorated to suit her taste, bought new curtains and chose which items she wished to take from the bungalow.

My husband went over to the UK (from our home in Australia) to help her with the move and, despite our concerns, she settled in to her bed-sitting room (which also had a small kitchenette and toilet) extremely quickly. In retrospect, it was to a large extent due to her positive outlook. Whereas we regarded the home with some trepidation, she regarded it as a bonus; she no longer had to worry about the bungalow, gardening, maintenance and snow clearing. She retained her independence and privacy, but had access to company if she wanted it. Added to this, she had the sense of security by having a 'warden' who was on call if she needed help.

Explanatory styles

Seligman (1975) and Rotter (1966) describe the difference in 'explanatory styles' relating to their mindsets. Some people have a pessimistic style and others an optimistic style based on three ways in which people explain events to themselves. Take, for example, a person who is out of work:

- *Internal*: 'It is all my fault'. *External*: 'My industry's in a depression'.

- *Stable*: 'The problem is permanent'. *Unstable*: 'I will get work eventually'.
- *Global*: 'My life is ruined'. *Specific*: 'This is a temporary setback'.

Depowered people tend to stay on the left side of the range of feelings illustrated above; empowered people tend to be on the right. Optimists tend to do better in study than expected and have less chronic illness, especially the ages of 45 to 60.

There are many factors that increase a person's propensity for pessimism:

- a parent's pessimistic outlook on life;
- criticisms from teachers;
- major shock events early in life – for example, the death of a parent in early childhood, which is taken as a stable, global loss;
- body chemicals and energy levels.

This does not mean to say that an outlook cannot be changed. It can, if individuals are prepared to work at it every day.

Combining visualization and prayer

A Muslim friend of mine who is involved in Human Resource Development in Kuala Lumpur recently told me how she combines the power of prayer with positive visualization. In a one-week training course, she uses the special Muslim Thursday-night prayer session to involve participants in praying for their goal – for example, to set up a prosperous new business.

Reframing negativity

The determination of the Tibetan people experiencing 'freedom in exile' has made them strong through more than 40 years of Chinese oppression. The expression 'freedom in exile' is a reframing of their predicament. I was astonished to see the Dalai Lama in an interview, where he was asked if he hated the Chinese, reply something like: 'No. After all, if they had not invaded Tibet I would not have been able to travel. This has enabled us to rewrite our constitution and address many of the changes that needed to be made'.

Creative visualization

Creative visualization is a process where you create a film or movie in your mind for the purpose of changing yourself and/or your surroundings. It is different from daydreaming as you are in conscious control of the pictures you generate in your mind. It is 'one of the most natural, gentle and safe self-help disciplines' (Fanning, 1988: 67).

Creative visualization has been used for over 10,000 years! Fanning (1988) suggests that the stone-age cave paintings indicate that people used creative visualization to ensure a successful hunt. The ancient Greeks used visualization for healing and to develop philosophical ideas. A detailed historical perspective is given in his book.

Activity: making a mind movie

A creative visualization exercise is useful for you to 'imagine and feel' yourself achieving your goals – for example, before having to give a talk or before going for a job interview. In both those scenarios you probably want to control nerves and to speak slowly and clearly.

A 'mind movie' is a positive visualization process developed by Hopson and Scally (1983), which may be remembered by the mnemonic RADAR (giving the first letters of each stage):

1. *Relax.* Lie on the floor; breathe slowly. Focus on the ingoing and outgoing breath to relax. Allow the stresses and strains of the day to drain out of you every time you exhale.
2. *Allow the pictures to come.* In your mind, visualize your future goal or dream, your job interview or talk.
3. *Direct the movie.* Concentrate on positive outcomes; edit out any negative images.
4. *Act in the movie yourself.* See yourself smiling: speaking slowly, clearly and confidently.
5. *Reward yourself for being successful.* Give yourself a treat after successfully completing the movie.

Positive mindsets and illness

Imagine a person going to the doctor for a check-up. The doctor asks for some tests, and when the results come out he tells the person that he/she has cancer. Before the check-up, that person may have been walking around feeling fine. However, after having been diagnosed as having cancer, the person becomes a 'patient' and frequently takes on the mindset that cancer is a metaphor for death. Hours beforehand the person had a mindset that he/she was healthy; then that changes rapidly.

Simonton believes that the emotional response directly affects the physical and spiritual responses and that these negative self-talk patterns actually suppressed the body's natural defence mechanisms. With others, he developed 'the Simonton technique' (1992), which involves patients in visualizing and drawing a picture of the 'good' cells in their bodies engulfing and destroying the cancer. The technique has been surprisingly successful.

Norman Cousins, the author, decided to attack his illness by changing the context. He left the hospital and booked himself into a cosy hotel and proceeded to watch non-stop Marx brothers and other comedy films. The results are described in his book *Anatomy of an Illness as Perceived by the Patient*. His cancer went into remission. Ancient Chinese texts speak of *fu-zheng* and describe the natural self-generated use of our disease-fighting powers in the mind (Fanning, 1988).

See also Power Card 12, Feelings.

40. PROBLEM SOLVING AND DECISION MAKING

Good problem solvers don't blame others if things go wrong. They just get on with solving the next problem.

Definition

Problem solving and decision making go hand in hand. You can solve problems in your head, but you need to decide which solutions you will put into action.

Rationale

We cannot expect to sail through life without some things going wrong. Problems are a fact of life. So, it is much better to view problems as a challenge to be solved than as being overbearing and/or unfair.

Activity: Combining intuition and reasoning

During the Age of Reason and the Industrial Era, feelings and intuition were suppressed as being unreasonable. Today, in the Information Age, things are changing radically and we need to use the potential of all our brains. Hopson and Scally (1986) suggest the combination shown in Table 3.8 for enhancing decision making, combining as it does intuition and reason. You could experiment with the content of this table to analyse a decision you need to make in the near future. Remember: you can and should use both intuition and reasoning in problem solving.

Table 3.8 Combining intuition and reasoning (from Hopson and Scally, 1981–86)

USE INTUITION	USE REASON
You choose what feels right; you play a hunch without thinking about it	Generate your options
	Gather information
	Clarify your values
	Analyse the risks
Decide on the best alternatives using both intuition and reason	Decide on the best alternatives using both intuition and reasoned alternative/s
Act	Act
Evaluate	Evaluate

Group decision making

Group decision making is more complicated than individual decision making, but for complex issues it is better to have input from many different perspectives. In group decision making a number of aspects need to be considered:

- Who is involved in the decision-making process?
- What issues are to be discussed?
- When should issues be raised, if at all? (Some hidden agendas never get raised in public. This may lead to anger later on as people feel that they have been deceived.)
- How are decisions to be made – by voting, consensus, expert, minority group or individual?

Some people think voting is the only way of making group decisions, partly because it *appears* quick and simple. However, quick decision making may lead to implementation problems later on. You can use 'straw voting' at various stages in trying to reach consensus; authority rule after discussion (eg a leader consults his/her team) or decision by a minority (eg an expert panel). Each mode has advantages and disadvantages, but the important thing is to let people know what process you are using: tell them the ground rules.

Technology as an aid to group decision making

Group problem solving and decision making in asynchronous time may be speeded up by using networked computers and programs such as PLEXUS, MEETINGWORKS and GROUPUTER. Electronic methods are now being used to enable groups to brainstorm anonymously and evaluate ideas. This means that ideas from senior executives are not automatically regarded as better than those of employees in other parts of the hierarchy. These methods enable the ideas of quieter people to be noted and discussed.

In my university we use MEETINGWORKS software to develop new curricula using the DACUM process (Hogan, 1994a), to enable students to evaluate courses in depth, and to involve staff in future departmental planning.

41. PUBLIC COMMITTAL

I am going to give up smoking.

Definition

Announcing something to friends and the public at large reinforces commitment. That is why politicians often shy away from speeches being taped or being put on the spot regarding promises in public. So this power card can be used in many different ways.

Rationale

Individuals may use this power base with colleagues in order to motivate themselves by making a public statement of a goal or action plan – for example, 'I am going to give up smoking'. At work, it is often useful to invite power-holders to make an announcement of their committal and support at the beginning of a project. Power-holders usually do not like to go back on what they have announced in public for fear of 'losing face'.

The power of dialogue

An example of using public committal for change is the 'power of dialogue' in the format of Alcoholics Anonymous (AA) meetings. In Australia, all members who are present are invited to speak at every meeting. As a visitor to an open AA meeting I was impressed by the strength that participants appeared to gain from being able to describe their thoughts, feelings and actions to a non-judgmental audience who actively listened and did not attempt to discuss, problem-solve or intervene. The whole recovery process is up to the individual. Even quieter members spoke – after all, everyone (including the session leader) had been through similar experiences.

See also the power of dialogue in journal writing in the Power of Reflection (Card 45) and the Power of Silence (Card 52).

42. QUESTIONING

There is no such thing as a stupid question. You have the right to ask questions.

Definition

There are many types of questions, for example:

- *Open-ended questions*: What do you do for a living?
- *Closed questions*: Are you a teacher or a student?
- *Probing questions*: Can you tell me more about your role?
- *Rhetorical questions*: What is the meaning of life? To me it is… (ie no answer is expected).

Rationale

I have observed that there have been many occasions in my life when I have wanted to ask questions, but did not know where to start; I also felt intimidated. Earlier, I stated that in writing this book, my value stance was that I hoped that increased self-empowerment would encourage dialogue and questioning. In the latter, I was referring to the need for us all to have the skills to question and find out more.

Activity: using the 'silent demonstration' process

By learning questioning skills, we are all released from the need always to have 'good' trainers or demonstrators. Downs and Perry (1981) developed a process to help students learn how to question. They proposed that, in a 'silent demonstration', students should learn new skills illustrated without a verbal commentary. The onus would be on students to question the presenter. Questions should be documented and classified under the headings shown below. The presenter would then be able to praise learners for the questions they have asked and show them what questions they should have asked or show them how they could have improved their questions.

QUESTIONING FRAMEWORK (AFTER DOWNS AND PERRY, 1981)

1. Purpose
What is this for? What does this bit do and why?

2. Procedure or order of things
Do I have to do things in any particular order?

---

3. Names and factual information
What is this called? How long will it last? Where was it made?

4. Measures and standards
Is this machine made according to industry standards? Is this equipment covered by a guarantee? What does the guarantee cover/not cover? How long is it valid? Does it cover all parts and all repair labour costs?

5. Manual (feels and holds) and perceptual (smell, colour, sound, look)
How tightly should I fasten this screw? What should the finished product look, taste or feel like?

6. Safety
Should I switch off at the mains before connecting all the leads? What if there is a power cut/thunder storm? Are there any safety precautions I have to take if I move this appliance around in my car? Are there any dangerous fumes?

Questions for action planning

The 5WH model can help you cover all aspects of action planning. WH stands for the initial letters of each question word:

- **What** is the project exactly?
- **Who** is going to be responsible for doing it and with whom?
- **When** does it have to be done by?
- **Why** is it important?
- **Where** do you start?
- **How** will you go about it?

Added to these is: And with what resources?

43. RECHANNELLING ENERGY

> If *satyagraha* is to be the mode of the future, then the future belongs to women.
>
> (Mahatma Gandhi)

Definition

Methods for rechannelling energy have been described in many ways: political *aikido*, *satyagraha*, transforming power.

Satyagraha

Gandhi called *satyagraha* the 'soul force' or 'truth force'. It is much more than just passive resistance, as described in some books; it is rather a positive energy relating to two attributes: fierce autonomy and total compassion. Marilyn Ferguson (1982: 217) quotes Gandhi as saying:

> I will not coerce you. Neither will I be coerced by you. If you behave unjustly, I will not oppose you by violence (body-force) but by the force of truth – the integrity of my beliefs. My integrity is evident in my willingness to suffer, to endanger myself, to go to prison, even to die if necessary. But I will not co-operate with injustice.

This philosophy forms the basis of many anti-nuclear groups, Greenpeace, etc.

Aikido

Aikido is based on the principles of martial arts, which aim to harmonize and harness energy rather than block it. *Ai* means harmony, *ki* means energy, *do* means the way, so *aikido* means 'the way of harmonizing energy'.

You cannot change others, but you may be able to channel their energies and talents in directions you want. This is the basic use of energy in Far Eastern martial arts, where energy is nullified or redirected rather than blocked, without harming the attacker.

Rationale

This power base is one of the cleverest as it actually transforms the powers and energies of others.

Growing respect

When I was a child, a young man called Alan moved in across the street. My father at once chatted to him. My father told me that Alan had been in his primary school class some years previously, and that he had been continually very naughty. My father had put him in charge of the class zoo (which included frogs, fish, small snakes and lizards). The boy had assumed his responsibilities well and woe betide any student who forgot to feed the animals etc. Also, his behaviour had gradually changed as he started to enjoy the trust and growing respect of his teacher and peers.

Similarly, there has even been some evidence in the training of children as mediators in

Northern Ireland that bullies make excellent mediators. This was evidence that their energies could be rechannelled productively!

Facilitating the channelling of energy

Facilitators often put noisy or dominating participants in charge of scribing on a flipchart or small discussion groups with the job of reporting back findings to the whole group. They thus get an outlet for their energy or need for recognition by the group.

Activity: rechannel energies

Think of ways you can rechannel the energies of people in your life at home, at work or in the community. Are there ways you can conserve your energies from dissipation by transforming the energies of others?

44. REDEFINING WHO WE ARE: GENDER ISSUES

A person is a human being first.

Definition

Steve Biddulph (1995) argues that the biological differences between males and females account largely for behavioural differences. Rod Mitchell of Liberation Management in Perth, Western Australia, on the other hand challenges Biddulph's contention that the difference between males and females is mainly biological and challenges the conditioning of both males and females. Mitchell believes that we should not stereotype human characteristics as being either male or female, but regard them all as potential human qualities (R Mitchell, personal communication 1999).

The activity set out below is an exercise he uses in workshops to enhance ideas of gender equity.

Rationale

'Redefining who we are' was added as a power base since many people nowadays are involved in their own self-development, and one area is the extension beyond stereotypical gendered behaviours that has in the past resulted from a conservative upbringing.

Activity: attributes you possess and wish to acquire

Question: What are the positive attributes in our society that are generally attributed to men and women? Complete Table 3.9 below, where some examples have already been given to start you off.

Then look at the list in Table 3.9 and circle the qualities *you* have that you admire and value in yourself. Now tick two attributes from either column that you would like to develop.

Mitchell then suggests that we look at the list. The entries are all human qualities, and all newborn babies have the potential to develop any of these attributes.

The conditioning process, however, imposes certain qualities in girls, even though they are already inherent. The conditioning process similarly imposes certain qualities in boys, even though they are already inherent. Girls who are inherently nurturing are scolded if they do not show that trait. Similarly, strength is attributed to masculinity, and if boys do not develop qualities of strength, they are scolded and bullied for not conforming to the norm, for not 'being male'. During conditioning, so-called 'female' qualities are systematically denied to men and so-called 'male' qualities are systematically denied to females (see Figure 3.9, indicating the process of conditioning, and Table 3.10, showing the impact of conditioning).

Table 3.9 Positive attributes of males and females

MALE	FEMALE
Strong	Nurturing
Decisive	Co-operative
Rational	Loving
Protectors	Good listeners
Technical and practical	Show emotions
Leaders	Peacemakers

Figure 3.9 The conditioning process

Table 3.10 The impact of conditioning

MALE CONDITIONING	Long-term effects	FEMALE CONDITIONING	Long-term effects
Be a man, don't be a sissy.	Terror of being seen as un-masculine.	Be ladylike and dainty.	Fear of not appearing feminine. Wearing clothing that limits movement or even harms the body – for example, high heels.
Show you are the boss; speak out; state your opinions.	Competition for status, power and air space in discussion.	Don't be brainy, men will be scared of you. Listen.	Playing down mental achievements. Lack of voice, fear of speaking out.
Hide your emotions.	Addiction to computers, sport, alcohol – anything to hide feelings. Isolation.	Be pretty, be slim.	Addiction to make-up, image, diets: anorexia, bulimia.
Take risks, be a hunk, be strong.	Addiction to body-building, fighting, bravado, risking life and limb.	Don't take risks; be careful.	Limiting activities and mobility in the community, lack of risk taking.

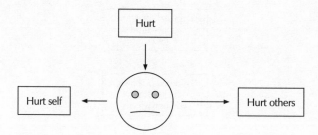

Figure 3.10 Displaced hurt and internalized oppression

This conditioning may be so oppressive and destructive that it takes our inherent human nature and destroys it almost beyond recognition.

The results of the above attitudes are hurt, anger and frustration in both genders. There is no point in blaming the other gender for the societal norms that have developed, because both are victims of imposed societal norms.

Unfortunately, the hurt is often acted out on others – see Figure 3.10, which shows how the hurt caused by some of these codes and mores is not only perpetuated by adults but also by children and teenagers in playgrounds and classrooms. Young males may also 'act out' certain tough behaviours on others or themselves as self-abuse or mutilation.

It is much more productive for people to work together to improve current and future norms. This has been done in both single-sex and mixed support groups, where people meet to express and release their feelings of frustration, anger, fear and embarrassment, and where they develop new ways of thinking and being. This may be a lifelong process because the conditioning from childhood may take some time to change.

At a societal level, many schools and parents are choosing reading and educational materials with more care. Children and adults are learning about stereotyping and encouraged to develop a wide range of positive human attributes and behaviours. Pressure is being brought on the media. But 'capitalism thrives on conditioned differences' (Mitchell, 1998). The fashion industry, sport, and the alcohol, drug and pornography industries all thrive on the ideal images portrayed to us by society. So there is still a long way to go.

Activity: self-exploration

Are there any ways in which you wish to expand your repertoire of skills or knowledge into areas that are non-traditional for your gender? If so, how will you go about this? Are there any issues raised above that have a bearing on your family life? If yes, how can you go about communicating your changing needs to your family?

45. REFLECTION

Sometimes I just sits and thinks, and sometimes I just sits.

Definition

Reflection is a conscious effort to cast the mind back over the past. It is not a passive activity, as is sometimes thought.

Rationale

Western society tends to focus on 'doing' rather than 'being'. We say 'How do you do?', not 'How do you be?' Even sitting at a desk in an open-plan office at work quietly reflecting, you may get challenged with, 'Haven't you got anything to do?' Yet, rushing from one thing to another may be both ineffective and inefficient 'busy work'. Indeed, the word 'business' is derived from 'busyness'. Perhaps we need to develop 'stillness studies' in order to complement 'business studies'.

Reason for reflection

Although 'reflection' is the second stage of Kolb's Experiential Learning Cycle (See Power Card 9, Experience), it is often neglected in our learning and in workshops. Why? I believe the reasons are threefold:

1. Facilitators and trainers often have a tendency towards 'activist' behavioural patterns. As a result, they tend to pack in as many exercises as possible instead of allowing the majority of time for reflection.
2. Facilitators and trainers want to give participants value for money, and they equate this with quantity.
3. Participants are often loath to slow down to undertake reflection, because in the workplace there is little time for reflection and it is not valued. They may be fearful of confronting real issues about real behaviour in their organization. Therefore they try to pressurize their facilitator or trainer into 'moving on'.

I have experienced instances as a facilitator when some participants have wanted to continue with activities without reflecting. I stopped proceedings in order to make visible

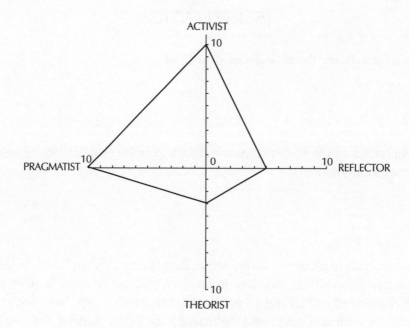

Figure 3.11 Learning Styles (after Honey and Mumford, 1986)

the group's process. I use two arguments to persuade participants for the need for reflection. After all, adult learners need to know why they are doing something.

First, I drew and explained Honey and Mumford's (1986) Learning Styles and the characteristics of each style (see Figure 3.11). That diagram shows a profile for an individual who has a very practical side who prefers to learn experientially rather than by reflecting and/or learning theory.

Honey and Mumford assert that we all have mixtures of each of the four learning styles, but many people have preferences and it is these styles in which we are most comfortable. In order to maximize individual and group learning, we need to ensure that we have developed a variety of exercises that include all four styles in order to keep up the interest of everyone and also to help people learn from all angles. The characteristics of each learning style are shown in Table 3.11.

Second, I drew Kolb's Experiential Learning Model (1984), as shown in Figure 3.12, explaining 'The model contains four areas shown in the boxes. If you miss out on one or more areas, 'deep' learning may not take place'. Third, I linked the two models so that learners could see the relationship. I added the learning styles in italics. With that explanation, the group settled down to reflecting before moving on to the next exercise.

Table 3.11 Learning style characteristics

Learning Styles	Characteristics
Activist	Jumps in first, loves experiential learning and doing before thinking.
Reflector	Sits and thinks things through first before acting.
Theorist	Likes to know where things come from, and who researched what.
Pragmatist	Of a practical bent: 'How will I use this at work or at home?'

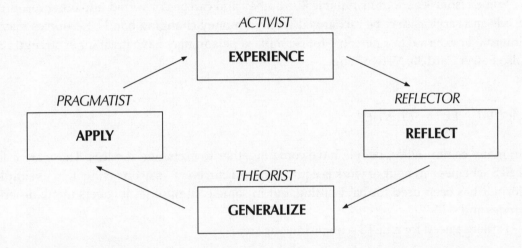

Figure 3.12 Links between the Experiential Learning Model of Kolb (**bold**) and the learning styles of Honey and Mumford (*italics*)

46. RESOURCES/RESOURCE EXCHANGE

It's more than my job's worth to bend the rules to give you extra disks...

Definition

Tangible resources include money, equipment and buildings. Raw materials such as minerals, timber, water and air are a gift given to us in trust by the earth. Intangible resources include goodwill, energy and enthusiasm, mutual support, skills and knowledge. These are built up over time. People have only finite resources of energy.

Rationale

Every person in a community or organization has control over some area, however small. Sometimes even the people in so-called 'lower' status positions may have extreme powers, and if you get on the wrong side of them they may choose to exercise their power in the manner of the quote above.

People who are guardians of resources have a strong power base. At work, who guards the budget, stationery, computing resources? Do you have easy or difficult access to these resources, and can you influence how they are distributed?

Some resources are transmutable like money and can be converted into other resources. Skills and services may be exchanged without money changing hands. Resources may be internal or external to a person – for example, a person may have great inner strength. See also Power Card 30, Networking.

Activity: LETS schemes

In many communities, people have come together to exchange services. These are called LETS schemes. An hour of work is equivalent to a currency – say one widget. In its simplest form it has been used for baby-sitting, but in some communities it covers many different trades and skills.

Is there a need for a LETS scheme in your area?

47. RESPONSIBILITY

Who will bell the cat?

(title of a US children's story)

Definition

Responsibility means being accountable for people, things and actions. It is part of growing up and part of the process of exercising citizenship. We all need to take responsibility for our own decisions and actions.

Rationale

One problem with Western society I believe is the way in which we often do not give enough responsibility to teenagers. In the developing world, there is hardly a recognizable adolescent phase since children leave school early and join the workforce. At the other end of life, some senior citizens are depowered, however lovingly, by relatives, friends or staff in retirement homes. Taking responsibility can be difficult and I use the US story 'Who Will Bell the Cat?' (see p146) because it humorously brings this point home.

CASE STUDY

Ellen Langer (1991) describes an experiment she conducted in 1976 when she explored the effects of decision making and responsibility on residents in a nursing home. She divided up the residents into an experimental and a control group. Health records of each group were similar. The people in the experimental group were actively encouraged to make more decisions:

- They had some say in where to receive visitors: inside the home, in the garden, in their personal rooms, in the dining room or in the lounge.
- When a film was available to be shown, they had to decide whether to view it or not and on what day.
- Each person was given a houseplant to care for, and he or she had to decide when to water it, where to put it, etc.

The people in the control group were given plants, but were told that the nurses would look after them. They were not encouraged to make any decisions for themselves and were encouraged to consult the staff who, they were told, were there to help them.

Measurements of behaviour and emotions were taken before and after the experiment, and then again 18 months later. The residents who had been given more responsibility were significantly more active, vigorous and sociable. Measurements of physical health indicated that there was a lower mortality rate in the decision-making group, at 15 per cent per year compared with 30 per cent in the control group.

Overprotectiveness

Overprotectiveness frequently leads to a loss of autonomy. Langer (1991) describes a discussion with an 80-year-old woman whom she met visiting her older 84-year-old sister in a nursing home. The nursing home resident had asked her sister to bring in some wooden laundry tongs so that she could put on her underwear without help as it was hard for her to bend over. When Langer asked if she had brought them in, the sister replied firmly: 'Heavens no! If she'd used them she'd probably have hurt her back!' In other words, well-meant protectiveness was undermining the inventiveness, initiative and autonomy of the sister.

Who will bell the cat?

Once upon a time in a far and distant land, there was a huge family of mice. They overran the whole household, peering out of cupboards and fireplaces and even making nests in the soft furnishings and beds of human beings. Then one day a cat arrived. It acted as if it owned the place! The poor mice were chased, mauled and – heaven forbid – even eaten. Life was just not the same any more.

So one day the mice called a meeting. One of the elders spoke first 'What are we going to do about the cat?' Lots of noise and muttering ensued. Another elder raised a paw. 'Wait. . . we will never get anywhere like this. Someone must get some flipchart paper so we can brainstorm ideas.' Nods of approval and scurrying of feet produced paper, masking tape and even felt pens. 'Right. Let's start again. What are we going to do about the cat?'

'Poison it!' 'Pull its fur out!' 'Get a dog' (much squeaking and laughter). 'Move house'. . . etc. A hundred ideas were suggested (for they were very creative mice!). Eventually the noise and energy died down a little and a tiny mouse at the back squeaked up: 'Why don't we put a bell on the cat so that we can hear it when it comes near, and then we'll have time to run away?'

Silence permeated the room. Then there was an eruption of 'Yes!' 'That's it!' 'Fantastic!' 'What an idea!' 'Give that mouse the Nobel peace prize'.

When the noise had died down, a baby mouse slowly raised its paw shaking and said 'Excuse me, but who will bell the cat?'

Activity: taking responsibility

Observe yourself and others at home and at work, and identify how many times no one takes responsibility, eg 'The ansaphone wasn't on'.

48. REWARDS

'Thank you so much for...'

Definition

Rewards are some kind of remuneration that we give to others for an action or behaviour. We all have many rewards we can give to or receive from others: praise, hugs, gifts, public acknowledgement. See also Power Card 38, Positive and constructive feedback.

Rationale

In the workplace, the use of reward power base has been changing. Where teams allocate work tasks, the supervisor loses control of this power base, with its ability to reward or punish people by giving them either the nice or disliked jobs. Team members often nowadays take on this responsibility. With the flattening of hierarchies, there are fewer chances for reward by promotion, and so managers have to think of other ways of rewarding a job well done.

Rewards do not have the same 'valence' or value for different individuals. As a result, it is useless to use the same rewards for all. In some organizations a 'cafeteria style' of reward system has developed. I recall a family friend, Phil, who walked into our band practice one night with a huge grin and a new electric bass guitar tucked under his arm. He quickly explained that he was due for a bonus at IBM and they showed him a list of items he could choose from. He noticed the guitar in the next level up and asked if he could have that if he paid the difference. His manager readily agreed and Phil was really pleased.

There are many types of reward – bonuses at work, chocolates or flowers at home – but be careful not to get the other person dependent on physical rewards. If we overuse material or food rewards at home, some children may come to expect a reward for 'good' behaviour – and the same applies to pets! Again, see Power Card 38, Positive and constructive feedback, for other insights into this topic.

49. SAYING 'NO'

'No', 'I'm sorry, but no', 'No thank you', 'No, not now, but how about later?'

Definition

There are many degrees of 'No' – from a definite 'No' to a not sure 'No'. The ability to say 'No' without causing offence is an art as well as an assertive skill.

Rationale

Many of us were raised to please others, and this remains ingrained in our adult behaviour. We feel that if we say 'No', we might be disliked or regarded as incompetent. However, saying 'No' may be a vital part of staying effective and efficient in our roles and responsibilities.

Activity: an exercise in saying 'No'

The stages are very simple:

1. Listen to what the person has to say.
2. Decide whether what the person is asking is important or urgent. If it is not, say 'No'.
3. Give reasons.
4. Offer alternatives.
5. Don't feel guilty – you cannot be all things to all people all the time.

Take a situation where you want to refuse a request and try to put the five-stage process above into effect – including, if necessary, practising not feeling guilty.

Two examples

For example, a male colleague walks into your office to ask for help. You are really stressed trying to finish something before a 4 o'clock meeting. You listen to his request, decide that it is not urgent (although it is important to him), and say something like: 'Look, I've only got 30 minutes to finish my report for the 4 o'clock meeting. I know this issue is important to you, so why don't we meet tomorrow at nine when we're both fresh. Meanwhile, you think about it overnight.' The chances are that your colleague will have solved the issue by the next day.

Some people suggest that we do not have to give reasons for turning down someone's request to us for our time or other resources. I believe it depends on the circumstance and whether or not we want to maintain an ongoing positive working relationship with that person. For example, if a person intrudes into my home space by knocking on my door in order to try and sell me something I already have, I do not hesitate to say 'No' and do not give any explanation. However, if my Head of Department asks me to do something that I feel is impossible, I would certainly go through all five stages mentioned above, including giving my reasons.

Here is an example of a different kind. I have a regular detailed correspondence with my cleaning lady. As we rarely see one another, we communicate through written messages in a small book. I asked her one week how her diet was going; she answered that she had lost over two stone. Surprised, I asked her the secret of her will-power. She replied, 'It's not a question of will-power but *won't* power.'

Cultural differences

Saying 'No' openly does not suit all cultures. In South-East Asia, for example, people are far less direct and often offer alternatives: in response to 'Would you like to come to our house at 5.00 pm?', instead of a flat 'No, that is not convenient' a more polite but indirect approach would consist of 'Perhaps 7.00 pm would be more suitable, especially as you have to work that day'.

I recall in Hong Kong that if I asked a secretary to do some typing saying 'Can you finish this by Thursday?' the reply was often 'I'll try' rather than 'No, I'm too busy but Friday is fine'. The secretary did not want to hurt my feelings by giving me a negative answer.

Tactics for refusing requests

Some less assertive people (or those who just want to block a request) often say 'Put your request in writing and I'll submit it to our committee'. In some ways, paradoxically, it may actually help the requesting person to put down his or her major issues. The committee then takes the blame for refusing the request. Some managers who do not like to take on responsibility or be held accountable for decisions use this strategy.

It appears that people appreciate being given a fair hearing. When the process and the explanation for a refusal seem fair, people are more willing to accept a negative decision.

When 'No' means 'Yes'

In sexual relationships, single women are usually trained by their parents to say 'No' to sexual advances. Misunderstandings occur when the 'No' means 'Definitely no' or 'No, not yet' or 'Yes, but later'. It is important that women listen to their intuition when dealing with unwelcome advances and that they remove themselves as quickly as possible from any threatening situation.

50. SENSES

The smell of baking bread takes me back to my childhood.

Definition

Our senses include sight, touch, taste, feeling, and hearing. Some of these have already been discussed under the Power of active listening (Card 1) and the Power of intuition (Card 19).

Rationale

This card has been included to remind you to use all your senses in learning and communicating with others. According to Richard Bandler (1979), some people relate to the world with one sense dominating. He called the study of people's language patterns 'Neurolinguistic programming' (NLP).

Neurolinguistic programming is a way of communicating using, and tuning into, other people's sensory preferences that are expressed through language – for example: 'I see what you mean', 'I heard someone in the group say…' or 'It touched me when he said…'. The suggestion is that people should use this methodology as a way of tapping into the listener's view of the world in order to communicate more effectively.

Smell

The effects of smells, noise, vibrations from refineries, abattoirs or factories, can be very depowering. Even the chemical smells from office cleaning processes can make some people feel ill at work and exacerbate disorders such as asthma. On the other hand, I have sometimes taken lavender into the training room because it is known for its relaxing qualities. I gave everyone a piece and noticed that frequently during the workshop individuals took a quiet sniff. It certainly induces a feeling of well-being.

Noise and sound

Sound can be measured, and certain levels may be painful to your ears. Noise, on the other hand, is 'unwelcome' sound and is subjective. Pop music to a teenager is sound, but to a stressed parent it may be perceived as noise and therefore a frequent source of conflict. See also Power Card 29 relating to the power of music, singing and dancing.

Touch

Touch can be used to make people feel more powerful – for example, a hand on the shoulder, a congratulatory handshake or a hug.

In Australia, until recently it was not customary for women to shake hands with men. However, coming from the United Kingdom, I find that hand-shaking is normal behaviour for me and something that I continue to practise because I find that it enables me to make an assertive introduction, especially with men.

Touch has to be used with care by facilitators, as some people do not like to be touched. Often, you can sense those who need more private, personal space. Or ask 'That's terrific news, can I give you a hug?' Touch also may be culturally inappropriate. Whilst living in Nepal I had to learn not to hug my Nepalese colleagues.

Activity: NLP in practice

Try utilizing some of the NLP language next time you are in a group: I see, I heard, I felt... . If you are developing marketing or advertising materials for courses or your work, try to include all the senses.

You can read more about NLP and its applications to the business and training world in Johnson (1996), Knight (1999) and Kamp (1996).

51. SEXUAL ATTRACTION

Wow! What a hunk!

Definition

Sexual attraction can vary from the magnetism between two individuals to the sexual act. What is the chemistry that attracts us to some people and not to others and vice versa? And how we respond to that chemistry depends on one's marital status and/or standards of morality.

Using sexual favours as a power base at work rarely works in the long run, as many men and women in public life (not least US presidents) have found to their cost. Like the power of coercion, the power of sex is usually only effective in the short term.

Rationale

In the workplace we need to be careful. It is impossible to turn the clock back and very difficult to return to a 'normal' working relationship after a sexual encounter has ended. After 102 interviews on power, Richard Brislin (1991) came to the conclusion:

Don't use sex as a resource in the power arena.

Sexual attractiveness and flirting

Sexual attractiveness does not necessarily involve sex and, as such, flirting in the workplace – provided it is wanted by both parties – can spark fun, productivity and motivation. It can also give energy to a 'wisdom affair' (see Power Card 34, Personal supporters).

Finding a partner

Clearly, if a person is using the card pack to help for either finding a partner or improving relationships, then this is a useful card to use. In pursuing a partner, a person may adopt many of the power bases described above – for example, the Power of perseverance (Card 32).

My sister and her friends went to ballroom-dancing classes after school. One friend was really attracted to the much older instructor. This girl continued with her lessons and entered competitions well into adulthood. She was always there to help and support the instructor. Eventually they married.

Cultural differences

In many cultures, marriages are arranged and the power of sexual attraction is often ignored. The arrangements are made frequently to increase the influence and/or prestige of families. Sometimes, huge dowries of land, money or goods are negotiated. Some friends in India told me that arranged marriages took away the stress and embarrassment of looking for, and possibly being rejected by, a potential partner. They saw the Western 'courting' process as very stressful and demeaning.

Facilitation and sexual attractiveness

Teachers/facilitators have legitimate power in their groups. We have thus to be careful not to abuse our position power. Some participants may see us in a somewhat glorified light and do not see us as real people 'warts and all'. It is important to maintain professional boundaries.

At one time I used abseiling as part of assertiveness training for women. I always hired a professional team of instructors. I was shocked one day when I realized that many of the women were not going over the edge through their own personal power, will-power or courage; some were looking doe-eyed into the eyes of the male instructor at the top of the cliff who was a good-looking, gentle hunk. They were going over the edge for him – as I also had done subconsciously the first time I abseiled! After that realization, I started to use all female instructors and achieved far better results in women empowering themselves and taking responsibility for their own risk taking.

52. SILENCE

The sounds of silence.

(Simon and Garfunkel, from a song of the same name)

Definition

Gandhi worshipped silence. He called it the 'still, small voice'. There are so many different kinds of silence. I feel 'contented, relaxed silence' when I sit with my spouse and watch the river flowing past our house. There is 'personal silence', the ability to be relaxed and contented with oneself. At my secondary school, silence was linked to misbehaviour and punishment. The harsh command 'Silence!' quickly warned us that something was wrong. It frequently heralded a drawn-out inquisition by a teacher who 'put us in silence' while waiting for someone to own up to some misdeed. So silence became an interruption to 'learning' and 'doing' in my mind; I wished for silence and it's associated tensions to end. 'Punitive silence' was used deliberately to depower us and to assert dominance by many lay and religious staff alike. 'Hallowed silence' was linked to the church, the sacraments and the priests. In religious classes we would listen in 'bored silence' to the monotonous tones of priests and nuns. Now I have learnt to appreciate the value of silence.

Rationale

I once assumed that there is no hierarchy in silence, but there is. I used to think that silence was an equalizer, but it is not. Silence can be a very powerful communication tool. Also, knowledge of the different cross-cultural meanings of silence is important.

Silence and culture

Ease with silence is culturally based. Some people (including myself) think and work best orally or by writing down ideas, drawing or orally piggy-backing in joyful brainstorming. Aboriginal people, on the other hand, find long periods of silence comfortable. An

Indonesian student in my class recently said, 'I would rather sit here in silence than say something badly that might hurt someone's feelings'. Western (particularly Anglo-Saxon and Latin) societies are in comparison noisy.

Uses of silence

Silence and speech making

Silence can be used for effect in a speech. Pauses after key statements allow the significance and meaning to sink in. A teacher who is speaking and who is also aware of a child talking at the back of the class can quickly draw attention to his/her displeasure by pausing in mid-sentence. Hitler sometimes stood for five minutes in front of a packed Munich stadium before launching into one of his rallying speeches; the silence built up a great sense of expectation and tenseness.

Silence and the Quakers

Silence is also useful for individual reflection. In our noisy Western society we seem to be almost afraid of silence. Quakers practise silence at their meetings and wait for some inner impulse to motivate someone to speak. They use 'the spirit of silence' and fellowship for group reflection and meditation.

I remember my first visit to a Quaker meeting-house near my home. I arrived early and chatted to people in the hallway. They invited me to go in and join the others. This I did and sat waiting for the meeting to 'begin'. After a while I became restless and thought 'They're late'. Then I realized that indeed they *had* begun, but each individual interpreted this in his/her own way. One person sat reading; another stared ahead; another had eyes closed. After half an hour a man got up and spoke. 'At last, I thought. Something is happening!' How wrong I was, since there were so many 'happenings' already.

All Quaker meetings are grounded in the use of periods of silence to open participants to guidance from the 'spirit', and this principle applies to all meetings, including business meetings. In the 18th century, Quaker John Woolman led many 'Clearness Meetings' with Quaker slave owners in the USA. Through these meetings, many Quaker slave owners came to the realization that they could no longer own and/or work people as slaves. This movement contributed to the abolition of slavery.

Silence and rebellion

In January 1998, I attended a course on 'Human Values in Management' in Calcutta, India. The course contained long periods of meditation, including an hour each morning at 6 am. I entered into this with determination, despite not being a 'morning person'. However, at first I found silence whilst walking and eating with others to be difficult, embarrassing and unnatural – it reminded me of school, and I played the 'rebellious child' at times, so much so that within three days the group had rebelled and the professor in charge of the course offered to change the norm he had imposed.

Interestingly, once our concerns had been raised, the group agreed to persevere; managing silence became easier; I later found it freeing, relaxing and healing. I had many spontaneous insights and new ideas. After four days of this 'retreat', I confided in a Danish participant that, 'I am no longer afraid of silence'. My colleague was surprised at the comment and so was I. During that course I learnt to enjoy 'solitary silence' in my room and 'group silence' when being around people or in collective meditation sessions.

Silence in business meetings

During business meetings a facilitator can help the group, if it is 'stuck' or in a heated repetitious debate, by invoking silence, not as a means of suppression but as a way of enabling everyone to catch their breath and their thoughts. One minute of silence between eight individuals is eight minutes of relaxation, thought and release of tension.

Does silence infer agreement?

When a leader or facilitator asks in a meeting 'Is there anyone who does not agree with this proposal?' and pauses, the facilitator sometimes mistakenly interprets the ensuing silence as agreement, that is, 'Speak now or for ever hold thy peace'. However, silence in that context may not indicate consensus, especially if there is fear of recrimination.

An assertive pause

An assertive pause is a reactive strategy to control knee-jerk reactions to verbal attack or hurt (Eales-White, 1994). It involves training yourself to pause before reacting. It can involve a deep breath, as opposed to our normal shallow breathing. It relates to the old expressions such as 'count to 10 before reacting'.

An assertive pause may also be used proactively for emphasis and effect. For example, in a meeting it is useful to let people argue back and forth and wait for a lull and then make a centred intervention along these lines:

I've been listening carefully to the arguments already discussed but I believe there is a vital factor that has not properly been considered. [Pause... then use strong eye-contact and demand full attention.] I think we need to...

Activity: using silence

Contemplate how you can use silence more effectively in your everyday communication and workshops.

53. SPACE; AMBIENCE

I just need my own space.

Definition

Our needs for space, distance and privacy are culturally defined. And individuals within cultures vary in their needs. Generally, Westerners tend to value their own 'space', meaning their privacy. Peoples in South-East Asia who live in 'collective' societies tend to yearn for the company of others.

Rationale

Your work and living area are important. The ambience or atmosphere of a room can influence how we feel. Do you have a space for yourself? Is there a relationship between your spaces and the functions they need to perform?

Your space

Think of a part of your home that is distinctly yours and expresses your personality. Most of us need at least a small area where we can express ourselves or escape for some peace if necessary. When we move into a new work area or home, we immediately make our mark on it, somewhat like a dog putting its scent around the perimeter of its territory.

Colour and light are important. Bright, cheerful surroundings uplift the spirit. It is important to be able to see the sky. In dowdy environments people frequently become depressed. In recent years it has been found that fluorescent tubes can be enervating.

Developments in lighting that reproduces the spectrum of natural light have shown dramatic results in lessening depression and SAD (seasonal affective disorder), in improving readability, and thereby in increasing productivity.

Constructing surroundings that are pleasing to you is powerful. If you want to stimulate your creativity, change your space. If you want serenity or a more humanized workspace, try to change your environment to provide it. If you need a more cheerful living area, decide what you can do to cheer it up. Have you got a private place to withdraw to if necessary?

The use of space can be functional or just plain frustrating. Most people are gregarious and, despite the benefits of home computers and Internet links, frequently prefer the structure of working outside the home. Others work at home because of the economy or to combine parenting and earning a living. In the latter case it is frequently necessary to delineate a separate 'work space'.

A friend of mine is a psychologist who works from home, but he has arranged his home so that clients enter and leave the consulting room from a door that is only used for that purpose. Another friend is a physiotherapist, but again her work area is kept very separate from the children and the family life space.

Activity: rearranging your space

More and more people work from home – some from choice and others for economic reasons to save on the cost of travel time or to save the cost of setting up a private workspace. If this is you, what is your workspace like? You have much more autonomy on room design than at work. What can you do to make your workspace stimulating? Or relaxing? Or invigorating? Can you compartmentalize your work and your home space so that you can remove yourself from work mode when necessary?

Is your room layout useful? Measure the walls and draw the perimeter to scale on a piece of graph paper. Measure your desk, book cases, filing cabinets, etc. Draw these to scale and cut them out. Now move the furniture around the room on your paper plan. Experiment. Have fun. Then when you are happy with the result, reorganize your furniture.

Open plan areas

Open plan offices are cheaper for employers to operate. However, there is another aspect to its use, and that is the control and surveillance factor. Notice that top executives often maintain their privacy at all costs, but are usually in favour of open-plan offices for their workers. Managers can oversee their workers. If there is 'too much' gossiping, it becomes noticeable straight away.

There are, however, drawbacks that are often unnoticed. For example, it is impossible for an employee to sit back and think. If the employee sits and stares into space, immediately people have a tendency to say 'Oh, haven't you got any work to do?' Thinking and reflection are not always part of the work norms, yet they may be essential for efficient and effective work.

Who is the space for? Whose interests are being served? Consideration needs to be given to such questions. For example, in high rise flats, children cannot go out to play unsupervised; in homes for senior citizens, elderly people often cannot potter in a garden or chat to passers-by.

Here is another example. A new building was opened in the mid-1990s in Perth to house the head office of a key government department. The architects were very proud of their open-plan interior, which was designed to give a sense of light and space. When all the employees moved in, immediately things changed as people moved around furniture, pot-plants, and cupboards to give themselves visual and oral privacy to conduct their work.

Lack of privacy caused by office layout or overcrowding can be very depowering for some people.

Activity: arranging space for meetings

How you arrange space for meetings is important. Consider the difference between a formal, long, oval board-room table and a U-shape with space for wall minutes. The latter redirects group energies to the issues under consideration rather than to antagonists facing one another. This may have a direct impact on the ambience of a meeting (Hogan, 1990).

Untidiness

Some people (myself included) find it very hard to be tidy. I used to feel bad about this until I learnt about left- and right-brain theory. A very simplistic way of analysing the brain is the division between right and left hemispheres. We know that people perceive the world very differently according to whether they are more right-brained (that is, more holistic, intuitive and specially aware) or more left-brained (that is, logical, analytical and organized).

Right-brained people are those who tend to prefer to live in a muddle. (I know, I am one – and my husband is more left-brained.) Right-brained people find beauty in surrounding themselves with lots of colourful, different things and can seem to tolerate any amount of mess. Left-brained people tend to prefer order and tidiness. The thing is to arrange your living/working space as best as you can to give you, your colleagues and family most peace of mind.

I worked once in an open-plan office. My corner seemed to be constantly in a mess despite my efforts to the contrary and resolutions to tidy up every Friday before going home. I told my colleagues about my concerns. They were really surprised. 'Oh, we don't mind because we know that lots of ideas come out of your corner of the room.'

54. SPIRITUALITY

> Pray as if your success depends on God; and work as if your success depends on you.
> (Sister John, my geography teacher)

A pragmatic nun at my school had a balanced approach to spirituality, and she would constantly remind us to pray before exams, but not to be too dependent on God for success. We had to use our personal power of hard work.

Definition

The power of spirituality covers a wide range of belief systems and does not necessarily relate to organized religion. It may relate to a sense of oneness with nature and all living things.

Rationale

It appears that the majority of people feel the need for some sense of spirituality in their lives. Indeed, this feeling appears to have increased as we have approached the new millennium. The spirituality may appear in many different forms for each individual – many people do not go to church and yet, when asked, say they pray or have their own belief system.

Religious faith and empowerment

For many, religion gives a meaning and purpose to life. Shared ritual and ceremony bring friendship and support. It also helps develop relationships through shared social activities and projects such as fêtes, raffles, coffee mornings, youth clubs, outings and car boot sales. Religion is often blamed for wars and bloodshed; however, I believe that religions have on the whole taught people positive behaviours. It is the differences between peoples that have led to warfare.

Prayer

Prayer is a multifaceted process. It is a reflective tool that may be used to:

- see: observe an issue;
- request help or intervention in an issue;
- unburden oneself and/or one's troubles;
- judge: apply one's values;
- act: act upon those values;
- overcome physical and/or mental pain and suffering;
- meditate, relax and slow down.

Prayer is often used magically to obtain what we want. In primary school I remember the nuns were raffling a doll's tea service. It was pale blue plastic, and for some reason I decided that I must have it. I prayed every night and lit candles to Our Lady. My parents became rather worried and sat me down and told me about the use and abuse of prayer. They were obviously worried in case I lost my faith if I failed to win the raffle. Well, the day of the raffle draw arrived and I won! Prayer is used to help win football matches, lovers and drive away disease.

Alcoholics Anonymous and spiritual awakening

Members of Alcoholics Anonymous and other similar self-help organizations freely talk of their illness as being a spiritual one as well as a mental and physical one. Alcoholics Anonymous is not aligned to any particular religious body. However, participants frequently admit to some form of spiritual awakening during the process of developing sobriety. To help individuals through the process the founders developed 12 steps. The first three are of interest in this context:

1. 'We admit we were powerless over alcohol – that our lives have become unmanageable.'
2. 'We have come to believe that a power greater than ourselves could restore us to sanity.'
3. 'We have made a decision to turn our will and our lives over to the care of God, *as we understand Him*.'

It is interesting in step 1 that alcoholics are encouraged to admit that, as alcohol is a disease of the mind (emotions) and the body (chemical reactions), an admission of powerlessness is the first step in the empowerment process. In steps 2 and 3, reference is made to a higher power; those who do not believe in a god form are encouraged to identify the AA group as that higher power.

Religion and communism

Karl Marx claimed that 'Religion… is the opium of the people' and yet in 1961, according to Celia Haddon (1985), there were 30 million regular churchgoers in the then USSR – less than half the number at the time of the Russian Revolution but still a very healthy number. Marxist sociologists accounted for this by explaining that people enjoy ritual and use religion to solve problems.

With the decline of communism in the 1990s, there was an immediate resurgence of religious practice in Russia and the newly independent countries that once comprised the USSR's satellite states.

Religion as oppression rather than empowerment

Christianity, Islam, Judaism and Buddhism all enhance the development of social relationships by promoting kindness and cooperation between people. It is unfortunate that in some groups the definition of 'neighbour' is taken as being a person of similar belief and that religious love like all love can be abused and/or restricted to a chosen few.

Members of a priesthood in any religion may nevertheless unfortunately act in a depowering way. Helda Camera in South America and Brian Gore in the Philippines enabled the rural populations there to break away from the church of the oppressors and landlords and helped the poor people take more charge of their lives thorough literacy programmes and forming co-operatives and better land management.

In relation to expressions such as 'God's will be done' or 'It was the will of Allah', for some people this may be depowering while for others it is comforting. (Refer back to Chapter 2 and review the reasons why people allow themselves to be depowered.)

Prayer, suffering and pain

Although I am no longer a practising Catholic, when my father was dying of cancer my mother and I would join him in prayers every night. It was not a cure, but it was a comfort to us all and made us feel less helpless. At school, we were taught that 'a family that prays together, stays together'. I doubt if there is any evidence for this; however, there is power in a joint activity.

During his last week my father was in St Joseph's Hospice in London. Each morning the nursing staff quietly filed into the ward and said prayers to help them and us through the day. It was strangely encouraging and I marvelled at their love and care of patients and their families. The collective focus on the day ahead and peace was very soothing.

There is a power of prayerfulness and this may be used to control pain. My father used prayer to overcome pain during his suffering with cancer. He refused painkillers, which he insisted didn't work. I later learnt that cancer of the bladder, which he suffered from for two years, is one of the most painful types. Ainslie Meares, a doctor who did research on alternative medicine, describes in *Relief Without Drugs* (1970) his fascinating journeys around the world discovering how people controlled pain through, amongst other things, positive self-talk, concentration on other things, and prayer.

Ritual

Ritual is important to human beings to celebrate success, mark transitions, mourn losses. It used to form the focus and structure of our lives. In many organizations various rituals are being revived. These rituals are more than a few drinks after work, but are more carefully orchestrated 'theatre' and ways of engendering a sense of belonging and spirituality in welcoming new employees, in celebrating successes and in saying farewell to departing employees.

In recent years I have been experimenting with 'ending' rituals in courses. Groups often work so hard in courses and yet sometimes their work is not celebrated. Indeed, as a society we tend to avoid mourning periods. This last stage of group development needs to be honoured as a happy–sad occasion – happy because it is celebrating achievements, and sad because a group is disbanding (see Hogan, 1994b).

Activity: developing your own rituals

In more recent times, some people have developed their own forms of ritual and of a sacred space in their homes. I have seen shrines with icons linking all the major religions of the world. Does this appeal to you? If the answer is 'yes', consider what you would place in your shrine.

55. STORIES AND STORYTELLING

There's nothing like a good story.

Definition

There are many different types of story: jokes, anecdotes and personal stories. On a deeper level, there are psychological stories comprising fairy stories and folk tales. Deeper still are the archetypal and mythological stories. Stories can be fact and/or fiction, serious and/or humorous. Adults as well as children love a 'good' story.

Rationale

Many different kinds of stories have been described in this book, because storytelling is the most ancient form of communication and teaching. Stories are powerful, because they unite us as human beings. When a story is being told, it is possible for the teller to use 'charismatic time' (see below) to woo people into a different time and space. As a result, storytelling can initiate deep responses and sometimes changes in the listeners (Finlay and Hogan, 1995; Hogan, 1997c; Parkin, 1998).

Charismatic time: bending time and space

For teachers, leaders and facilitators there are two main sorts of speaking time: clock time and 'charismatic time'. These are illustrated in Figure 3.13.

The former is rapid speech and is most frequently used; it is the norm in Western culture. It means the rapid shooting of words and ideas and is subtly tense. We have so many messages telling us 'don't be late', 'time is money', 'don't waste time', etc that we have to do some unlearning in order to use charismatic time effectively.

'Charismatic time', described by Heron (1993), is slow. It incorporates extremely long pauses and lulls the listener into a different time and space. It enables the storyteller to tap into different levels of consciousness using 'distress-free authority'.

Normal speech, in contrast, is often fast and somewhat jerky (Heron, 1993; Hogan, 1994d).

The essence of charismatic speech is that it is *anxiety-free*. The speaker is totally centred in himself/herself and totally living in the present. Intentional silences and pauses are used. This use of silence is very different from a simple pause in speech. Recall the 'I have a

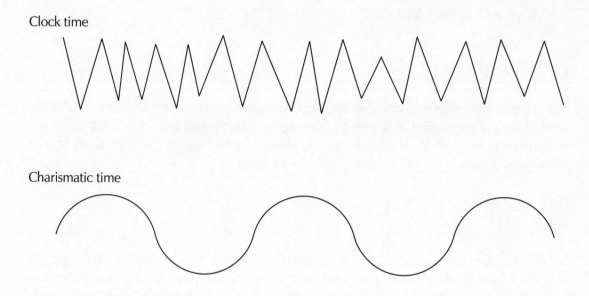

Clock time

Charismatic time

Figure 3.13 Speech in clock time and in charismatic time (from Heron, 1993, p 50)

dream' speech delivered by Martin Luther King in 1963 at the Lincoln Memorial in Washington DC to 200,000 civil rights marchers (reproduced in McCroskey, 1986). Inflection, silence, pauses, passion and commitment made King's message meaningful, exhilarating and memorable for generations to come.

Speech in charismatic time may be used intermittently for a number of purposes:
- explaining key points;
- emphasizing issues of moral or ethical importance;
- confronting a group about inappropriate behaviour;
- giving meaningful positive and constructive/change feedback.

Beware of an inappropriate use of this technique. Do not overuse charismatic time or your message may appear pedantic, pompous and patronizing. Using charismatic techniques and 'centring' techniques, a storyteller can alter the listeners' perceptions of time and space.

Influence and persuasion

Storytelling is a very useful tool in the workplace. Participants in meetings can use a powerful story to influence and persuade. Managers frequently have to use 'transformational' or 'charismatic' leadership skills to motivate workers to follow a mission or goal (Conger, 1989 and 1992).

Mission and vision statements are often clinical and non-motivating and eminently forgettable. If they are expressed as a story, however, the impact is very different as illustrated by the great leaders of the past. Anita Roddick is highly skilled in enthusing Body Shop workers by the stories of her travels and experiences with tribal peoples. She has her own video company so that monthly 'newsletters' containing not only her own stories but those of employees and their innovations are sent out to over 1,000 Body Shops in 30 different countries. When customers buy Body Shop products, they often buy because of the environmental stories linked to the products.

56. STRESS MANAGEMENT

Burnout is a major disease of the 20th century.

Definition

Stress is the name given to a variety of emotional and physical responses that occur when we feel that our needs and/or goals might not be met. It can result in feeling engulfed by life events and a perceived lack of ability to cope. There is also 'eu-stress' or good stress, for example, a certain amount of stress that we feel before giving a talk to a group of people energizes us to prepare thoroughly. However, we need to manage that stress so that it does not become dysfunctional and interfere with our ability to give that talk.

Rationale

Frost and Robinson (1999) comment that organizations have always generated some stress (toxicity) as well as joy and fulfilment, but they cite the current focus on market-based economies and shareholder profits as causing psychological, professional and physical burnout and illness.

Stress management is a life skill, since prolonged stress can lead to bouts of depression, heart palpitations, migraines, chronic sleeplessness, ie personal and professional burnout. The costs of burnout to families, organizations and communities are immense.

Stressors

There are two main categories of 'stressors' or causes of stress. First, major life events, for example, the death of a close relative, divorce, injury, redundancy or sexual harassment

(Holmes and Rahe, 1967). Second, there are daily hassles that can also cause stress, for example, preparing meals, shopping, too many things to do, loneliness, money worries, noise and local crime (Lazarus *et al*, 1985).

Individual reactions to stress

No two people respond to stress alike, so what might be a stressor to one person may have little impact on another. Outlook is important too: optimists tend to be more stress resistant than pessimists. Some people who are more stress resistant or hardy view stresses as challenges to be overcome, rather than problems. However, we need to identify our stressors and how these are manifested in our bodies (see exercise below).

Organizational toxicity and toxic handlers

Frost and Robinson (1999) raise concerns about 'toxic handlers': compassionate individuals who listen empathically, suggest solutions, and work behind the scenes to prevent pain in organizations. These people often reframe harsh messages from power handlers and carry the confidences of others. They provide an organizational need, as some organizations are highly toxic as a result of change, downsizing and toxic bosses. Unfortunately, toxic handling is often regarded as women's work and in many organizations it is not acknowledged, supported or rewarded.

Exercise: Are you a toxic handler?

Identification of body reactions

If you are a toxic handler you may need to review periodically the impact of toxic handling on your body.

In the drawing below, highlight the areas of your body that react when you are feeling stressed. You may feel a headache or stomach ache. Your palms may feel sweaty or you may get cramp in your toes. You may feel sleepy as a way of getting away from your stress.

Figure 3.14

Exercise: Are you looking after yourself?

Check the list below to identify the ways in which you handle toxicity. Are there any strategies that you need to add to your repertoire or are there some things you do that you need to add to the list?

According to Frost and Robinson (1999), effective toxic handlers:

- network, support and exchange strategies with others in similar positions;
- learn to say 'no', but offer other people alternative modes of help;
- know when to get help with administrative things;
- know when to ask for counselling help for themselves;
- take holidays, ie they schedule two- to five-day holidays with their families per year;
- exercise two to three times a week;
- model healthy toxic handling, ie they maintain calmness and take deep breaths in tense situations;
- keep a balance between work and personal life.

Exercise: Planning breaks

Be kind to yourself and plan holidays. When you get away, you can look at life more objectively. Sit down with your family and/or friends and plan two to five breaks each year; pre-book and make a commitment. After all, when you are busy it is tempting to cancel arrangements, but if you have made a financial commitment or promise to family and/or friends, it is harder to renege.

Exercise: Stress placebos

In the 1960s it became popular for people to learn to control the physical responses of the bodies – for example, heart rate and brainwaves – through biofeedback equipment. Through trial and error a person can learn to control 'involuntary responses'. Placebos may achieve the same effect, even though the placebo is not a drug, but a replacement for a drug. For example, a person may eat an apple instead of smoking a cigarette in a stressful situation. If I am on my way to give a talk to a very large, strange audience, on the way I frequently pull my car in to the curb and eat a very strong peppermint (a placebo) and say to myself, 'OK, you've done all your preparation, take a deep breath and enjoy yourself'. The effects of placebos are powerful, but not fully understood.

57. TIME MANAGEMENT

What is the best use of my time right now?

Definition

Time is an invaluable but finite resource. It is regarded as a linear entity in the West, but in many Eastern societies it is regarded as a more cyclical phenomenon, based on the seasons, and some even consider it multidimensional.

Rationale

We cannot create more time; we can only learn how to manage it. To do this, it is useful first to establish our values and then spend our time appropriately (see the story of the millionaire in the Power of Goal setting, Card 13). Time management is also closely related to stress management: having established values and goals, it is useful to prioritize, as the story below shows.

Some valuable advice

A millionaire did not have time to go on a time-management course and he asked a consultant to give him a 'quick' lesson. The consultant said 'I will give you just one main hint, and if it works for you within one year pay me $20,000. Do you agree?'

The millionaire agreed. The consultant said 'Here is the key to it all. Write on a card above your desk the words: "What is the best use of my time right now?"' One year later, the consultant received a cheque in the mail for $30,000 – that is, more than he had asked for.

Activity: simple time management

Based on the story described above, find a piece of card and write on it: 'What is the best use of my time right now?' Hang this in a prominent position at home or at work. This is not a tool to make you feel guilty. If you have planned a weekend at the beach, having finished all your work, then you should turn off this question in your mind. If the question pops up again, just reply to yourself: 'Yes, playing with my family on the beach is the best use of my time right now, as we need to spend time together having fun'. Do not feel guilty for using some planned time to have fun and relax properly with family and friends.

The timing of change

Successful change agents are good at timing. When things get really desperate, people are ready to unfreeze. New employees often make the mistake of trying to change things too quickly. Often, it is better to let people get used to you and even to plant new ideas in the minds of power-holders. After all, provided that your ideas are accepted it doesn't always matter who gets the kudos – though you wouldn't want that to happen all the time! Choose your battles and your timing. For example analyse:

- the pendulum of public opinion;
- when to introduce a new idea;
- the feeling within a meeting.

Problems with time-management courses

There are numerous time-management courses, time-management books, filofaxes, palmtop diaries and electronic systems. One aspect that most of them ignore is that they are really only catering for people who are predominantly 'left-brained' – that is, those who are at ease with logical, analytical, organized thinking and problem solving. The systems emphasize goal setting, breaking down tasks into 'to-do' lists and setting deadlines and timetables. These strategies are fine for predominantly left-brained people, but they ignore the right-brained people who find these rules too restricting and are more visually and intu-itively oriented. These are the people (like me) who file in piles on their desks and like to see everything in front of them.

Another problem is that time-management courses frequently are so goal-focused that participants are not really given time to think about their desired lifestyles and values (see Power Card 13, Goal setting).

People who are dominantly left-brained (logical and analytical) usually respond better to time-management courses. More right-brained people, who like to see things around them and who think holistically and creatively, usually thrive in messy situations. Seibert and Kleiner (1991) quote the research work of Dr McGee-Cooper at Colombia University and recommend that right-brained people should:

- take trouble to create a motivating, non-structured atmosphere in which to work;
- incorporate a sense of fun into the workplace and workspace;
- divide time strictly into work and break periods;
- develop a colour-coded filing system;
- use attractively coloured calendars for organizing time;
- buy coloured note pads, pens, etc;
- bring fun into the way they structure their life;
- capitalize on being 'whole-brained', maximizing the best of both outlooks.

Many of these strategies would also benefit left-brained people, because it is useful for all of us to work in a more whole-brained way. The main thing is to empower yourself to use the strategies that help you manage your time best.

Activity: estimating time and creating deadlines

I always make unrealistically short deadlines and then get stressed as a result. My husband's advice (after years of surveying on building sites and setting deadlines) is, 'Think of the longest time the job could possibly take you. Now double it'. It works. Why don't you try it?

58. UNCERTAINTY MANAGEMENT

He who does not expect the unexpected will not find it.

(Heraclitus)

Definition

Our lives are becoming increasingly unpredictable. Uncertainty is becoming the norm for many of us. Our era has been described as a time of turbulence and change. This has led to a great deal of uncertainty.

Morgan (1986) describes two types of uncertainty: *environmental uncertainty* (in markets, resources, supply of materials, skilled people, finance, the state of the dollar and interest rates, the stock market) and *operational uncertainty* (the breakdown of computer systems, through physical crashes or viruses; the breakdown of production).

Rationale

Uncertainty can be useful for 'unfreezing' situations that previously seemed to be static, aligning with the status quo. During periods of uncertainty, we are often at our most open and aware for new learning. We are almost like children, turning to new events and circumstances in a refreshing and new way.

Using uncertainty to one's advantage

Some people use unfreezing tactics on purpose to unfreeze individuals, groups or organizations. Kurt Lewin (1951) described this as a three-stage process: 'unfreeze–change–refreeze'. Of course this is now seen as a gross oversimplification because the process is not linear. However, a period of unfreezing and uncertainty is guaranteed with most changes. Indeed in some instances 'unfreezing' the status quo may lead to 'freezing' as people try to hang on to what they 'know' in an attempt to maintain a bit of certainty in their lives.

The problem is that, in many organizations that have been repeatedly restructured, there is very little – if any – time to 'refreeze' and settle before the next change comes along. In organizations where people are losing their permanency status, there is frequently a change in outlook and behaviour, in that contract staff are less likely to take innovative risks or speak out about issues as they fear resulting job loss.

Operational uncertainty is sometimes orchestrated because it unfreezes people from their traditional ways of doing things. In some cases you may be able to make use of uncertainty that has been created by, for example, the current poor economic situation, which has resulted in so many cuts in funding. I spoke to the counsellor at a hospice in London and she described the cutbacks in their funding. I commiserated. She replied brightly 'Oh no, I'm not worried, a period of austerity is not a bad thing. It will give us the chance to really look at what we are doing and how we are doing it, and to make some changes. We had got too complacent'.

Uncertainty can be artificially created in other circumstances. A maintenance worker may exaggerate the time needed or difficulty of a repair job. Computer programmers may develop programs without putting in inline documentation or 'comments', with the aim of preventing others from getting into 'their' program.

There is a certain amount of uncertainty produced when someone starts a new job. Some people make active use of this to generate the 'new broom' image and change the job role radically within the first few months. However, this tactic has to be used with care. Entrenched workers can quickly react if not treated carefully, and a newcomer can be quickly put back into his or her box.

Uncertainty management is a valuable skill

Skills of managing during times of uncertainty enhance a person's power base. It is like riding the waves of turbulence and getting to the shore in one piece. Management authors such as Tom Peters (1989) teach people how to 'thrive on chaos'. (It's not as easy or as simple as it sounds.) If we accept that we are living in times of uncertainty, then it makes sense to learn to 'go with the flow' to some extent and learn to cope with frequent changes rather than fight them. (See Power Card 27, Mind flexibility.)

Helping people deal with uncertainty

Managing a career change frequently means having to deal with a number of unknowns or managing risks. Robert Frost wrote a beautiful poem called *The Road not Taken*, which describes a traveller standing perplexed in a wood trying to decide which way to go. The poem ends with:

> Two roads diverged in a wood, and I –
> I took the one less travelled by,
> And that has made all the difference.

An ancient Sufi story entitled 'The Tale of the Sands' (described in Finlay and Hogan, 1995), may be used to assist people to go through the rebirth that uncertainty and change may require. In addition, see also the model of 'The Hero's Journey', an effective framework for change, developed by Joseph Campbell (1975), described in Chapter 5.

The tale of the sands

This is a story of a stream that normally flows to join the sea, overcoming everything in its path. One day it reaches the desert and it notices that as it flows over the burning sands it disappears, yet it knows that its destiny is to cross to the mountains on the other side. It doesn't know what to do.

The sands whisper and suggest that the stream should allow the wind to carry it across. The stream is scared and protests: 'What if I'm never the same again? Where will the wind drop me?'

The sands respond, 'You will never stay the same, no matter what. If you stay here you will become a quagmire.' The stream finally agrees and give itself up to the welcoming arms of the wind, who carries it gently to the mountain top where it falls as rain. The stream again becomes a river.

Activity: reflection on 'The Tale of the Sands'

Refer to the 'Tale of the Sands'. Ask yourself:

- 'How does that relate to you personally?'
- 'Tell a story about another time when you experienced that?'
- 'How does that reflect your position in the organization?'
- 'Tell a story about another time you were at this point. What did you do then?'
- 'What are your next steps now?'

In reflecting on previous experiences, successful and unsuccessful coping strategies become clearer.

59. WHOLE PICTURE/GESTALT

Oh, now I get the whole picture.

Definition

'Gestalt' is a word introduced into psychology by Christian Ehrenfels in 1890 to indicate the perception of unity, form or shape of the whole, in which each individual part affects every other, rather than the whole being the sum of the parts. For example, in writing a book, to begin with, everything appears a disconnected muddle of ideas and then suddenly everything appears to fall into place and the structure or form of the whole work becomes clear.

The same phenomenon appears to occur for students during their learning process. At the beginning of a course they often say 'I can't see the wood for the trees', (a very depowering state) but then at the end the concepts and structures become clear (hopefully) and the students express themselves in words like 'Now I can see the whole picture'.

Rationale

Power is lost through fragmentation and ignorance of the whole picture. Indeed, our Earth is suffering because of our lack of realization of the interconnectedness of life as described in the biological concepts such as the 'web of life', by authors such as David Suzuki and organizations such as Greenpeace, and by the Buddhist doctrine of self-likeness to the universe. The pictures taken of the whole Earth from outer space help us to see the gestalt of our planet.

Mind-mapping and the whole picture

The power of the mind-mapping process is that it enables people to see the whole picture on one page, as well as interconnections between the parts. When planning for the future, it is useful to do a SWOT (strengths, weaknesses, opportunities and threats) analysis on a single page as a mind map – see Figure 3.15.

The SWOT process was developed for organizations, but you can also use it on yourself. When I introduced such an exercise in management training, I was delighted when participants said how useful the exercise had been. One person commented: 'This is the first time I have seen the whole organization and the strategic planning process as a whole picture on one piece of paper'. Indeed, drawing a SWOT mind map enables you to see whether a strength can also be a weakness – for example, a very successful and charismatic boss with

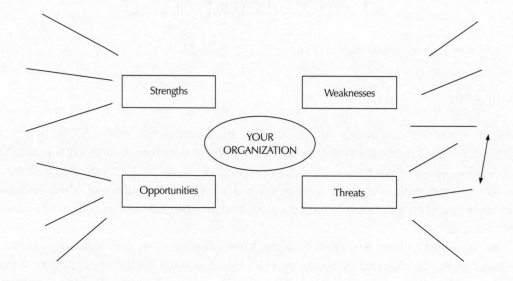

Figure 3.15 A SWOT analysis represented as a mind map

lots of contacts may also create a weakness. If he or she was taken ill or suddenly left, the organization could be at a disadvantage.

Activity: *do a SWOT analysis*

Do a SWOT analysis of your organization on a single sheet of paper. Join up the strengths and weaknesses that are linked with arrows around the outside of the mind map. Do the same with opportunities and threats etc.

60. WOMEN/FEMALENESS

Women hold up half the sky.

(Chinese proverb)

Definition

The stereotypical characteristics of 'femaleness' are linked to the ancient roles of gatherer–nurturer, which required patience, nurture skills, cooperation and compassion. What is defined as 'femaleness' varies from society to society, and is currently changing in the West.

Rationale

Statistically, women not only outnumber men but also do far more than 50 per cent of the work in the world. As with the Men's Movement, the Women's Movement has resulted in many books published by women who are redefining the meaning of femaleness.

The Women's Movement

The Women's Movement has helped women to see the power of supporting and networking with each other far beyond the traditional networking that has always occurred in the area of home and childcare – for example, campaigns for human rights, career rights, peace work and domestic violence. But taking on more roles has taken its toll.

Women have made many gains and widened the options open to them. However, many now realize that they have to be careful. In gaining access to more roles in life they are sometimes overworking, taking on full-time jobs and yet continuing to manage the family and home affairs (with little change in male roles and responsibilities in the home). Health and stamina may then be severely undermined.

In some instances they are also taking on the hazardous behaviours and attributes that men have had to take on to operate in a male world, and as a result women are suffering the consequence of increased rates of stress disorders and heart disease.

Societal norms

Helen Ernington, at a Women in Education conference (1991), encouraged women to make their own reality and be proud of it:

> Equality does not mean being like males, it is about liberation for men and women. It's time for both sexes to remove the confining boxes and redefine what 'maleness' and 'femaleness' means. The simplistic yin–yang divisions are no longer acceptable. Nor is the concept of 'androgyny' (a mix of male and femaleness) developed by Sandra Mem in 1974.

Understandably, women often want to do things 'their way', but the accepted societal norm is how things are done in a male world. Women have been given permission culturally to develop different ways of doing things to men – for example:

- ways of bonding;
- ways of developing individualism and group support;
- ways of using and expressing feelings and intuition.

Women need to make their own conversation about themselves and their lives and history ('herstory'). Codes of behaviour that are socially male-constructed can be changed. If the Berlin wall can come down, then we can redefine male and femaleness and create a different ways of doing things.

Helen Ernington also encouraged women to be empowered to:

> damage people's perceptions about what we can and cannot do by living 100 per cent of our lives 100 per cent of the time. The doors may be open but we need to push them open even further. . . To create a 'meaning system', you need more than one person alone; therefore women need to get together to share their meanings of education, people roles, etc.

Ernington argued that it is harder for women to confront meanings of femaleness than for men to confront meanings of maleness because men are confronting accepted norms whereas women are developing and affirming new norms. On the other hand, it is hard for men too, because redefining maleness means giving away some of the power that men have fought and worked so hard to achieve.

Having a voice and being heard

The work of Dale Spender in South Australia (1980) confirmed that males tend to dominate the 'air space' in classrooms, conversations etc. She proved this by placing tape recorders in many different meeting rooms and encouraged those who did not believe her to do the same. The results are surprisingly similar: in mixed company men talk more. Women are not quiet on purpose 'What's the matter? Did the cat get your tongue?' No. As Ernington continues:

> It's socialization that has bitten women's tongues. From the days we were in our pink booties, we need to speak out no matter how nervous we all get. Empowerment skills are critical skills and behaviours in a bureaucracy.

Activity: observing use of air space

Next time you are in a mixed group at work or socially, take note of the number of times males and females talk. Notice who takes up most 'air space' and who gets interrupted and by whom. Observe also what happens if you point out your observations to the group!

Women and power

Women use power differently from men (Kirner, J and Raynor, M, 1999). I have observed that women respond very positively to using this power card sort. The reason for this is so far unclear, but for some reason it appears to make talking about power more palatable. The card pack also includes many power bases that hitherto women have used, but these power bases have not been acknowledged in the business world.

Power flows through all relationships. But it is not a simple question of men on the one side and women on the other and power flowing between the two. It is necessary to consider class, age, culture, values and nationality.

It is interesting to note that communist regimes in China and Russia, which have supposedly given equal opportunities to males and females, have few women visible in politically powerful positions. Robert Connell (1987) points out four components whereby women in most capitalist and communist countries are almost excluded from the policy-making centres:

- the hierarchies of institutionalized violence – for example, the military, the police and the prison system;
- the hierarchy of the heavy industry labour force – for example, the mineral, steel and oil companies;
- the hierarchy of the high-technology industry – for example, the IT and aerospace industries;

- the working class milieu that emphasizes physical toughness and men's association with machinery.

Major areas that need to be added to this include:

- the medical profession, especially research into contraception, fertilization and reproduction;
- the sciences: maths, physics and chemistry.

Instigating relationships between the sexes

In starting up relationships, there are many power differences, although these are changing.

In the West, the generally accepted norms are that the male usually: approaches the female, takes her out, asks to take her home, gets a phone number and the female waits for a call. At a recent 'Women in Education' conference I attended, these social customs were discussed. One woman said, 'Oh, it's all different now because my daughter gets messages on the ansaphone. The problem is that before we had one if we were all out my daughter could come home and pretend to herself that he may have rung. Now my daughter complains "I know he didn't ring"'. Note that even with modern technology the onus is still often left to the male to make the call! Perhaps with the increasing ownership of mobile phones among young women for safety, the responsibility of 'who rings who' is changing.

Activity: working together

We have to work together as human beings to overcome conditioning, gender stereotypes and the resulting hurts. So I have chosen another power card to represent this – see Power Card 44, Redefining who we are: gender issues. Go to this power base and do the activity entitled 'Attributes you possess and wish to acquire'.

CONCLUSION

This chapter contains information on each Power Card. It is possible to write a book on each one. The stories, case studies, quotes and narrative included here have been designed to provoke thinking. This chapter is a reference for the cards. Finally, if you ever get into a fix, it is useful to remember:

Whatever makes you strong, provided that you do not harm others.

4

Case studies

INTRODUCTION

Having considered some alternative exercises on empowerment, this chapter focuses on case studies that illustrate the profiles of people from different walks of life who have used the power cards in very different ways:

1. an executive in a marketing company trying to improve his interpersonal skills;
2. a change agent introducing new technology to a university;
3. a cross-cultural team trying to reduce conflict and improve relationships at head office;
4. a woman attempting to take charge of long-term illness;
5. a lecturer designing a new course of study;
6. community workers facilitating a group of long-term unemployed young adults.

REASONS FOR THE CASE STUDIES

These case studies have been included in depth for a number of reasons:

- analysis of case studies enables others to analyse what power bases they might use in similar situations;
- you can compare their projects with the ones described;
- pragmatic learners like to know how others have done things in practice;
- facilitators can learn from the ways that participants interpret the cards.

CASE 1: USING THE CARDS TO SOLVE AN INTERPERSONAL PROBLEM AT WORK

An empowerment workshop was facilitated with a Marketing Company. Tony Johnson, one of the four principal directors, attended and contacted the facilitator after the workshop with a story about how he had used the cards.

Tony is a very creative and sociable person with an extensive network of skilled acquaintances in the marketing field. The company regularly needs to take on extra staff when taking on short-term projects like conference work. Rather than taking on full-time staff, the company policy is to use a number of short-term contract staff.

Because of having a wide network of friends and acquaintances in the trade, Tony frequently recommends names of people for his co-directors to interview. In order to ensure that he does not bias their decisions, he leaves them to make the final choices on whom to employ. Tony was nevertheless aware that Ian, a fellow director, was continually irritated by this procedure and probably regarded him as practising nepotism. Communication between Tony and Ian had almost broken down to a few grunts at meetings.

During an empowerment workshop, Tony described his frustration with the atmosphere at work and decided to use the power cards to address this problem. He reframed his problem as a project entitled 'How can I improve my interpersonal relations at work?' He worked through the cards and then decided to work on action plans for the following cards:

1. The power of active listening (Card 1)
    'I really do need to listen to the others more. Often I am too wrapped up in my own ideas and who I think is the best person for the job. The trouble is I know a lot of talented people around town. Still, things can't go on the way they are at the moment. I really need to listen to the meaning behind their words and not be such a bull in a china shop. I need to find out more about active listening and maybe even do a short course on it.'

2. The power of questioning (Card 42)
    'I need to ask our creative designers what kind of skilled people they really want for their short-term projects before I start mentioning names. In some ways, the fact that I recommend someone for interview seems to bias some of the others against them.'

3. The power of body language (Card 2)
    'I need to be more aware of what Ian's body language is saying and try and sort things out. I also need to communicate better with the support staff. I know I don't say "please" or "thank you" enough when I give them work – and I certainly don't spend time telling them about the aspects of their work that particularly please me. I will make time on Monday to chat to Linda and ask if she has got any suggestions for me. I know she has trouble with my writing sometimes.'

4. The power of the whole picture (Card 59)

'We really need to do some longer-range planning – or as much as is possible in this business. We need to list the dates of forthcoming contracts and conferences and work on a schedule of part-time staff to cover these events. The chopping and changing that we do at the moment is actually quite inefficient at times, and we frequently lose talented staff as they go off and get themselves more permanent employment.'

The following week Tony rang the facilitator saying 'Hey, I've got a surprise for you. Guess what I did with the cards? I got to work really early on Monday, and no one but Ian was around, so I made two cups of coffee and we sat down for a chat. I admitted that I had been a bit heavy-handed lately regarding staffing and other things and had made some resolutions. I spread the cards out and explained how I had sorted them at the workshop the previous week. Ian was pretty quiet and then said, "Well, yes, I can see that some of those cards refer to me too".'

Outcomes

The result was that the two of them talked more openly than they had done for months. Because they were sorting the cards out in front of them on the table, the problems of the company were highlighted in a more depersonalized way; there was less blaming in their talk. In fact, they started working together on attempting to solve common problems that had been worrying both of them for some time.

The staffing issue was discussed and a wall planner introduced at their next main meeting, and some careful medium-term plans were developed. Part-time staff were also contacted to find out what their commitments and needs were over the next 12 months. Tony also made a start on treating the support staff more like people and less like robots. Six months later, Tony went on an active listening course, and is much more aware of the impact of his communication on others.

The strategy used by Tony worked well. The cards can indeed be used by teams to sort out joint problems. On interpersonal issues, it may be necessary to consider 'appropriateness' – ie the appropriate time and place and the right person to confront with an issue.

CASE 2: USING THE CARDS IN WORKING AS A CHANGE AGENT

In 1992, I was approached by the head of the Teaching Learning Unit in Curtin University to undertake a nine-month secondment as change agent to set up video conferencing technology (PictureTel) at three campuses: Bentley Campus, Perth, Western Australia; Kalgoorlie School of Mines, 700 kilometres east of Perth; and Muresk Institute of Agriculture, 120 kilometres east of Perth. The case study has been documented in greater depth in Hogan (1992).

The specific aims of the project were to:

- increase communication between the three campuses by providing intercampus teaching and learning, staff and management meetings, and staff–student support;
- provide an outreach programme from Curtin, both Australia-wide and internationally;
- initiate 'fee for service' for external clients and users in the community.

I used a number of strategies to bring in the desired changes:

- the power cards;
- an electronic diary to record ideas on my computer;
- force field analysis;
- video-recording of my own use of the videoconferencing equipment.

The first step was to obtain a large sheet of coloured card, which I pinned to the back of my office door. Onto this I temporarily attached all of the power cards. As a result, I had a movable model. I intended to use the cards first alone and then with colleagues who, I hoped, would help me to identify strategies that I had not thought of.

I used many cards during the nine months. Here are some examples.

1. The power of questioning (Card 42)
    My first inclination was to search outside myself for learning about this new system. Having looked carefully at this card, I also realized I had to sit and contemplate my own approach and creativity to videoconferencing. As a result, it occurred to me that most people in this field were concentrating on the technical side, ie training people to use the keypad, and they were focusing on evaluating whether or not people could see, hear, etc. These are important aspects, but I realized that less attention was being given to the *social* impact of this medium and the new group norms it engenders, or to what needed to be developed. As a result, I developed an information sheet on 'vid-e-quette' of desirable individual and group norms of behaviour.
2. The power of illusion (Card 15)
    I wanted to create the illusion that the technology was user-friendly and has human attributes. I gave each camera unit a name: the biggest and most complex was called 'Cardea', after the Roman goddess of Door Hinges. The second and smaller camera was called Janus after Cardea's consort. Janus was the god of Doors and the first month of the year. I thought these names were apt as this technology was opening new doors to the world. This rather absurd 'job description' of these gods appealed to my sense of

humour and also to participants in training workshops. It was also far easier to refer to Cardea and Janus rather than camera 1 or camera 2.

3. The power of goal setting (Card 13)

    I set concrete goals of 20 hours of usage per week on average after six months of my work and employed Kurt Lewin's Force Field Analysis (1951) to analyse the forces for and against achieving this goal. (See Chapter 3 on the power of goal setting (Card 13) for explanation of force field analysis process.)

4. The power of facilitation and group skills (Card 11)

    I designed a training workshop to encompass the socio-technical approach (Trist, 1981) described above. I was determined that:

    - the learning should be non-threatening – I have had many embarrassing experiences whilst being a participant on computer training programmes;
    - learners would have maximum 'hands on' use of the equipment and I would keep my demonstrations to the minimum;
    - I would only use the minimum of technical terms;
    - learning should be fun, exploratory and creative.

5. The power of positive mindsets (Card 39)

    Working with new technology can be both invigorating and exasperating. Early on, I realized that there were going to be times when the technology broke down. Therefore I had to disassociate my own ego from the success or failure of the equipment. I also developed in the training manual strategies for dealing with breakdowns.

6. The power of perseverance (Card 32)

    Perseverance was hard to maintain at times. There were times of frustration when I could have screamed and wished the project had ended. I know however, that this is part of being a change agent. I used expressions like 'take every day at a time', and relied on the support of my friends when I got frustrated.

7. The power of networking (Card 30)

    Curtin University and three other educational institutions set up a networking group called Friends of PictureTel. We agreed to meet once a month for mutual problem-solving and resource-sharing, which was invaluable.

8. The power of influencing powerful people (Card 16)

    The power of influencing powerful people was important because, without the support of the campuses, the school and departmental heads, no funding would be approved for use of the equipment. As a result, I spent considerable time presenting at staff meetings, giving demonstrations and lobbying for support. The country campuses were the easiest to motivate – after all, there were far more advantages for them.

Outcomes

The use of the videoconferencing facility built-up over a year and was monitored and documented (Hogan, 1992, 1993a, 1994b). One unexpected comment was from my boss, who introduced me to a visiting academic saying 'This is Chris. She is doing some very creative work setting up interactive teaching with the videoconferencing. But you'd better watch her, she's doing research on empowerment'.

CASE 3: A CROSS-CULTURAL TEAM TRYING TO REDUCE CONFLICT AND IMPROVE RELATIONSHIPS WITH HEAD OFFICE

While on study leave in Nepal, I was based in an International Non-Government Organization (INGO). At one point there was considerable frustration by both Danish and Nepalese staff with INGO's head office in Copenhagen. As experienced development workers, they all had understanding of, and skills in, 'empowerment'. They agreed to meet to try out the card process on this issue, and reframed it into a project entitled: 'How can we improve the understanding of and communication with the Copenhagen office?'

Six people were present, and so they decided to split into groups and work in separate rooms and then compare the results. There were Nepalese and Danes in each group. I clearly could not be present in each room, but here are some of the cards that were discussed:

1. The power of influencing powerful people (Card 16)
    This was a key issue because the Copenhagen head office has the final say on projects, staffing and budgets. One suggestion was put forward to include in correspondence something like the following:

    > After consulting with people at village level, we strongly believe your decision could have negative long-term repercussions and could ultimately be disastrous for the reputation of INGO. If you order us to go ahead, then of course we will have to comply; however, if it goes wrong, then it is you who will have to shoulder the blame and responsibility.

    If they didn't agree with Head Office, another strategy discussed instead of saying 'no' was to keep offering alternatives, ie indirectly saying 'no' (which is more appropriate in Nepalese society). Another strategy was that of referring the problem back to Head Office, acknowledging the problem but asking for more information before jumping to conclusions.

2. The power of passive resistance (Card 31)

    At this stage there was quite a lot of humour as one participant suggested that they could soon sort out Copenhagen by *not* spending the allocated aid money. (Denmark spends 1 per cent of its gross national product on aid). As this deviousness was humorously discussed, there was an interesting turn in the discussion, as is shown in the next power card.

3. The power of mind flexibility (Card 27)

    The group realized that every time a problem arose they perceived it as 'Copenhagen's problem'. This seemed to be quite an eye opener and turned the discussion around. They realized they were slipping into the trap of an 'us and them' approach to conflict resolution, and they identified that both parties had the same superordinate goal, ie the development of Nepal. They used 'role reversal' and attempted to imagine how administrators in Copenhagen perceived the problems.

4. The power of networking (Card 30)

    The INGO has good computing facilities and the discussion focused on ways of improving networking, not only with Copenhagen but with other Danish development workers in Africa, so as to identify how they resolve issues with their head offices. The Internet is going to have a major impact on networking between countries in the South (ie the developing world) rather than between south and north head offices, because that is the most common flow of communication at the moment.

End of the workshop

Neither group had time to look at all the cards, there had been so much discussion. In the last part of the workshop the two groups rejoined to share their ideas. Observations included the following:

- A changed attitude to conflict developed, away from the 'us and them' model to an improved *esprit de corps*.
- One group rejected one card and the other group discussed it in a way the others hadn't even dreamt of.
- Having two small separate groups increased the 'air time' or 'speaking time' of the Nepalese, who tend to get dominated by the more vociferous Danes.

Outcomes

Some of the anger and frustration with the head office in Copenhagen subsided as the development workers had a proactive plan to deal with the demands and challenges – they could channel their energies more positively. The workers were also more mutually supportive when they realized that both the Nepalese and the Danish groups shared a common frustration with the demands of Head Office.

CASE 4: USING THE CARDS TO TAKE CHARGE OF LONG-TERM ILLNESS

Joan Wright is a senior citizen who has had emphysema for the past two years. She lives in an old-established suburb in London surrounded by neighbours she has known for 30 years or more. As she lives alone, the local community rallies round to help with shopping and to give her moral support. She rarely goes out because even short walks to the local shops had become impossible, since the return journey included a hill that made her extremely breathless and understandably frightened.

At one stage Joan was quite depressed. She broke down and wept, frustrated and angry with the debilitating effects of the disease. She turned this anger into a project entitled: 'How to take charge of my emphysema, rather than vice versa'. Joan sorted the cards and chatted aloud, identifying the following power cards that she was already using:

- 'The power of spirituality, I am using that already; I can't get to church but the priest visits me every week.'
- 'The power of women – the neighbours are terrific, we have a "girls" night every couple of weeks, and we see a lot of each other.'
- 'The power of questioning – I use that a great deal, I always write down all my questions before going to the doctor.'

When all the cards had been discussed, the facilitator prompted her to extract power bases that were useful to help her take more control of the emphysema. Each of these was then turned into an action plan. Here are some examples.

1. The power of positive mindsets (Card 39)
    Joan suggested some phrases: 'I need to be more positive. I'll say to myself, "I can do it" and "I can take the ventilator and I can do it"'; 'I need to be more careful planning my day, to do things straight after I take the ventilator'. Later, she said: 'I'll write up the sayings and put them on the bathroom mirror'.
2. The power of information and its retrieval (Card 17) and networking (Card 30)
    'I want to know more about emphysema. I'll contact the Breathe Easy Association for asthma sufferers and send in my address so that I can correspond with other people who have got emphysema and find out how *they* cope.'

3. The power of physical strength and well-being (Cards 35 and 36)
    'I need to go out to the shops every day and start doing my lung exercises again first thing in the morning.'
4. The power of expert knowledge and skills (Card 10)
    'I want to get more information about alternative medicines from Neal's Yard in Covent Garden. I also need to get all my drugs sorted out – I feel as if I am rattling.'
5. The power of goal setting (Card 13)
    'I want to go on the cricket tour to Tewkesbury (in the South-West of England), and so I'll have to get fitter for that. I also need to lose some weight.' 'How much and by when?' prompted the facilitator. A target was fixed. 'And I want to get a shower fitted upstairs over the bath. It's very awkward sometimes getting in and out.'

Outcomes

The process was not as smooth as this appears. However, six months later Joan had fulfilled many of the goals stated above. Here are some:

- 'It is my birthright to live fully and freely. I love life and I love me' was written on a card and stuck to the bathroom mirror.
- Joan joined the Breathe Easy Association and regularly received its newsletter.
- She went regularly to the shops throughout the summer, although in October the cold weather started to affect her breathing. Instead, she tried to exercise regularly indoors.
- The alternative medicine clinic in Neal's Yard was not contacted. During her daughter's visit, Joan saw a lung specialist and was hospitalized for a few days for tests. She was diagnosed as having diabetes and her drugs were monitored and changed. A physiotherapist visited her home and encouraged her to do daily exercises to increase oxygen flow to the heart and improve circulation.
- Joan went on the cricket tour in August and her friends complimented her and said she looked and acted healthier than the previous year.
- Moderate weight loss occurred and four months later Joan was seven pounds lighter.
- A new shower was fitted and the local occupational therapist fitted a special seat in the bath. In October, Joan rang her daughter in Australia and said that she had achieved most of her goals and was going to consult the cards again and set some more goals.

The card sort cannot remove the problems of coping with long-term illness, but information on the potential powers available can help individuals take a more objective look at their problems – when they are ready. The decision must be theirs in their own time.

CASE 5: USING THE CARDS FOR CURRICULUM DEVELOPMENT

John was a senior lecturer at a college. He saw the need for a new unit of study in the field of Facilitation and Group Process Skills in a postgraduate course in Human Resource Management. Although he had expertise in the area, he was keen to gain input from the community and students. He had the support from the Head of School to develop the unit. After sorting the cards, John decided on the following power bases:

1. The power of facilitation and group skills (Card 11)
    As John was experienced in curriculum design and already knew the DACUM process (DACUM stands for Developing A CUrriculuM), which could be used with groups for developing new courses. However, he knew there was a way of speeding up this process by using a computer laboratory with networked computers.
2. The power of information (Card 17)
    John returned to the literature about the DACUM process (Centre for Continuing Education, undated; Hogan, 1994a, 1999) to check the stages. The DACUM process was developed at the University of British Columbia and was originally used in the hospitality and tourism fields. It has been used successfully in technical and further education and at Curtin University of Technology in Western Australia. The DACUM Process is used when a need is identified for a new training programme or for the revision of one that is outdated. The process may also be used to generate job descriptions or to generate information for positions that are becoming multiskilled. It is a process in which a specially selected group of current practitioners in the job, or in just the skills to be analysed, interacts face-to-face to develop a set of behavioural objectives related to a specific job or occupation. The end products of the process are:
    *   a skill inventory and behavioural objectives for a specific job;
    *   information that may be used for performance appraisal systems or competence profiles;
    *   useful data for HR managers, where learning booklets may form the basis of future courses.
    John set about contacting skilled facilitators. He selected participants according to the following criteria recommitted in the DACUM literature. They were people who: had full-time involvement in the occupation; who were articulate and open-minded; who were creative and forward-thinking; and who could be present throughout the whole workshop.
3. The power of charisma (Card 3)
    As a keen networker, John already had contact with many people in the facilitation field. When he rang them, he used the power of charisma to persuade them to

volunteer their time. He cited the vision and challenge to be involved in creating a new and different type of course for facilitators.

4. The power of resource and resource exchange (Card 46)
    John also offered the invited facilitators a copy of the data generated. (The beauty of using a networked computer lab is that a one-day workshop can be completed in half a day *and* everyone can get a printout of the data before they leave.) John also cited the opportunity to network with other facilitators and to talk about current resources trends in the marketplace etc. In other words, even though he was asking them to volunteer their time, he was offering them a quid pro quo.

Outcomes

Ironically, an unexpected outcome from the workshop was that John found that the facilitators were interested in supporting the unit further and offered their services as guest speakers or participants in role play. Other useful outcomes were that the list of competences developed by the workshop participants provided students with a useful before-and-after self-assessment questionnaire. It also enabled John to design assignments and tests to check whether or not his teaching and resultant student were successful.

CASE 6: USING THE CARDS WITH THE LONG-TERM UNEMPLOYED

Jane was a community worker who was responsible for facilitating courses for unemployed young people between the ages of 16 and 24. The courses lasted 18 weeks and involved a series of workshops on life skills, which included issues of empowerment and depowerment. The course catered for 16 students, but varying numbers would turn up each day. Many members of the group had very low self-esteem and suffered from bouts of depression and hopelessness, which manifested itself in outbursts that included lots of put-downs on their peers. When Jane confronted them over their behaviour, they said 'But this is how we always talk to one another. It's not a problem'.

She nevertheless pondered how to break the downward spiral. She planned a session with a colleague, Ann, on 'How to manage unemployment – with attitude'. Jane and Ann knew that the job-seeking skills sessions were all very well, but the employment statistics in their area indicated little hope for young people with few skills and qualifications – there were in reality only so many suitable job vacancies.

Jane and her colleague wanted to hit a balance between educating the group members about structural and cyclical unemployment and leaving in place their motivation and energy to keep looking for work. They knew that it would be difficult to strike the correct balance, and that they would need to keep the session as light as possible, involve the students with a variety of activities, and have frequent breaks to keep up their energies and concentration.

The planning of the workshop took a while. Jane and Ann had worked together for a long time as co-facilitators, but they knew that they had to carefully work out the sequence of activities to gain maximum impact and shifts of thinking. They knew that most of the participants were streetwise and had a great deal of skills and knowledge to manage on the streets.

The facilitators decided to show a video clip from the film *Brassed Off* because they believed the group would identify with the hero, played by Robert Carlyle. From this video clip, discussion led into the concept of 'choice' and the idea of identifying a project that the young people could all be involved in. Some understandably were cynical: 'Come off it, get real! What choices have we really got?' Lots of discussion ensued about the ups and downs of being one of the long-term unemployed, including the expectations of family, friends and society. The concepts of structural and cyclical unemployment came out in context of the discussion. The group discussed elements that helped them to feel empowered and depowered.

Eventually, Jane and Ann moved the participants on to the cards and gave everyone a pack. Ann reminded them of the workshop title: 'How to manage unemployment – with attitude'. Some decided to work alone; others worked through the cards in groups of two or three. It is not necessary to comment here on who chose what and why; however, power bases that required further discussion and exercises were:

- Personal power (Card 33);
- Positive mindsets (Card 39);
- Perseverance (Card 32);
- Information and its retrieval (Card 17);
- Crisis (Card 6).

CONCLUSION

The purpose of this chapter was to describe case studies and stories of how different people from different walks of life have used the power cards in very different ways. The next chapter describes further exercises on power.

5

Other activities using power

INTRODUCTION

This chapter includes some further exercises on empowerment. A wide variety of interactive activities have been included:

- a creative exercise on limitless power and change;
- an exercise to log daily uses of power bases;
- an analysis of where you feel empowered in your life at the moment;
- an analysis of the content and tone of written communication in an organization;
- group discussion questions;
- a poem;
- 'The Hero's [Heroine's] Journey', which may be used at the end of empowerment projects;
- film analysis: *Brassed Off*, *The Full Monty*, *Dead Poet's Society*;
- hassle lines: when there is an imbalance of power;
- a myth: 'Women's Choice'.

EXERCISE 1: CREATIVE USE OF LIMITLESS POWER

[This exercise can be used as an ice-breaker to lead into more serious work.]

If a magician called to see you and gave you limitless powers to do all the things you ever wanted to do in your home, organization or community, what would you do? The sky's the limit!

EXERCISE 2: LOGGING DAILY USES OF POWER

[Try this exercise for one week. I'm grateful to Michael Ashford from the Department of Commerce and Trade in Perth for the idea for this exercise.]

Draw up a table of all the 60 power bases (see example in Table 5.1 below). At the end of each day, take some moments to reflect on events at home, work and in your community. What sources of power did you use and why? What were the results? What did you do well? What do you need to improve on? What other sources of power would you like to try out?

Table 5.1 Daily power log

Power Bases	Mon How used	Tues How used	Wed How used	Thurs How used	Fri How used	Sat/Sun How used
1. Active listening						
2. Body language						
3. Charisma						
4. Choices						
5. Coercion						
etc						

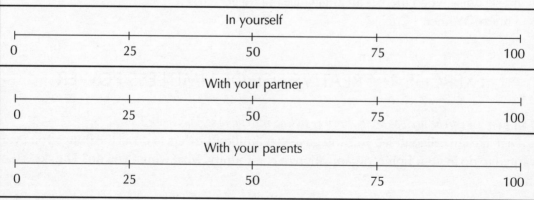

How empowered do you feel at the moment?

1. Put a dot to indicate your perception at present: 0 = nil, 100 = excellent.
2. Decide which area of your life you want to work on.
3. What strategies will you use, based on other exercises in this book?
4. What action plans do you need to make?
5. Come back and redo this exercise in three months' time.

In yourself

| 0 | 25 | 50 | 75 | 100 |

With your partner

| 0 | 25 | 50 | 75 | 100 |

With your parents

| 0 | 25 | 50 | 75 | 100 |

Figure 5.1 Monitoring the empowerment process

EXERCISE 3: HOW EMPOWERED DO YOU FEEL AT THE MOMENT?

[This exercise is most suitable for self-development groups with people from a variety of different backgrounds. It helps people to identify projects and monitor change.]
Fill in the form shown as Figure 5.1.

EXERCISE 4: EMPOWERING COMMUNICATION METHODS IN ORGANIZATIONS

[Dafna Eylon and Susan Herman facilitated a workshop at an Organizational Behaviour Teaching Conference in the United States in 1993. One part of their workshop included a variation on the 'in-tray exercise', showing how communication by memo, fax or e-mail could be either empowering or depowering. In this exercise it is best to use internal written communication from within the organization you are working with. It may also be tactful to remove names of senders and receivers, or to generate them beforehand with the help of employees.]
Compare the two internal memos shown as Figures 5.2 and 5.3. Think about the patterns of communication in your organization that come to light from your considerations.
[An alternative exercise is to hand out a number of depowering memos and ask participants to rewrite them.]

EXERCISE 5: DISCUSSION QUESTIONS

[It is useful to generate questions that you would like to raise about the empowerment process.]
Here are some examples of discussion questions that have been generated in the past:

1. Is it possible to have 'overempowerment'?
2. 'I know plenty of people who are empowered and all they do is tread on others to achieve their goals.' Aren't these power cards dangerous, therefore?
3. 'I only use four of these power bases – that's all I need.' Discuss the advantages and disadvantages of only having a limited number of strategies in your toolkit.
4. What are the differences between 'power over' and 'power with'?
5. Describe the reasons for the changes in the way power is perceived in our society.
6. With reference to power-holders that you know, describe the power bases that they use or misuse.

To: Department Heads

From: D Rhodes

Date: 3 October 1999

Congratulations! We have just heard that we got the big contract with Dynamo that we have all been working on. However, this information is still confidential – just wanted to make sure you knew about it since I knew you would be excited about it.

Figure 5.2 Sample memo (1)

To: Department Heads

From: D Rhodes

Date: 3 October 1999

Sorry, I'm afraid I'm not at liberty to disclose any information regarding our contract with Dynamo to you. Until it is finalized, information is only available to director level and above. If you have any specific decision that needs to be made in this regard, outline the issue and I will help you with the decision. By the way, once you see a press release in the papers from our company, I can then share this information with you.

Figure 5.3 Sample memo (2)

EXERCISE 6: A POEM

[A poem can be useful to invoke feelings.]

Read this poem to participants and then take a few moments to jot down the thoughts ideas and feelings it triggers in you. The poem was written by Martine Gohl, a friend and multi-talented woman. She wrote the poem after attending a writing workshop.

You, who are looking in the past.
You, who are always certain that what you think and what you do is right!
You, who are holding rigidly onto patterns and boundaries of old.
You, who are afraid of change.
You, who are afraid to walk into the future without the yardstick of the ages!
You are looking into your future in the mists of time.
How long are you going to repeat the mistakes of yesteryears?

You, who have no freedom, you never met the same!
How can you????
You, who see everything through the filter of the thoughts of your forebears.
You, who can put your rightness onto the wind of change,
and it will fly away.
You, who lust for riches
And yet you are so poor in spirit!
You, who are afraid of the unknown,
And so you should be!!
You, who think it is the devil, and yet you glorify him,
Because you pay homage to the lived.

You, who are committing the sin of leaving and yet go quickly back to the old and tried.
Your patterning will not allow you the freedom of leaving, every step and turn you make,
you move towards the past in the future and towards the future in the past!
You follow a book of scripts,
And find it a cardinal sin to think for yourself,
You, who are afraid of shadows,
And yet, you are too afraid to be without.
You, who make the future, but only repeat the past.
And you expect it to last for ever.

Be your own Phoenix, believe it! It is not a Myth!
Step forward to the future so new
You can not conceive it yet to be.
Make your choices of being,

Make your choices of living,
Without a concept to know now, what you and it will be.
Take a chance!
Life gave you the ball, run with it not to the goal,
Run, not fly off the playing fields of rules and grooves of time gone by.
Fly to the game where you can play life according to your rules and choices.
Grab your limitless life and make it your own.
Be daring, to think, to be and do different.
Dance your new rhythm
Sing your new song
You will find it in the wind of change.
Soar above the clouds not yet formed,
Outfly the eagle and become a new kind of bird
More brilliant than any bird of paradise.
More glorious, more luminous than any sun that shines,
Let life teach you and you teach life,
Minute to minute, moment by moment,
What and who you can and will be.

Fly away from past patterns and leave them far behind
'The truth!' 'The rightness!' will set you free.
Life will be your wind of change,
It will carry you deeply into the oceans of life and yet lift and blast you higher and deeper
into the universe of the unknown.
With a sureness and knowing of ordered synchronicity,
the very tapestry of new life itself.

You will love your life untouched by anyone's hands
Created by you, without the guild of the past.
Created by you, who dared to leave it all behind,
Created by you, who dared to make the first step in your own mind.
First forgive yourself and then forgive the others.
There is more to life than lust, greed and the whole spectrum of negatives.

There is fulfilment of dreams, yours!
There is love, yours!
There is freedom, yours!
There is life, yours!
And you will be able to touch 'The face of life itself'.

Martine Gohl, *The Breaking of the Chrysalis*
(written 15 July 1992; reproduced with her permission)

What are your reactions to the poem? List them and ponder them.

EXERCISE 7: THE CHANGE PROCESS AND 'THE HERO'S [HEROINE'S] JOURNEY'

[Getting involved in an empowerment journey involves many 'ups and downs'. This is a normal sequence of life events which Joseph Campbell called 'The Hero's Journey' (Campbell, 1973) – which could, of course, apply equally well these days to a heroine.

'The Hero's Journey' may be used to enhance the empowerment of others, so that they can see their situation in a different way, as an archetypal journey. Archetypes are deep and abiding patterns in the human psyche that remain powerful and present over time. Joseph Campbell first wrote about 'The Hero's Journey' in The Hero With a Thousand Faces *(1973). He describes the stages of the universal journey and the adventures, joys, mistakes, challenges and dangers that faced the hero at each stage. The hero/heroine is the person who takes off on a series of adventures beyond the ordinary, either to recover what has been lost or to discover some life-giving elixir. See Figure 5.4 below.]*

Exercise

Think back over your past and recall stories of when you have experienced hero or heroine's journeys. Ask your friends and/or colleagues to tell you about their major journeys or quests.

Campbell advocates 'follow your bliss', a phrase borrowed by Anita Roddick (1992) of The Body Shop. Campbell's meaning of the phrase was different from the 'do your own thing' catch-cry of the counterculture movement of the 1960s and 1970s. Campbell's exhortation was to choose something that compelled you and that required a lifelong, almost sacrificial, commitment. I have chosen to incorporate the myth of the hero's journey, as myths are pervasive in everyday life – not just in language but in thought and action (Vogler 1992). Myths evoke emotion, energize and inspire me to act, and help me to make sense of my place in the universe.

Joseph Campbell first wrote about the concept of the hero's journey in *The Hero With a Thousand Faces* (1973). He dismissed the modern idea of myth as attractive falsehoods or fiction and went on his own journey of discovery to seek out the meaning of myths across the world. As a result, he postulated that myths were deep meaning-inducing patterns that talk to the human soul, and therefore have the potential for guidance in our lives and for the future of the planet. He explained that myths across the world are attractive to us because they are metaphors that help us understand human sensibilities. Seeing them as scholarly tools, Campbell promotes the use of myths as guiding tools to enable us to make sense of our lives and the world (Larsen, 1996).

Campbell describes the stages of the universal journey and the challenges and dangers that faced the hero at each stage. The hero is the person who travels off on a series of adventures beyond the ordinary, either to recover what has been lost or to discover some life-giving elixir. I first encountered Campbell's work in 1994 and was thrilled by the sense that

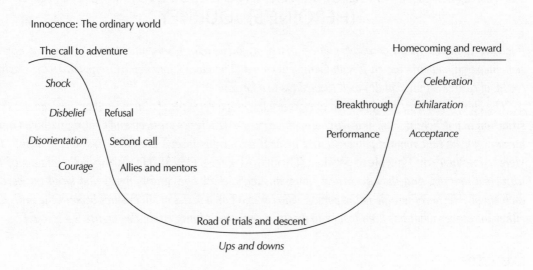

Figure 5.4 The stages of the hero's [heroine's] journey

metaphors such as the hero's journey were universal and could link all peoples of all cultures through time. When I started writing this book, I viewed the hero's journey somewhat like that shown in Figure 5.4, based on a workshop I attended on Campbell in 1996 (Larsen, 1996) and used it in an article I wrote with a storyteller friend, Marie Finlay (1995).

The term 'archetype' was employed by the Swiss psychologist Carl Jung meaning 'ancient patterns of personality that are the shared heritage of the human race' (Vogler 1992: 33). Jung suggests that these archetypes reflect different aspects of the human mind – that our personalities are divided up into the main parts we play out in the drama of our lives. He proposes that these archetypes come from a deeper source, the 'collective unconscious' of the human race, and that these in turn are linked to our own unconscious (Jung, 1968).

The stages marking the hero's journey are as follows, and match the critical points marked in the diagram in Figure 5.4:

- innocence, where all is well and stable;
- the call to take on a new project, where someone is called to be more than he or she currently is;
- refusal or resistance because of fear or shock, denial and disbelief;
- a second call, which often comes with a 'push' – eg a lost job, or an accident that results in a commitment to act;
- initiation, the acquiring of the skills to undertake the journey;

- allies and mentors, for the hero/heroine doesn't go it alone, with allies being human, technical or spiritual;
- the road of trials/the descent. Acceptance of the challenge and the obstacles to be overcome
- breakthrough, which is the moment when the change becomes conscious and clear, the hero/heroine having 'come through' through discovery and development;
- celebration of successes: reflection and integration of the changed situation;
- homecoming: the hero/heroine returns changed and/or with a gift for the 'tribe' – in modern terms, the project is completed.

Exercise

Are there any life transitions and/or problems that you are experiencing at the moment that you can re-frame as hero/heroine's journeys? It may help to identify what stage you are at in Figure 5.4. If you feel you are in the Road of Trials and Descent, it may comfort you to know that this stage will not last forever. Refer to the Card Pack in Appendix C to see what power bases you have already used and what others may help you.

I now query the model of single hero in today's world. Although the model pays heed to mentors whom one meets along the way, I support the ideas put forward by Reich (1987), who calls for the promotion of new myths of the 'team as hero'. Gilligan *et al* (1982) also saw women's journeys more in terms of nets or webs of human interconnection. I also see the heroine's journey as a circle, like Jean Houston's interpretation of Campbell's metaphor (1992), but I would like to be able to draw it in three dimensions like a spiral of upward growth as opposed to the U-shaped, linear trough described above. Within this spiral are many smaller spirals (see Figure 5.5).

Using this model to guide and support the change process can enable people to build up a repertoire of learning and stories about their empowerment journeys. This imagery brings the journey to life as compared with complex lifeless change models found in some texts.

Exercises

The hero/heroine's journey may be used in a number of ways:

- you can tell your past empowering stories before embarking on new projects;
- you can take solace in the fact that all heroes and heroines make mistakes at times;
- you can wallow in the road of trials and descent;
- you can tell your empowering hero/heroine's journey in order to celebrate your successes!

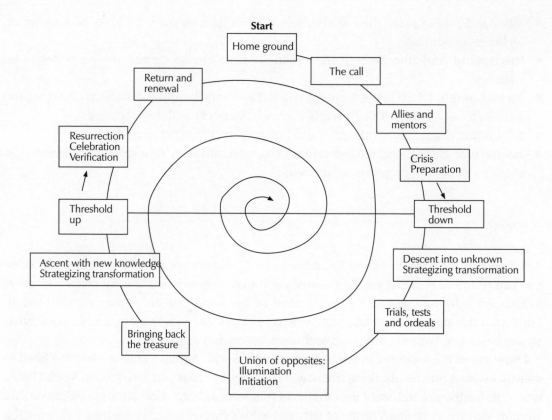

Figure 5.5 The heroic cycle

Celebration is a very important part of the empowerment process.

EXERCISE 8: VIDEO/FILM ANALYSIS

[Nowadays, many people relate to films and enjoy seeing short clips from well-known releases. Films are a form of 'observational learning' and, as with any story, characters can touch our souls. It is easy to hire videos, and so the cost outlay is not great. They provide a welcome change of pace in a workshop. Many learners (particularly those who are more right-brained) find watching pictures a useful learning strategy.]

I have briefly described three videos below (and cited a number of others) that can be used for various illustrations of empowerment and depowerment. But, first, I describe a few general guidelines about the use of videos in workshops.

General guidelines

Like all communication tools, the success of videos as a learning strategy can be enhanced by facilitation and debriefing skills. The amount of learning that occurs in any workshop that you run depends on how you prepare participants beforehand and how you help them process the information in the video. Watching the television at home is a passive pastime; you need to get participants to engage their brains when watching a video and make it an active rather than a passive learning experience. After lunch is a low-energy time, and so it is best not to show videos straight after people have eaten.

Prepare beforehand

Preview the video before the official showing, and ask yourself the following questions:

- Does it cover what you want to accomplish?
- Is it suitable for your audience?
- Is it too long?
- Would it be more useful to show a small part of the video only?
- Will the video interest participants, or will they find it boring?
- Is the video culturally appropriate?
- What is the purpose of the video?

In relation to the final question in the list above, there are many ways in which you may use videos. For instance, you can use them to: introduce a new topic; stimulate a discussion; reinforce or summarize a topic you have taught; or engage students' feelings on a topic. Note down questions to focus the attention of participants on specific aspects of the video.

Introduce the video

At the beginning of the session, help the participants to 'tune in' to what they are about to see. Example openers are:

- 'This video is called…'
- 'I'm showing it to you because…'
- 'It was made in the UK by…'
- 'The video was made in the 1970s. It is, however, still relevant to us today because…'
- 'I will stop the video at intervals so we can discuss some of the issues it raises.'

Give a handout with questions, or write questions on the board, in order to stimulate thought on the video:

- What three main things did you get from the video?
- Did anything surprise you?
- Did anything confuse you?
- What do you agree with? Why?
- What do you disagree with? Why?
- What questions would you like to ask about what you saw?
- What did you like about the video?
- Do you have any new insights? If yes, what are they?
- Did you react to anything? Did anything disturb you? If so, why?

After the video

If participants are slow to respond, ask them to stand up and move arms and legs. This re-energizes everyone. It is useful to start with questions like 'Any comments on what you've seen?' or 'Any reactions?' Pause and allow silence or 'think time'. Go through the pre-set questions.

An alternative strategy is to ask participants to generate questions that they think should be asked in order to analyse the video as fully as possible. This strategy helps participants learn how to frame clear, open, thought-provoking questions.

Learning transfer

If you are looking for learning transfer back to the work or home environment, ask questions like:

- What will you do differently as a result of seeing this video?
- What will you tell people tomorrow at work/home about this video?
- Would you show this video at work/home? If yes, why? If no, why?

Facilitator reflection

After the video, ask *yourself* whether you would use the video again and, if so, whether and how you would use it differently.

Make your own videos

If you have a video camera in your organization or if you can borrow one, how could you or your participants use it to make your own videos about empowerment?

The Full Monty

The title, 'The Full Monty' is taken from a phrase that developed during the Second World War. Field Marshall Montgomery, a famous leader in the British Army in North Africa, always insisted on a full English breakfast – ie eggs, bacon and sausages – despite the desert heat and the wartime dearth of supplies. This became a joke amongst his troops and a phrase developed: 'The Full Monty' meaning going the whole way.

The film, *The Full Monty* illustrates the depowering impact of long-term unemployment on communities, families, adults and children. The film gives a superb example of 'emergent leadership' where an unlikely hero gets an idea, emerges with a vision, and motivates his friends to achieve a superordinate goal – a goal that one person alone could not have accomplished. He ropes in his friends and also learns to bring in extra skilled people to enable the group to make the vision (of an all-male striptease act) happen.

What is interesting about the film is the way various characters at times behave as 'victims' or 'losers' (with due cause) and the impact on those around them. Likewise, when they do manage to 'get their act together' they are treated differently by those around them.

Brassed Off

The film entitled *Brassed Off* also focuses on the theme of unemployment, but this time with the threat to a brass band and a community as a whole when the local coal-mining pit closes. Again, clips from this film can provide useful focal points for discussion. And even the sound track from *Brassed Off* (and *The Full Monty*) can provide useful music for workshops.

Dead Poet's Society

In *Dead Poet's Society* the teacher, John Keating, takes a very different approach to teaching English. He is a charismatic person who exhorts his students with phrases such as 'Carpe diem' ('Seize the day').

The film is an interesting study of the very different group norms in Keating's classes compared with that of the rest of the schoolteachers. It can also be used to illustrate problems with going against the grain; indeed, as a change agent Keating did nothing to cover himself or his students with the governing hierarchical members of the school.

An interesting area for discussion is Keating's relationship with a student, Neil Perry, who wants to become an actor. The boy's father has very different ideas. Keating supports Neil, who takes the part as Puck in Shakespeare's *A Midsummer Night's Dream*. Keating encourages Neil to tell his father his real career aspirations. The father, who has strong legitimate power in an overbearing, autocratic father role (based on his military background) overrides his son's impassioned pleas. Neil takes what he sees as the only way out and commits suicide.

Interesting discussions can be triggered on the need for a mentor like Keating to stay with a young person like Neil – ie in this instance encouragement was not enough, Neil did not have enough 'personal power' to make his father change his attitude. It could be argued that Keating should have stayed with Neil to support him in telling his father what career he really wanted to follow.

Other films

Having cited three of my favourite films, which are also very useful for workshop use when considering empowerment, I realized that they all focus on males. Here are the titles of films with female heroines and/or lead roles:

- *Shirley Valentine;*
- *Norma Rae;*
- *Silkwood;*
- *Steel Magnolias;*
- *Thelma and Louise;*
- *The Craft;*
- *The Miracle Worker;*
- *Broadcast News;*
- *Julia;*
- *Elizabeth;*
- *Isadora.*

There is a company in the United Kingdom that was set up in 1993 by two disillusioned television producers and two environmental and social justice activists. They specialize in making documentaries about political and environmental issues: 'the news you don't see on the news'. For more information, contact Undercurrents Productions, 16b Cherwell Street, Oxford OX4 1BG, UK (fax: 00 44 (0) 1865 243562; e-mail underc@gn.apc.org; Web site www.undercurrents.org).

Other videos on political action include *From Missouri to Memphis* and *Mississippi Burning*.

EXERCISE 9: HASSLE LINES: WHEN THERE IS AN IMBALANCE OF POWER

[This exercise was developed by the Quaker 'Turning the Tide' programme in London and explained to me by Steve Whiting. (This programme advances the understanding and use of active nonviolence for

positive social change by making use of the experience and insights of previous non-violent movements. I will first describe a role play and then describe an 'active nonviolent' action that made legal history in 1999.) The exercise was designed to help participants experiment with various scenarios when there is a distinct difference in power and/or where there is oppression ie a gross imbalance of power.

In one example, the Quakers used a role play involving a Mafia 'heavy' who was collecting imposed 'dues' from a frightened shopkeeper. In another instance, they used the example of a boss who was sacking an employee unfairly, and it is this one that I shall describe below. It helps to give participants two brief but different role plays because the second time around they can swap roles and get a chance to experiment with a wider range of behaviours.

There are two stages. The first is the role play and the second is a discussion about the relative power strengths and weaknesses of each of the 'players'.]

Divide up the participants into two equal lines so that each person is facing a partner. Give one row the name of Toni, a worker. Give the other row the name of Chris, the boss (try to use names that are used by both sexes.) Brief each side about their respective roles. Toni is the latest person to join the company and has been trying hard, but at times has not been given proper training. He/she has not received any feedback to suggest that the boss is not satisfied. Chris has been pressured from above to cut costs and can only think of laying people off as work is slack at the moment.

Some people may feel awkward and resist playing the 'baddy' in a role play, and so it is useful to 'give them permission' to be bad along the lines of: 'You will all learn more from this role play if you act the part. Remember you are acting under a pseudonym and will return to your own persona later.' Further, at the end of the role play ask participants to shake hands with their partners and shake off the personas they were playing.

It is useful to document the debriefing discussion on a flipchart in the following sequence (ie ending up on the sources of strengths for the oppressed):

1. *What are the sources of weakness for the boss? Where is he/she not powerful?* For example:

   - lack of training;
   - lack of feedback;
   - no concrete evidence, only hearsay;
   - may feel bad about having to dismiss someone.

2. *What are the sources of strengths for the boss? Where is he/she powerful?* For example:

   - position/legitimate power;
   - the power of illusion, eg formal or expensive clothing;
   - the power of ambience, eg a large office, a large desk.

3. *What are the sources of weakness for the worker? Where is he/she not powerful?* For example:

   - caught by surprise, and has to think on his/her feet;
   - lack of knowledge of his/her rights;
   - new to company, and so may not have the support of other workers.

4. *What are the sources of strengths for the worker? Where is he/she powerful?* For example:

- labour laws regarding training and feedback on the job;
- personal power, namely standing ground, keeping eye contact and asking for specific feedback;
- power of persuasion and negotiation;
- a request of specific feedback to be gathered (ie buying time);
- the power of collective action as a last resort.

For a more detailed description and historical examples of nonviolent action, see volume 2 of *The Politics of Nonviolent Action* by Gene Sharp, in Finkelstein (1974). 'Nonviolence' is a word that may be interpreted in many different ways. Some interpret it as conveying gentle, harmless or non-confrontational actions. For many activists it means 'people power', typified by social and political movements that use the power of demonstrations, non-cooperation or direct action to change a situation. Marshall Rosenberg describes non-violence as a mode of four stages of communication between people (described further in the Power of Positive and constructive feedback (Power Card 38) in Chapter 3).

For Quakers, the term 'active nonviolence' has a more spiritual meaning, to do with the ultimate goal of the nonviolent action and the spirit in which it is carried out. It includes dialogue with people and resistance to the structures to compel change. I observed an exercise facilitated by Quaker friends where they asked small groups to complete the sentence: 'An action is nonviolent if …'. The exercise caused great debate.

Even within the Quaker community, the term 'nonviolence' has been re-evaluated and redefined over the centuries and today includes destruction of property. For example, in June 1999, three activists from the Trident Ploughshare 2000 group were remanded in custody for causing £80,000 of damage to the *Maytime* Trident submarine floating laboratory complex in Loch Goil in Scotland. Angie Zelter, one of the accused, conducted her own defence, claiming:

> I have tried every other reasonable method to prevent nuclear catastrophe over the last 25 years before disarming *Maytime*. I did not disarm the nuclear research laboratory on a whim or in anger. It was not the act of a vandal or terrorist. I had tried everything else and, in the circumstances, there was no other reasonable legal alternative.
>
> (*Guardian*, 8 September 1999, p 5)

In October 1999, the women were acquitted in a landmark decision by Sheriff Margaret Gimblett, who accepted their defence that Britain's Trident nuclear submarine programme was illegal under international law and that their destruction of property had been acting simply to prevent a greater crime, ie a major loss of life. The results of this case bring a whole new meaning to the interpretation of nonviolent methods.

EXERCISE 10: THE WOMEN'S WISH

[The story of 'The Women's Wish' can be traced far back to the Arthurian legends and Sir Gawain. It also appeared in 'The Wife of Bath's Tale' in Chaucer's **The Canterbury Tales.** *I have seen the story recounted by one person at length, or it can be performed by two people as a role play after some rehearsal. I have summarized it here. If you tell it in public, please use your imagination and add embellishments.]*

The women's wish

Once upon a time, there was a young knight at the court of King Arthur. The knight was full of pride and strength. One day he saw a maiden in the forest. He was so overcome with her love-liness that he tried to carry her off by force. But other knights heard her cries and the knight was seized and brought before King Arthur for trial.

Arthur was furious and sentenced him to death, but Queen Guinevere sought mercy for the knight and succeeded in her pleas. But she did not want to let the knight off lightly, and so she gave him one year and a day to earn his freedom – on one condition, that he must find the answer to the riddle 'What is it that women most desire?' If he failed, he would receive the death penalty.

The knight set off with great speed, but as he searched the kingdom he was confused by all the conflicting answers; no two people agreed. Some said 'honour', others 'riches', and others 'fine clothing'. But no answers seemed to feel right somehow. He wandered far and wide seeking the advice of others. At length the year was up and he sadly rode his horse through the forest towards the castle.

In the dusky light he saw a circle of 24 maidens dancing. But as he drew nigh, they vanished and an old, ugly woman appeared. He told her his problem and she promised to help as long as he agreed to do anything she asked. He gave his word (he was desperate, after all).

At the court, the crone demanded that the knight should marry her in return for the answer to the riddle. He begged and begged (he was horrified and repulsed), but she said he must keep his word. He was distraught, but – understandably – he reasoned he would do anything to escape the death penalty.

The ceremony took place and he resigned himself sadly to his fate. That night he crept into the bridal bedroom hoping his bride would be asleep. As the door squeaked open he saw a stunning young maid, who greeted him lovingly. She explained that she was the victim of a curse and that he could either have her as a young, beautiful woman in their bedchamber and a crone in public during the day, *or* a beautiful young woman during the day and a crone in their bedchamber: he must choose.

He was overcome with sadness at the decision before him. He paced up and down. Eventually he said 'My dear wife, I put myself in your hands. Choose for yourself which you think is best'. The young woman almost wept for joy. 'At last the spell that was cast on me has been broken and you have found for yourself what women most desire: dominion over our own affairs.'

Discussion

This story can be used in many different ways to discuss:

- archetypes: maid, woman, crone, hero, anti-hero, queen;
- heroic qualities: quests/journeys;
- dominion over own affairs: what does this mean to you? Is it too individualistic?
- choice;
- myths and modern stories.

CONCLUSION

A wide variety of experiential activities have been included here, because learners like to be stimulated in many different ways. No doubt you have many of your own that you can add in the box below.

KEY POINT SUMMARY

This chapter has included a wide variety of exercises.

There are many different exercises, films and stories that you can use to provoke your thinking about power and empowerment.

Be creative when deciding upon and evaluating your own activities.

There are many films, stories and poems to provoke thought.

The Hero's [Heroine's] Journey/Cycle is a useful model to explain the stages in the transition and/or change process.

Your own points

6

Reflections on empowerment workshop processes

INTRODUCTION

The purpose of this chapter is to:

- reflect on the different uses of the power cards;
- describe serendipitous learning from the power cards;
- describe the importance of the action planning and sharing stage;
- describe how you can use these exercises to increase awareness;
- identify when and how power can be used unethically or against an individual;
- describe the contextual influence on individuals and empowerment;
- reflect on future directions of empowerment.

The process of card sorting was chosen for this book because it presents individuals and/or groups with a number of choices coming from a simple-to-use portable model. It enables participants to 'play and experiment' in a non-threatening way with a number of alternatives before deciding on suitable action plans. It is important that facilitators ask participants to consider their reasons for including or excluding a particular power base. Requesting participants to show a partner or small groups their card sort encourages serious questioning and discussion of previous assumptions.

People often say 'But I always do things this way'. This answer may need to be challenged with the question 'Why?' and a re-examining of the reasons why individuals either assume that there is 'no choice' (as described in Chapter 3) or that they cannot use certain power bases.

Some participants may need help to rewrite their 'script' (or 'repeated internal learnt messages' in transactional analysis terms (Harris, 1969)). For example, an individual might normally think 'I can't speak up to powerful people' and change to saying 'Until now, I have chosen for a variety of reasons never to use the 'power of influencing powerful people [Power Card 16]. However, I can change; and in this circumstance I choose to use this power base because…' .

SERENDIPITOUS LEARNING FROM THE CARDS

Serendipitous learning refers to unanticipated, pleasant and unexpected discoveries. The word 'serendipity' was coined by Horace Walpole in 1754, when he wrote a fairy tale entitled *The Three Princes of Serendip* (Serendip was the old name for Sri Lanka, even before it was Ceylon). The three princes went on adventures and learnt many things (*The Concise Oxford Dictionary*, 1982).

My experience is that serendipitous events occur even during my workshops: some participants suddenly learn surprising things about themselves or others. For example, one person confided that she suddenly realized that she was not as empowered as she once thought. She wrote:

> I discovered that although I always felt empowered, deep down I am not. I felt disconcerted. It made me really think… Like with monster issues at work, I feel in control and have taken action in the past. But on a daily basis, like little things when normal people ask favours, I tend to conform to what they want rather than thinking about what I want.
>
> (Public Affairs Officer)

This participant, though rather disconcerted about the revelation about her own level of empowerment, quickly started working positively on this serendipitous piece of learning.

THE 'PMI' PROCESS TO EVALUATE CHOICES AND MAKE DECISIONS

In Chapter 1, the definition of empowerment is linked to the concept of choice. In Chapter 3, the power of choices (Power Card 4) illustrates how to generate different choices through the process of brainstorming. Alvin Toffler in *Future Shock* (1970) talks about the stress of 'overchoice'. This implies that we have access to all the available information – which is often not the case (for example, in patient–doctor relationships).

It is necessary, therefore, to have an evaluation process in order to enable us to make informed choices. If empowerment is about recognizing choices, then it follows that we have also to make decisions. This may not be as easy as it first appears. We make thousands of decisions every day: starting from when we wake up, we decide to get out of bed, what to wear and in what sequence to put our clothes on, what to have for breakfast, and so on through the day. Luckily, a lot of these decisions are made almost subconsciously. We have to make most everyday tasks routine in order to conserve time and energy.

One useful process, which enables us to map out and compare many options, is the 'PMI' process developed by Edward de Bono (1987). The letters 'PMI' stand for **P**luses, **M**inuses and Interesting points (where 'interesting points' are aspects that are neither particularly positive nor particularly negative, but are just unusual or interesting features of that item).

Let's take the example of a career decision. First of all, jot down as many alternatives as possible without evaluating any. For example:

- Go back to full-time study and change careers.
- Stay in the same job/career.
- Stay in the same job and study part-time for a new career.
- Stay in the same job part-time and study part-time for a new career.
- Go on a working holiday for a year.
- Look for another job in the new career area.
- Look for another job in the old career area.
- Ask for leave without pay to go travelling for three months.
- Ask for leave without pay to experiment working for yourself.

Then draw up a table and compare the pluses, minuses and interesting points of each option – an example is given in Table 6.1 below. Add feelings and hunches. Show your ideas to a partner or 'critical friend' who you know will give you constructive feedback.

Table 6.1 Evaluation of alternatives: PMI process

Options	Pluses	Minuses	Interesting points
1. Go back to full-time study	Be great to be a full-time student again. Get away from work pressures	Can I afford it? Would I be able to keep up with younger students?	Work and study both create pressure and it depends on how I respond to them
2 Stay in same job and study part-time	Less risk	I'm fed up with my job. Stress and time	Doesn't feel right
3 Stay in same job part-time and study part-time	Less stressful	Could be difficult financially	Could be possible if I can hang in with my job just part-time
4. Go on a working holiday for a year	Sounds romantic	The problem will stilll be there on my return	I need my friends around me at the moment

THE IMPORTANCE OF THE ACTION PLANNING AND SHARING STAGE

Since the identification of alternative sources of power is only a first step in the empowerment process, it is very important that participants complete an action-planning sheet (see Appendix B). Transferring power bases into appropriate actions requires skill and needs to be thought through by you before returning to work or college to change the world.

> I was delighted when I saw there were more than just five power bases [referring to French and Raven's work]. Last week I used some new ones. I hope I will have a job next week.
>
> (Staff Development Educator)

Yes, this participant was still in her job at the time of writing some months later, even though she had assertively confronted her boss on some issues.

The sharing stage at the end of the workshop (either in small groups or to the whole group) is a vital part of completing the 'reflection' stage of the experiential learning model. As participants listen to one another's plans, they invariably add ideas to their own plans and make constructive suggestions to one another.

THE CARDS CAN BE USED AGAINST INDIVIDUALS AND GROUPS

Whilst the cards (see Appendix C) may be used as a means of marshalling potential power resources, participants need to be made aware that power bases can be used in a *depowering* way or could be abused. For example, the devolution of power from centralized bureaucracies can empower agencies; however, in the healthcare field in Australia, Hicks (1985: 687) points out that:

> Devolution is offered as a way of helping people in the regions to accept cuts in health resources. The underlying rationale for regional devolution is that participation by those most closely affected will result in more acceptable and efficient policies concerning the allocation of scarce resources than would occur if decisions were imposed from a central authority. Federal governments push the responsibility for health services onto the states, the states push it onto the regions and so no one in the chain is easily made responsible to the user population... If your goal is not achievable, then make it someone else's responsibility.

Legitimate power may become illegitimate power in the hands of an unscrupulous user, or when it has been obtained through bribery or nepotism. The power of alignment to powerful people may be depowering if a person only aligns to one person and that person falls from grace.

CONTEXTUAL FACTORS IMPINGING ON THE EMPOWERMENT PROCESS

The argument described at the beginning of this book, namely that empowerment is ultimately the responsibility of the individual, now has to be taken a stage further. Wilson (1987) describes a continuum of images, ranging from a person who is behaving in a self-empowered way to one who is behaving like a victim. Images range from that of a proud, independent self-sufficient person to that of a helpless, powerless individual who suffers as a result of his or her own personal inadequacies.

But, first, the empowered behaviour may not be permanent, depending on life events. Secondly, the disempowered behaviour may not be the result only of a person's 'inadequacies'. The individual may have very little 'room for manoeuvre' within the confines of the surrounding culture (as with the women in Afghanistan during the administration of the Taliban). Furthermore, a feeling of empowerment may be due to the body chemistry of those affected, which will also impact on their mental state. Whatever the cause, a person should never be made to feel inadequate or he/she is not trying. An American Indian expression states that we should not judge someone until we have walked in their moccasins for three weeks.

The empowerment process also needs to be placed in its wider context:

- the 'readiness' of the individual and/or group;
- the mental state of a person;
- the cultural background of participants;
- the culture of the organization;
- the current societal structures.

These attributes are described further below.

Readiness

Relating to 'readiness', one participant has commented:

> I am still very much constrained by a particular incident. I would like to do this again next week [referring to the mind map of empowerment factors] when I feel stronger.
>
> (Technical and Further Education Course Manager)

The decision 'not to act' may be just as empowering as the decision 'to act'. If a person is feeling vulnerable, it may be a very powerful and sensible strategy to wait until inner strength returns. The decision 'not to act' is very different from wallowing in indecision.

Mental state

Some individuals may be feeling very depressed and depowered, and they may need specialized help. Others may have a medical condition that results in depression. In countries that have long dark winters, some people suffer from seasonal affective disorder (SAD), a recently recognized medical condition where the nerve centres in the brain controlling our daily rhythms and moods are insufficiently stimulated because of the lack of light entering the eyes. During the night, the pineal gland produces melatonin to make us drowsy. In the morning, the bright light causes the gland to stop producing melatonin, but on dull winter days – especially if a person is indoors – not enough light is received to trigger the waking-up process. Norman Rosenthal (1991) has experimented with full-spectrum lighting systems that mimic daylight to offset this phenomenon.

Cultural background

Readers from different cultures may be confused by some of the Western values inherent in the power bases described above. Individual goal-setting is a Western phenomenon. In many cultures in South-East Asia, goals are traditionally set by parents for their children, or by whole families who may collaborate – for example, aunts and uncles agree to help a niece to go abroad to study, on the understanding that when she returns she will help them in achieving security or medical help in their old age.

In the developing world, social systems often exist that depower some groups of the population from birth: the caste system, the poverty trap, the monetary system, land ownership systems. To talk glibly about 'choices' to people who are on a starvation diet in the poverty and indebtedness trap is an oversimplification of the issues involved. In these instances there are no easy answers, and the empowerment of individuals may have to go hand in hand with substantial social change.

There are many students from South-East Asia in my university in Perth, Western Australia. I used the power cards with a first-year class, and one male student from Sarawak approached me in my office later. He had been using the cards to try to resolve his inner conflict: he wanted to do a course in art, but his parents had made him enrol in a management course. We discussed his family background. A number of family members had collected to support him financially to come to Perth; it was a group investment. As a result, he decided to use the power of the individual to make sure he could use his creativity whilst still doing the management course: he specialized in marketing in his course, making use of his uncle's computer so that he could become expert in computer graphics and use these creative skills in the marketing field.

The culture of an organization

There appears to be a gap between the perceptions of managers and those of employees. Messmer (1990) describes a survey in the United States that was designed to measure the extent to which employee empowerment is being practised within US business. Messmer found that 88 per cent of the managers who responded believed that they were giving employees more authority to make decisions and take action than they were five years ago. In a survey of employees, however, only 64 per cent said that management has given them more authority to make decisions and take action than they were given five years ago.

The first important step in closing any gap between perception and reality is to determine if the culture of the organization is 'ready' to change. If management and the organizational culture do not nurture the value of empowerment, then it will be stifled. So there may need to be some extensive preparation work before an empowerment workshop.

Wider societal factors

I believe that it is important for facilitators to spend time identifying the wider societal and contextual factors that may prevent workshop participants from achieving their goals. Arnstein (mentioned in Chapter 1 for her ladder of participation) relates participation to the redistribution of power thus:

> The idea of citizen participation is a little like eating spinach: no one is against it in principle because it is good for you. Participation of the governed in their government is, in theory, the cornerstone of democracy – a revered idea that is vigorously applauded by virtually everyone. The applause is reduced to polite handclaps, however, when this principle is advocated by the have-not blacks, Mexican-Americans, Puerto Ricans, Indians, Eskimos and whites. And when the have-nots define participation as the redistribution of power, the US consensus on the fundamental principle explodes into many shades of outright racial, ethnic, ideological, and political opposition.
>
> (1969: 176)

Without wishing to disillusion you or your participants, it is my opinion that it is immoral to use exercises such as the ones described above without ensuring that individuals are aware of the wider societal constraints and spend time on developing action plans to take these into consideration. For example, when I have facilitated workshops with the long-term unemployed, I believed it was important to address the structural societal constraints that were in part preventing young people from getting a job. The more the unemployed were informed about these issues, the more I believed they were likely to:

- use less self-blame;
- use positive self talk that we taught them;
- structure their time;
- develop hobbies and interests;
- create some form of self-employment;
- find work experience or voluntary work.

ETHICAL ISSUES REGARDING EMPOWERMENT

There appear to be at least two areas where ethical use of empowerment needs to be addressed: the facilitator and the participants.

Facilitator and ethics

There are some training programmes that advertise and promise the world. I believe it is unethical to use these materials in this way to raise expectations unrealistically. As I described above, the societal and physical constraints need to be addressed without putting major negatives in a person's way.

Participants and ethics

Skills – in whatever form they take – can be used in many different ways. It is the motives and results that may be unethical. Of course, what is ethical to one person may be unethical to the next, and so there are no definitive rules on this point.

Empowerment should not be passively enjoyed. According to Hamelink (1994), it has to be actively achieved and guarded. So once individuals start to feel more empowered, they have an ethical responsibility to contribute actively to the rights of others in this regard, rather than to use their power skills to depower others. Neither can individuals expect others (the state, the media, action groups, etc) always to defend their rights:

> If people do not actively engage in the battle for their empowerment, they should not be surprised to find themselves one day totally disempowered.

> (Hamelink 1994: 12)

VALUING THE JOURNEY

In Western societies today, we tend to value outcomes and achievements rather than the processes used to reach goals. Some people look at books, theories and ideas and have the expectation that the creators produced these products quickly, easily and alone. The process of learning and the journey contributing to the production of ideas, books and theses is rarely valued. I remember I fell into this trap when I started research for my master's thesis.

Katrin, my friend and mentor, said to me: 'Just start reading anything and everything on the topic. Don't start making headings or assumptions in your mind yet'. I was confused and frustrated, for I was not prepared for the almost space-like weightless state of confusion and drifting. My mentor consoled me: 'Don't worry. This is natural. It's all part of it'. For some reason I had made the assumption that my research questions would just flow. But I was not prepared, either intellectually or emotionally, for the frustrating and disorientating process that occurred to me.

In retrospect, in fact, that was when some of my major learning took place. In the West we are taught to think 'logically and deductively'. This can limit our thinking; allowing a wider space to think inductively often gives us unanticipated learning and/or information. Empowerment is a journey not an end state. It requires constant co-operation.

There follows a story that is useful for demonstrating the change in attitude or spirit necessary to create a more co-operative and civil society.

'The Good Man': the power of co-operation

A man was given a reward for his goodness. He chose to 'see heaven and hell' *before* he died. An angel accompanied him, first to hell, where he saw richness and plenty, but the people were so miserable and cursed the Lord. He saw they were tied up with chains of steel and they had chains of steel on their arms, so although they could reach out and take the food, they could not put it into their mouths.

Then he travelled to heaven, where he saw the same scene, with people tied up in the same way. 'It's the same', he said. 'But just a moment. It *is* different'. And as he watched, he saw the people in heaven reach out, pick up the food, and feed each other.

Group synergy

At school we were often told 'Get on in silence. You must complete this exercise alone, and woe betide anyone who cheats'. The inference was that to talk to a fellow student about a problem or issue was wrong. The inability to complete a task alone was often considered a mark of individual failure.

However, if you consider the workplace today, the complexity of problems requires not only the pooling of information but also the pooling of ideas in a creative and problem-solving atmosphere. During such sessions many ideas may be 'sparked'. This triggering can often lead to the identification of creative solutions that no one may have thought of alone. This is called 'synergy' and may be expressed as: $1+1+1+1 = 7$, indicating that four people together may generate the work of seven individuals working alone.

Empowerment in organizations is a complex phenomenon that requires co-operation and commitment from everyone. It is a change of values and mindsets. Therefore this type of organizational change should not be undertaken without considerable forethought and a united long-term effort by all levels of management and employees. Where this commitment is lacking, some people have justifiably become cynical of such endeavours. The current trend to flatten hierarchies and to introduce downsizing or rightsizing – or whatever euphemisms are used – frequently mean that people lower down the hierarchy are being asked either to leave or to take on more responsibility than ever before.

In order to make this change palatable, some top managers are promoting the requirement as 'empowerment'. In reality, what is happening is that workers are being asked to undertake unstable nomadic careers or take more responsibility and stress than ever before, sometimes with little or no training for the new job roles and certainly no expectation of any kind of rewards. Extra responsibility with no extra power causes increased stress. Recent studies suggest that it is not top management that gets most stressed, but middle and lower managers.

Despite all these warnings, I still firmly believe that this is the way organizations and indeed nations have to go. John Heron in a workshop in Perth in 1993 commented: 'there is now an inexorable process for human rights right across the planet. This process began in the 17th century and is gaining momentum, both in developed and developing countries'. If this process is going to progress in a peaceful way, then empowerment is going to be a necessary part.

CONCLUSION

As Paulo Freire has emphasized, no education is ever neutral. His liberating teaching and empowering literacy programmes ended in his imprisonment and exile from Brazil, illustrating that education may be used for liberation *or* domination. There are no simple formulas for empowerment, but there is an underlying values base of participation and power sharing, plus associated tools and strategies. I hope that the ideas and processes described in this book have stimulated your thinking and energized you to adapt and create your own strategies.

In conclusion, I will end with comments made from workshop participants:

> Doing the card sort at home made me think of ways of solving the problem which I would not normally think of.
>
> (Training Development Executive)

> I found it interesting that some power bases are not necessary in some situations. Some are totally useless. I need to work on positive thinking power.
>
> (Staff Development Officer)

> Where does empowerment stop? Is there overempowerment?
>
> (School Development Officer)

> I was amazed to see all the ways of using power. It started me thinking about a problem. I found it useful to discuss the card sort with my 'study buddy' partner and share ideas. It really jolted my thinking.
>
> (Psychologist)

> I could incorporate the cards into my learning journal. I put up the cards at home on the wall and ticked them every time I used them.
>
> (Computer trainer)

One last quote to end up with is a favourite of mine:

> If I am not for myself,
> Who will be for me?
> If I am for myself only, what am I?
> If not now – when?
>
> (Talmudic saying Mishnah, Abot)

KEY POINT SUMMARY

The card sort process is a non-threatening activity that enables people to play and experiment.

The card sort process generates serendipitous learning.

The cards may be used against a person, but being able to recognize this is empowering in itself.

It is important to allow plenty of time in empowerment facilitation for open discussion, feedback and follow-up.

The context may need to be taken into consideration during action planning in respect of:

- the readiness of the individual;
- the mental state of a person;
- the cultural background of participants;
- the culture of the organization;
- the societal background.

Discussing the contextual background enables participants to make more informed action plans.

Empowerment is inexorably linked to the march for human rights across the planet.

Your points

Appendix A

An empowerment workshop framework

INTRODUCTION

This Appendix has been written for workshop facilitators. It highlights the possible stages in a one-day workshop based on the 'Empowerment Cycle'. The suggested framework is encapsulated in a set of instructions to workshop participants, and the pack of power cards used for facilitating empowerment is given in Appendix C.

There are, of course, many potential variations in the workshop framework and structure that can occur, and any workshops you plan to run should be designed according to your facilitation style and the needs and context of the group.

Each stage of the workshop is cross-referenced to relevant detailed explanations in previous chapters.

SAMPLE WORKSHOP FRAMEWORK

A sample workshop framework is shown in Table A.1 below using the headings 'Content', 'Process' and 'Time' developed by Doyle and Straus (1986). The contents of the Table are only intended as a guideline and, in fact, the timing of exercises regularly deviates from this depending on the requirements of the organization and levels of discussion generated by the participants. The day is meant to be highly interactive, and so it is important to build a trusting environment at the beginning.

John Heron (1989) describes three facilitator power modes of workshop design:

- *hierarchical*: the facilitator alone decides the content and process;
- *co-operative*: the facilitator plans the content and process with the participants;
- *autonomous*: the facilitator delegates the planning of the content and process to the participants but is available for consultation and back-up help.

If the workshop on empowerment is to be fully empowering, it should be designed ideally in the co-operative mode. Follow-up workshops should then operate in autonomous mode.

Table A.1 Framework for a sample workshop on empowerment

Content	Process	Time
What is being covered?	How will the content be addressed?	How long will it take?
1. Introductions and ice- breakers.		
What is the purpose of the workshop in relation to the goals of the organization?	Various processes.	9.00–9.10
2. Contracting for group needs. Why are you here today?		
Do the workshop outline and processes meet your needs and those of the group?	Paired interview, round robin, dot voting	9.10–9.30
3. How can we get the most out of the day?	Contracting for desirable group ground rules	9.30–9.40
4. What does 'power to the people' mean?	Whole group listens or accompanies the John Lennon song 'Power to the People'	9.40–10.00
5. How are the meanings of 'power' and 'empowerment' changing?	Facilitator presents information and group in discussion	10.00–10.30
	MORNING TEA	10.30–10.50
6. What is the 'Empowerment Cycle'?	Discussion of the empowerment model	10.50–11.05
7. What experiences have group members had that were empowering and depowering?	Mind-mapping in small groups	11.05–11.15
8. Group feedback.	Feedback to whole group and generation of main themes	11.15–11.45
9. What rationales/excuses do people use to avoid making choices or taking action?	Discussion of 'ego defence mechanisms'	11.45–12.30
What societal constraints stop people from being more empowered?	Discussion of societal constraints	
Over lunch, participants are requested to discuss possible problems/projects that they may wish to work on in the afternoon.	LUNCH	12.30–1.15
10. What power bases are available? (French and Raven, Ferguson, etc)	Presentation	1.15–1.30
11. Introduction of 'Your Personal Power Pack'.	Questions and discussion on the meaning of the power bases	1.30–1.50
12. What problem or project do individual participants or small groups wish to work on?	Individual/group reflection	1.50–2.00

Table A.2 A Framework for a sample workshop on empowerment (continued)

Content	Process	Time
What is being covered?	How will the content be addressed?	How long will it take?
13. What power bases are useful?	Card sort process and self reflection and questioning: individually or in pairs	2.00–3.00
14. How can participants make it happen?	Action planning	3.00–3.15
	AFTERNOON TEA	3.15–3.30
15. Feedback of plans to whole group. What implications do these action plans have for the wider organization?	Discussion and feedback between staff and management	3.30–4.30
16. What did you think of the day?	Short-term feedback	4.30–4.40
17. Where to from here? How can participants be involved in the planning and facilitation of the next workshop?	Action planning	4.40–5.00

WORKSHOP STRUCTURE

The day is organized to start with very generalized contextual information and whole-group work. This is followed by small-group work, where participants start to free up in talking about their past experiences. The next stage, ie the card sort, consists of either individual or small-group work. At the end of the day, the whole group meets again to discuss individual and group plans and wider organizational issues which need to be considered to support making things happen. Figure A.1 shows these four aspects in broad diagrammatic form. In addition, the 17 stages of the workshop, as set out in Table A.1 above, are described in more detail in the sections below.

Stage 1: What is the purpose of the workshop in relation to organizational goals?

The purpose of the workshop should have been made very clear in either pre-workshop briefings or internal memos/e-mails. However, a statement of desired intentions at this stage is important in relation to the goals of the organization.

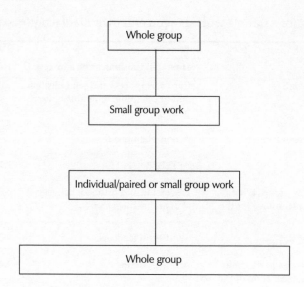

Figure A.1 The four aspects of workshop structure

Stage 2: Contracting for group needs: Who are we and why are we here today?

Rather than presenting a workshop outline as fait accompli, I prefer to contract with the group because it gives me a more detailed indication of group needs than I can usually get from prior needs-analysis research. Figure A.2 shows a suggested set of questions that should be raised at contract stage. I use the 'paired-interview' technique, where the participants are divided into pairs and are required to interview each other with the three questions shown in Figure A.2.

As described by Arnstein in Chapter 6, it is deemed unethical to contract for group needs if you are not prepared, if necessary, to reshape aspects of the workshop. The golden rule is: never invite people to participate if your mind is already made up.

The reason for this stage is that participants will be most motivated to work on issues that directly affect them. This stage also enables the facilitator to identify 'resisters' – those people who are attending but for some reason may not want to be there. Their answers and body language are likely to give some clues as to what is unsettling them and what hidden agendas may need to surface during the workshop.

After the set of paired interviews, ideas are generated on flipchart paper. Each participant is invited to contribute one item in turn in a round-robin process. When ideas seem to be exhausted, each participant is given three self-adhesive dots and asked to place them on three different items from the generated ideas that they believe are important. This ranking of needs is then discussed and compared with the workshop outline, and changes are made where appropriate.

NAME _____

Please interview the person beside you. Put his/her name at the top of the page and when you have finished give the sheet to him/her.

As a result of this workshop on 'Empowerment':

1.   What do you want to get out of the day?

2.   What do you want to know?

3.   What skills do you want to learn?

4.   How do you want to feel at the end of the workshop?

Figure A.2 Questions to raise at contract stage

Stage 3: How can we get the most out of the day?

This stage involves the whole group listing ground rules. This gives an opportunity for the participants to actively listen to each other; one person speaking at a time; shout if you need a stretch break.

Stage 4: What does 'power to the people' mean?

In order to warm people to the topic of empowerment, I play the John Lennon song 'Power to the People' and display the words on an overhead projector. I also have a box of musical instruments (tambourines, cymbals, drumsticks and a conductor's baton) and invite participants to choose what they would like to use to accompany the song.

When everyone is satisfied with his or her choice of instrument, I invite someone to conduct from the front with the conductor's baton. This produces much hilarity. I start the music and usually an incredible din ensues. Some people dance; others stand somewhat awkwardly. At the end everyone sits down in noisy disarray. Then the debrief starts and I ask what had that exercise to do with empowerment? The discussion usually generates the following points:

- Empowerment means doing some things you don't normally do.
- It stretches your comfort zone, I felt embarrassed.
- It was great! It was fine for me. I could have gone on longer.
- I had to choose what to play and whether to participate. I felt very odd
- It was easier to participate because everyone was doing it… I didn't feel so odd.
- I noticed that no one was taking any notice of the conductor. I guess that could happen to managers if we all went off in different directions at once. Empowerment needs co-ordination.
- The song is rousing, but a bit simplistic. It isn't as easy as that.
- Empowerment means having choices.

As I have said before in this book, facilitators need to choose techniques with which they feel comfortable. At this stage there is a need to 'warm' participants to the tasks ahead. The choice of ice-breaker is up to you, but preferably it should have some link to empowerment.

Stage 5: How are the meanings of 'power' and 'empowerment' changing?

The information and depth of discussion in this stage depends on the background knowledge and needs of the group. Detailed information about these concepts is provided in Chapter 1.

Stage 6: What is the 'Empowerment Cycle'?

This model is presented in detail in Chapter 2, and it is set down diagrammatically here in Figure A.3. In the workshop I give participants a handout of the model.

For a more detailed explanation of this see Chapter 2.

Stages 7 and 8: What experiences have group members had that were empowering and depowering?

This exercise enables people to discuss in small groups some of the issues that they may not like to divulge in the whole group. Small groups of four or five individuals plot ideas in colour on a mind map on flipchart paper. To save time, I usually plot the main headings on the paper first, ie:

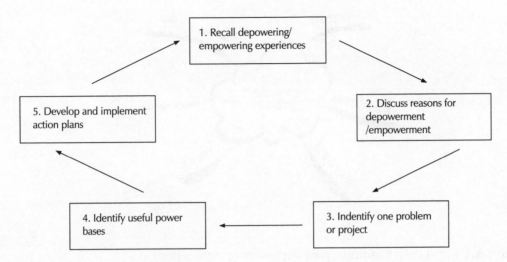

Figure A.3 The Empowerment Cycle

- yourself;
- your cultural traditions from your country of origin and/or residence;
- other people;
- organizations/institutions;
- events;
- things spiritual and material.

The foregoing headings have been developed after many workshops and I find they help to trigger discussion, which should be kept very broad at this stage. These headings may, of course, be adapted according to the focus of your workshop.

I usually give some examples of each heading from my own life – normally the depowering event when my sister was once totally embarrassed by the school principal who called her up in front of the whole school to point out the error in the design of her summer dress uniform (which our mother had made to save money). My sister still talks about that incident to this day! This quickly prompts participants to tell their own stories. This stage requires close monitoring to get people started.

A detailed explanation of mind-mapping is not appropriate here, although the basic maps for use at this stage of the workshop are given in Figures A.4 and A.5. I am surprised in workshops nowadays that there are always a few individuals who are familiar with the technique and I ask them to intersperse themselves amongst different groups. If you want to find out about the technique it is well worth while reading Buzan (1974, 1993) and Hogan (1994c).

Each group is asked to feedback the key points of their mind map to the whole group. An alternative process is to display all the mind maps together and if the group is not too large to get people to gather around and talk about key insights.

Figure A.4 Mind map headings: past depowering experiences

Figure A.5 Mind map headings: past empowering experiences

Taking this activity further, it is useful to ask participants to reflect on what they do that contributes to the depowerment or empowerment of others. This would highlight how the pecking order in human society frequently means that no matter how depowered people may feel, they may frequently use 'put-downs' and 'insults' to gain self-esteem (ie I'm better than you) or status in a group.

The whole group is asked to identify common key points eg:

- different stages of an experience can be both empowering and depowering (eg divorce);
- the state of mind at the time of an experience can influence an individual to react in an empowered or depowered way;

- empowerment is about identifying choices and deciding which way to act to preserve health and well being.

In conclusion for this stage, it is useful to go back to the theme of choice:

> There is always an alternative and we can choose. . . None of the alternatives in some situations may be desirable, but it is the knowledge that there is *always* a choice that heralds the beginning of self-empowered thinking.
>
> (Hopson and Scally, 1981: 57)

Stage 9: What rationales/excuses do people use to avoid making choices or taking action?

This stage gets people to look at two major factors that impinge on the empowerment process, namely 'internal' excuses (described in depth in Chapters 1 and 2) and 'external' or societal/organizational constraints (described in depth in Chapters 1 and 6).

By identifying these constraints at this stage I am not wanting to demotivate people merely to address some of the issues that are involved in the wider context. In this way I try to motivate people to address the excuses they make for themselves and help them to at least be aware of the societal and organizational constraints on them. If need be, some of these issues can be addressed in the action planning later. Everybody makes excuses and it is important that the facilitator does not 'blame' people as some excuses may be very sensible.

Before lunch I invite participants to think and talk about the projects they would like to work on in the afternoon, if necessary lobbying others if they want to work as a group on one topic.

Stages 10 and 11: What power bases are available and what is 'your personal power pack'?

A detailed explanation is given here of how I expanded the card pack based on reading about power and from suggestions from workshop participants. It depends on the type of group you are facilitating as to how detailed you want to be here, but it does help to explain some of the power bases. I show an overhead transparency of the list of all the power bases and ask people to identify the power bases they would like explained further. (See Chapter 3 for explanations of these power bases.)

If appropriate, at this stage participants are introduced to the changes in management thought about power. This also gives people a chance to gain explanations of power bases that they do not understand. The instructions for participants are given in Appendix B and the power card pack is included in Appendix C.

Stage 12: What problem or project would you like to work on, alone, in pairs or groups?

I invite some participants who have identified their projects to tell the rest of the group their topics (if they wish). This is useful because some individuals may want to amalgamate and/or some individuals may still be having difficulty in defining the real problem and framing it as a project. It also enables the facilitator to give feedback, particularly where some 'either/or' or 'closed' questions are not suitable for the card sort process.

In some instances it is useful for a person to work on an issue with another person who will challenge him or her to look at the power cards in a different way. In one workshop, I saw a woman who had been recently diagnosed with multiple sclerosis. She was in a state of crisis and she distrusted her doctor (who had not fully informed her of the issues). I watched her holding back tears as she worked through the power cards with a friend. This seemed to give her emotional support: she was not alone and the friend challenged her thinking.

If I am working as a sole facilitator with a large group, I usually say: 'Choose a problem that you feel is appropriate to work on today in these surroundings and with this group of people. You do not have to tell others about your project if you don't wish to.'

Frequently, identification of the real cause of the problem may take a participant some time. In one workshop, a team spent the whole session trying to define the real problem which we all agreed later was time well spent. I make it clear that it is best to ask for help at this stage if anyone is stuck. Having identified a problem, it is necessary for the participants to turn it into a project, because problem solving is reactive but working on a project is empowering and proactive. Other people naturally focus on a project, which they may have just started or have wanted to start for ages.

Please go through all the instructions verbally before allowing the participants to start anything! In my experience there are often many participants whose predominantly 'activist' learning style results in them jumping into the exercise without reading and/or fully understanding instructions. And ask participants to look at the power cards and check that they understand them all – there are always some questions at this point. Explain that the reasons for the number of cards is that they will stimulate thinking about their projects from many viewpoints. Draw the group's attention to the blank cards numbered 61–64 so that they can name or rename their own power cards.

Explain that the participants need to:

- spend time clarifying *one* problem to work on;
- write down a situation at work, college or home, or a project they would like to initiate or make happen, and if they have a problem (eg a potential career change), they should try to reframe it as a project;
- choose *one* project that they and you feel is suitable to work on in the workshop. Write down a brief scenario of the project such as place, people, circumstances and the desired outcomes;
- add some extra power bases on the blank cards where necessary;
- find a large space on a table or on the floor to spread out the cards.

Stages 13 and 14: What power bases are useful? How can you make it happen?

The card sort exercise is highly engrossing. At this stage, participants are working on real projects – usually with great enthusiasm. I make frequent walks around the room in case people get stuck and need a 'sounding board'.

During the card sort process, I always play some unobtrusive background music. This seems to work well, because the process is very absorbing and some peaceful music provides privacy for those who wish to talk without eavesdroppers, and it also provides calm for those who wish to be absorbed in their own concentration.

ACTIVITIES FOR LATER

There are many different activities that may be appropriate later on. For example, if participants have worked alone, invite them to discuss their ideas with a partner who is required to act as a 'critical friend' or sounding board. The roles of the partner are to challenge assumptions regarding the discarded cards and to elaborate on uses of the chosen cards.

Role play some of the cards with participants, ie let them try out some of the power bases and see how they feel. For instance, what would you say to someone if you were using your power to say 'no'? Invite constructive feedback. Discuss the serendipities that arose from the exercise. There are usually quite a few 'eye openers'.

When participants have finished, suggest that they pin up their action plans in an appropriate place at home or at work as reminders to themselves.

Stage 15: Feedback of plans to the whole group. What implications do these action plans have for the wider organization?

A general plenary session like this is the culmination of the day's work. It is important for senior managers to be present to listen to action plans and to give their perspectives and ideas and, where possible, to lend their support to the projects.

Stage 16 What did you think of today?

Short-term evaluation can be conducted via a number of processes: written questionnaires, card sorts or verbal discussions. This should provide useful feedback for planning future workshops. I like the use of card sorts. Here is a brief outline of how I use them. You need a thick black felt pen per participant and packs of large Post-it Notes in two colours, eg yellow (for positive ideas) and green (for growth/change improvement ideas).

- What were the major things you got/learnt from this workshop?

On the green Post-its ask participants to respond to the question:

- What improvements could be made to this workshop?

Ask participants to note as many responses to the questions as possible in silence, one per Post-it. Up to 15 minutes may be needed. This allows individuals to reflect on their ideas in a competition-free atmosphere where premature decisions do not have to be made. Invite participants to stick Post-its on separate walls, one for the yellow and one for the green. Ask them to cluster the Post-its and then clarify their thoughts. This process gives far more honest feedback than discussions as it is almost anonymous, ie it is very difficult to tell who wrote each Post-it. I also like it as it enables the facilitator to clarify problems and suggestions. Written questionnaires can leave a facilitator feeling frustrated as they do not enable discussion and clarification of ideas.

Stage 17: Where to go from here? How can participants be involved and take responsibility for the next workshop?

As described above, there are three modes of 'facilitator power'. In order to keep within the philosophy of 'empowerment', it is appropriate to use the 'co-operative' or 'autonomous' mode to plan the next workshop.

INVOLVEMENT OF SENIOR MANAGEMENT

Organizational change of any nature must have the support and participation of senior management. If possible, managers should be present for the duration of empowerment workshops. It may be necessary to brief them beforehand to ensure that however well-meaning their intentions, they do not dominate proceedings. Whatever happens if recommendations are made at the end of a workshop they should if possible be acted upon as quickly as possible – as the following case study illustrates.

CASE STUDY: BUILDING TRUST

I was engaged to facilitate a one-day workshop each month with six different shifts of men in a glass-bottle foundry. At the end of the first workshop, the first shift group whom I worked with recommended that the demountable training room should be shifted as we were constantly interrupted by noisy fork-lift trucks passing by. (Hundreds of rattling bottles make an incredible din.) The shift leader was asked to take this idea to management. When I phoned the manager the next day, he started making many excuses: 'We can't move the training room as it will be too far for the men to go to the toilets' etc etc. I let him finish and then added my argument: 'Many of the older men suffer from industrial deafness. Any background noise makes things far worse for them. Walking to the toilet would, I am sure, be a minor inconvenience – but, above all, moving the training room would be concrete proof that you mean what you say, ie you are willing to listen. If you move it immediately you will really start to build trust!'

When I visited the organization the following month to meet the next group of shift workers, I was directed to the new site of the training room. Not only was it well away from the fork-lifts, but the men had also stacked a wall of crates with empty bottles about 6 metres high and 15 metres long as a sound barrier. It was most surreal. I welcomed the group and the first discussion was about the site of the training room. Some of the men were still cynical – after all, a change in management style does not happen overnight. 'Oh, they only moved it because you were here, Chris.'

I decided to work on this point and discussed with the group that trust has to be built-up slowly on all sides and that they should take this example as a sign of good faith. Obviously not all their ideas would be taken on board, but this was a start. With nods of agreement, we started the workshop proper. Each month the succeeding shift group came up with ideas and slowly changes started to happen.

CONCLUSION

This Appendix has been written to give you an overview of a one-day workshop on empowerment. It is not meant to be a template, merely a reference for facilitators. All workshops have to be tailored to the needs of the group, the organization as a whole, and the skills of the facilitator. There are some exercises in Chapter 4 that incorporate workshop activities, and I refer you to them.

KEY POINT SUMMARY

The concept of participation has different meanings for different people.

Preparation is required before launching into empowerment workshops with an organization.

It is useful to plan workshops under the headings of 'content', 'process' and 'time'.

The facilitator has three power modes in workshop design: hierarchical, co-operative and autonomous.

Do not contract at the beginning of a workshop if you are not prepared to change your programme.

It is useful to contract for 'content' as well as 'desirable group process'.

When possible, participants should be actively involved in the design and facilitation of follow-up workshops.

Involve senior management actively throughout the whole empowerment/change process.

Allow plenty of time for groups to pool their key points from past experiences.

Always go through the instructions verbally with participants before they start.

Monitor the group carefully as questions arise as people start sorting the cards.

Quiet music is useful whilst people are sorting the cards.

Check that participants complete the action-planning stage properly.

Allow enough time to enable participants to share their action plans and contribute to one another's learning.

Your own points

Appendix B

Instructions for workshop participants

INDIVIDUAL ACTION

The following is a set of six activities for workshop participants to undertake under the supervision of their facilitator.

1. Write down a situation at work, college or home, or a project you would like to initiate or make happen. If you have a *problem* (eg a potential career change), try to reframe it as a *project* (eg 'What career should I take up next?').

2. Choose one situation that you feel happy to work on. Write down a brief scenario of the project (eg place, people and circumstances).

3. Write down the outcomes you want from the exercise.

4. Check the list of power cards – see the control list for all 60 near the start of Chapter 3, reproduced below as Table B.1. If there are any that you do not understand, refer to the detailed explanations of the relevant cards in Chapter 3. In a workshop setting, it is worth taking a few moments with the group perusing and discussing the list of cards, displayed for instance on an overhead transparency. See if you have some extra power bases and add to the pack on the blank cards.

5. Cut up the cards along the guide lines. Hold the pack of cards in your palm and turn over each card at a time. Consider each in turn in relation to your project. Transfer your actions to your Action Planning Sheet (sample later in this Appendix). Answer the questions on the Action Planning Sheet so that you can identify thoughts and behaviours to go with each power base. Note that not all the questions are applicable to every project or problem.

    Are there any surprises?

6. In pairs, discuss your ideas with your partner, who will act as a sounding board. The role of your partner is also to challenge your assumptions regarding the cards you have rejected as 'not useful'.

GROUP/TEAM STRATEGIES

If you want a team to pull together to change or create something, team members can sort the cards together and then divide roles and responsibilities for action planning according to the power bases and/or power skills of each person.

ACTIVITIES FOR LATER

Role play some of the cards, in other words, try out some of the power bases and see how they feel. For example, what would you say to someone if you were using your legitimate power?

Involve your team or family in working on a project together. A set of individuals will generally have different power bases, and they can use the variation to help everyone achieve a common goal.

A skeleton Action Planning Sheet follows hereafter.

Table B.1 List of power cards

1. Active listening
2. Body language
3. Charisma
4. Choices
5. Coercion
6. Crisis
7. Cross-cultural communication
8. Delegation
9. Experience
10. Expert knowledge and skills
11. Facilitation and group skills
12. Feelings
13. Goal setting
14. Humour/laughter
15. Illusion
16. Influencing powerful people
17. Information and its retrieval
18. Inspirational totems
19. Intuition
20. Law
21. Letting go
22. Love
23. Media literacy
24. Mediation
25. Meditation
26. Men/maleness
27. Mind flexibility
28. Money
29. Music/singing/dancing
30. Networking
31. Passive resistance
32. Perseverance
33. Personal power
34. Personal supporters
35. Physical strength
36. Physical well-being
37. Position
38. Positive and constructive feedback
39. Positive mindsets
40. Problem solving and decision making
41. Public committal
42. Questioning
43. Rechannelling energy
44. Redefining who we are: gender issues
45. Reflection
46. Resources/resource exchange
47. Responsibility
48. Rewards
49. Saying 'No'
50. Senses
51. Sexual attraction
52. Silence
53. Space; ambience
54. Spirituality
55. Stories and storytelling
56. Stress management
57. Time management
58. Uncertainty management
59. Whole picture/gestalt
60. Women/femaleness
61. Blank:
62. Blank:
63. Blank:
64. Blank:

ACTION PLANNING SHEET FOR YOUR PROJECT

Name of your project _____

1. Choose the power cards that you need to work on and enter their names below.

2. NB: Not all the questions are applicable to every power base.

Action power card	What will you say to yourself?	What actions will you take?	How will you behave?	What will you say to others?	How will you know if you are successful in using this card?
eg					
Power of Feelings	I feel depressed and sad about this. I've got to pull myself out of it.	I will ring up my best friend and chat about it.	Authentically to my friend.	'I'm feeling a bit low at the moment so please treat me with care'.	I have identified and worked on my depressed feelings and replaced them with optimism.
1. Power of					
2. Power of					

3. Power of

4. Power of

Notes

When you have finished completing this form, it is useful to pin up this action plan in an appropriate place at home or at work for reference.

Appendix C

Power card pack

1. Power of **Active listening**	**2. Power of** **Body language**
3. Power of **Charisma**	**4. Power of** **Choices**
5. Power of **Coercion**	**6. Power of** **Crisis**
7. Power of **Cross-cultural** **communication**	**8. Power of** **Delegation**

9. Power of **Experience**	**10. Power of** **Expert knowledge and skills**
11. Power of **Facilitation and group skills**	**12. Power of** **Feelings**
13. Power of **Goal setting**	**14. Power of** **Humour/laughter**
15. Power of **Illusion**	**16. Power of** **Influencing powerful people**

17. Power of **Information and its retrieval**	**18. Power of** **Inspirational totems**
19. Power of **Intuition**	**20. Power of** **Law**
21. Power of **Letting go**	**22. Power of** **Love**
23. Power of **Media literacy**	**24. Power of** **Mediation**

25. Power of Meditation	26. Power of Men/maleness
27. Power of Mind flexibility	28. Power of Money
29. Power of Music/singing/ dancing	30. Power of Networking
31. Power of Passive resistance	32. Power of Perseverance

33. Power of Personal power	34. Power of Personal supporters
35. Power of Physical strength	36. Power of Physical well-being
37. Power of Position	38. Power of Positive and constructive feedback
39. Power of Positive mindsets	40. Power of Problem solving and decision making

41. Power of **Public committal**	**42. Power of** **Questioning**
43. Power of **Rechannelling energy**	**44. Power of** **Redefining who we are: gender issues**
45. Power of **Reflection**	**46. Power of** **Resources/resource exchange**
47. Power of **Responsibility**	**48. Power of** **Rewards**

49. Power of Saying 'No'	50. Power of Senses
51. Power of Sexual attraction	52. Power of Silence
53. Power of Space; ambience	54. Power of Spirituality
55. Power of Stories and storytelling	56. Power of Stress management

57. Power of **Time management**	**58. Power of** **Uncertainty management**
59. Power of **Whole picture/gestalt**	**60. Power of** **Women/femaleness**
61. Power of	**62. Power of**
63. Power of	**64. Power of**

References

Adair, M and Howell, S (1989) The subjective side of power, in *Healing the Wounds – The promise of ecofeminism*, ed J Hant, New Society Publishers, Philadelphia

Adler, N (1996) *International Dimensions of Organizational Behavior*, 3rd edn, Wadsworth Publishing Co, Boston MA

Albert, D H (1985) *People Power – Applying non-violence theory*, New Society Publishers, Philadelphia

Arnstein, S (1969) Ladder of Citizen Participation in the USA, *Journal of the American Institute of Planners*, July, pp 216–26

Aung, S S K (1991) Freedom from fear, *Oxford Today – The University Magazine*, **4** (1), pp 26–28, Oxford

Bandler, R (1979) *Frogs into Princes: Neurolinguistic programming*, Real People Press, Moab, Utah

Bartol, K M *et al* (1995) *Management: A Pacific Rim focus*, McGraw-Hill Book Company, Sydney, Australia

Belbin, E, Downs, S and Perry, P (1981) *How Do I Learn?*, Further Education Curriculum Review and Development Unit, Department of Education and Science, Stanmore, England

Belloc, N B and Breslow, L (1972) Relationship of physical health status and health practices, *Preventative Medicine*, **1**, pp 409–21

Biddulph, S (1995) *Manhood: An action plan for changing men's lives*, 2nd edn, Finch Publishing, Sydney, Australia

Bilodeau, L (1992) *The Anger Workbook*, Hazelden Educational Materials, Minnesota

Block, P (1990) *The Empowered Manager – Positive political skills at work*, Jossey-Bass, California

Bond, M H (1986) (ed) *The Psychology of the Chinese People*, Oxford University Press, Oxford

Boomer, G (1982) *Reading and Writing*, Macmillan, South Melbourne, Australia

Brislin, R W (1991) *The Art of Getting Things Done – A practical guide to the use of power*, Praeger Publishers, New York

Brislin, R W *et al* (1986) *Intercultural Interactions: A practical guide*, Sage Publications, Beverly Hills

Brown, P (1999) Deadly serious, *Guardian*, 8 September, p 5

Burton, J (1990) *Conflict: Resolution and prevention*, St Martin's Press, New York

Buzan, T (1974) *Use Your Head*, British Broadcasting Corporation, London

Buzan, T (1993) *The Mind Map Book*, British Broadcasting Corporation, London

Campbell, J (1973) *The Hero with a Thousand Faces*, Bollingen Series xvii, Princeton University Press, Princeton, NJ

Centre for Continuing Education, University of British Columbia (undated) *DACUM Series 1–6*, Geoid Media Service Ltd, British Columbia, Canada

Clavell, J (1983) The Children's Story... But Not Just for Children, Coronet Books, England

Concise Oxford Dictionary, The (1982) 7th edn, The Clarendon Press, Oxford

Conger, J A (1989) *The Charismatic Leader – The art of transforming managers into leaders*, Jossey-Bass, San Francisco

Conger, J A (1992) *Learning to Lead – The art of transforming managers into leaders*, Jossey-Bass, San Francisco

Connell, R W (1987) *Gender and Power – Society, the person and sexual politics*, Stanford University Press, California

Coren, S (1997) *Sleep Thieves – An eye-opening exploration into the science and mysteries of sleep*, Free Press, New York

Creighton, J and Simonton, C (1992) *Getting Well Again*, Bantam, New York

Cushner, K and Brislin, R *et al* (1995) *Intercultural Interactions – A practical guide*, 2nd edn, Sage Publications, California

Darwin, C and Amy, J (1991) *The Social Climbers*, Pan Macmillan Publishers, Sydney, Australia

De Bono, E (1987) *The CoRT Thinking Process*, Pergamon, London

Dick, B (1987) *Helping Groups to be Effective: Skills, processes and concepts for group facilitators*, Interchange, Queensland

Downs, S (1995) *Learning at Work – Effective strategies for making learning happen*, Kogan Page, London

Downs, S and Perry, P (1982) Research Report: How do I learn?, *Journal of European Industrial Training*, **6** (6), pp 27–32, Occupational Research Unit, Department of Applied Psychology, UWIST, England

Downs, S and Perry, P (1984) Developing Skilled Learners, *MSC Manpower Services Commission Research and Development*, (22), pp 13–14

Doyle, M and Straus, D (1986) *How to Make Meetings Work: The new interaction method*, Jove Publications, New York

Doyle, M and Straus, D (1993) *How to Make Meetings Work: The new interaction method*, Berkeley Publishing Group, New York

Dunford, R W (1992) *Organisational Behaviour an Organisational Perspective*, Addison- Wesley, Sydney, Australia

Eales-White, R (1994) *Creating Growth from Change – How you react, develop and grow*, McGraw-Hill Company, Maidenhead

Ellis, A and Harper, R (1975) *A New Guide to Rational Living*, Prentice-Hall, London

Emery, E (1976) Searching for new directions in new ways for new times, *Occasional Papers in Continuing Education*, No 12, Australian National University, Canberra, Australia

Ernington, H (1991) Opening Speech, *Women in Education* conference, Perth, Western Australia

Fanning, P (1988) *Creative Visualization*, Bantam Books, New York

Ferguson, M (1982) *The Aquarian Conspiracy – Personal and social transformation in the 1980s*, Paladin, London

Finlay, M and Hogan, C (1995) Who will bell the cat? Story-telling techniques for people who work with people in organizations, *Training and Management Development Methods*, **9**, pp 6.01–6.18

Frankl, V E (1959) *Man's Search for Meaning*, Beacon Press, Boston MA

Freire, P (1972) *Pedagogy of the Oppressed*, Penguin, Harmondsworth, England

Freire, P (1974) *Education: The practice of freedom*, Writers and Readers Publishing Cooperative, London

French, J R P and Raven, B (1959) The bases of social power, in *Studies in Social Power*, ed D Cartwright, University of Michigan Press, Ann Arbor, Michigan

Fromm, E (1960) *Escape from Freedom*, Harper and Row, New York

Frost, P and Robinson, S (1999) The toxic handler: organizational hero – and casualty, *Harvard Business Review*, July–August, pp 97–106

Fry, W F and Salameh, W A (eds) (1987) *Handbook of Humor and Psychotherapy – Advances in the clinical use of humor*, Professional Resource Exchange Inc, Florida

Gilligan, C *et al* (1982) *In a Different Voice: Psychological theory and women's development*, Harvard University Press, Cambridge MA

Goldberg, P (1983) *The Intuitive Edge – Understanding and developing intuition*, Jeremy Tarcher Inc, Los Angeles

Green, R and Elffers, J (1998) *The 48 Laws of Power*, Hodder & Stoughton, London

Gyatso, T (1992) *Compassion and the Individual*, Wisdom Publications, Boston MA

Gyatso, T (1995) *The Power of Compassion*, Indus HarperCollins, New Delhi, India

Haddon, C (1985) *The Powers of Love*, Michael Joseph, London

Hamelink, C J (1994) *Trends in World Communication – On disempowerment and self-empowerment*, Southbound Third World Network, Penang, Malaysia

Harris, T (1969) *I'm OK – You're OK*, Harper and Row, New York

Heider, J (1986) *The Tao of Leadership*, Wildwood House Ltd, Aldershot, England

Henkel, A G, Repp-Begin, C and Vogt, J (1993) Empowerment-readiness survey: foundations for Total Quality Management, in *The 1993 Annual: Developing human resources*, ed J W Pfeiffer, Pfeiffer and Co, San Diego, California

Heron, J (1989) *Facilitator's Handbook*, Kogan Page, London

Heron, J (1993) *Group Facilitation: Theories and models for practice*, Kogan Page, London

Heron, J (1999) *The Complete Facilitator's Handbook*, Kogan Page, London

Hicks, N (1985) Formula funding and regional planning of health services in Australia in Milbank Memorial, *Fund Quarterly*, **63** (4), pp 671–90

Hofstede, G (1980) *Culture's Consequences: International differences in work-related values*, Sage, California

Hofstede, G (1991) *Cultures and Organizations: Software of the mind*, McGraw-Hill, Maidenhead

Hogan, C F (1984) *Participatory Planning, Participation and Equity Programme, Technical and Further Education*, Western Australia

Hogan, C F (1988) Student participation in the planning, implementation and evaluation of a participation and equity programme. Master of Education Thesis, Curtin University, Perth, Western Australia

Hogan, C F (1990) Taking the board out of board meetings, in *The Effective Board*, The Department for the Arts, Perth, Western Australia

Hogan, C F (1992) Confessions of a change agent, *Training and Management Development Methods*, **6** (5), pp 5.07–5.24

Hogan, C F (1993a) Simultaneously teaching facilitation skills to students at separate locations using interactive videoconferencing, *Training and Management Development Methods*, 7, pp 5.17–5.32

Hogan, C F (1993b) How to get more out of video conference meetings, *Training and Management Development Methods*, 7, pp 5.01–5.16

Hogan, C F (1994a) Course design in half the time: how to generate ideas using a network of computers, *Training and Management Development Methods*, **8** (2), pp 5.01–5.14

Hogan, C F (1994b) Empowering ethical endings, *Management Development Review*, 7 (1), pp 32–40

Hogan, C F (1994c) Mind mapping – some practical applications, *Training and Management Development Methods*, **8** (1), pp 3.01–3.18

Hogan, C F (1994d *The Search Conference Process*, Curtin University, Perth, Western Australia

Hogan, C F (1994e) Using charisma to enhance your personal communication and leadership style, *Training and Management Development Methods*, **8** (3), pp 3.31–3.43

Hogan, C F (1997a) Murmuring from Mongolia: Lessons to be learned from running programmes overseas, *Training and Management Development Methods*, **11**, pp 8.37–8.56

Hogan, C F (1997b) The Study Buddy System: You are not studying alone, *Training and Management Development Methods*, **11** (1), pp 7.17–7.22

Hogan, C F (1997c) The power of story telling in learning about conflict resolution processes, *Training and Management Development Methods*, **11** (1), pp 8.01.–8.18

Hogan, C F (1999) *Facilitating Learning: Processes for college and university*, Eruditions Press, Melbourne, Australia

Hollier, F *et al* (1993) *Conflict Resolution Trainers' Manual*, Conflict Resolution Network, New South Wales, Australia

Holmes, T H and Rahe, R H (1967) Social readjustment rating scale, *Journal of Psychosomatic Research*, (11), pp 213–18

Honey, P and Mumford, A (1986) *The Manual of Learning Styles*, Peter Honey, Maidenhead, Berkshire, England

Hopson, B and Scally, M (1981) *Lifeskills Teaching*, McGraw-Hill Company, Maidenhead, England

Hopson, B and Scally, M (1981–86) *Lifeskills Teaching Programmes 1,2,3,4*. Lifeskills Associates, Leeds

Hunter, D, Bailey, A and Taylor, B (1992) *The Zen of Groups*, Tandem Press, New Zealand

Hunter, D, Bailey, A and Taylor, B (1995) *The Art of Facilitation*, Fisher Books, *where

Hunter, D, Bailey, A and Taylor, B (1998) *Co-operacy: A consensus approach to work*, Gower, England

Hunter, D, Bailey, A and Taylor, B (1999) *The Essence of Facilitation*, Tandem Press, Auckland, New Zealand

James, W (1953) *The Philosophy of William James*, Modern Library, New York

Janis, I L (1972) *Victims of Groupthink*, Houghton Mifflin, Boston MA

Jeffers, S (1987) *Feel the Fear and Do It Anyway*, Harcourt Brace Jovanovich, Florida

Johnson, R (1996) *40 Activities for Training with NLP*, Gower, Aldershot, England

Jung, C (1968) *The Collected Works of C G Jung*, 2nd edn, Routledge and Kegan Paul, London

Kamp, D (1996) *The Excellent Trainer: Putting NLP to work*, Gower, Aldershot, England

Kaplan, F (1994) The art of anger: imagery, anger management and conflict resolution, *The Canadian Art Therapy Association Journal*, **8**, pp 18–29

Kirner, J and Rayner, M (1999) *The Women's Power Handbook*, Viking, Ringwood, Australia

Kiser, A G (1998) Masterful Facilitation: Becoming a catalyst for meaningful change, AMACOM, New York

Knight, S (1999) *NLP Solutions: Neuro Linguistic Programming: How to model what works in business to make it work for you*, Nicholas Brearley Publishing, London

Knowles, M S (1980) *The Modern Practice of Adult Education: From pedagogy to andragogy*, Collett, Chicago

Knowles, M S (1984) *The Adult Learner – The neglected species*, Gulf Publishers, Houston TX

Kolb, D (1984) *Experiential Learning*, Prentice Hall Inc, Englewood Cliffs, NJ

Langer, E J (1991) *Mindfulness – Choice and control in everyday life*, Harvill, London

Larsen, S R (1996) The life of Joseph Campbell, in *68th Annual Summer School*, University of Western Australia, Perth, Western Australia

Lazarus, R S *et al* (1985) Stress and adaptational outcomes: the problem of confounded measures, *American Psychologist*, (40), pp 770–79

Lewin, K (1951) *Field Theory in Social Science*, Harper, New York

Long, D G (1990) *Learner-Managed Learning: The key to lifelong learning and development*, Kogan Page, London

McClelland, D (1984) The Two Faces of Power, in *Organizational Psychology: Readings on human behaviour in organizations*, 4th edn, ed D Kolb, I Rubin and J McIntyre, Prentice-Hall, pp 59–72

McCroskey, J C (1986) *An Introduction to Rhetorical Communication*, 5th edn, Prentice Hall, New Jersey

Meares, A (1970) *Relief Without Drugs*, Fontana Books, Sydney, Australia

Messmer, M (1990) How to put employee empowerment into practice, *Woman CPA*, **52** (3), pp 1–25

Milgram, S (1963) Behavioral study of obedience, *Journal of Abnormal and Social Psychology*, pp 371–78

Morgan, G (1986) *Images of Organisation*, Sage, California

Muller, W (1996) *How Then Shall We Live? Four simple questions that reveal the beauty and meaning of our lives*, Bantam, New York

Parkin, M (1998) *Tales for Trainers: Using stories and metaphors to facilitate learning*, Kogan Page, London

Peters, T (1989) *Thriving on Chaos*, Pan Books, London

Raven, B H and Kruglanski, W (1975) Conflict and Power, in *The Structure of Conflict*, ed P Swingle, pp 177–219, Academic Press, New York

Rawlinson, J G (1981) *Creative Thinking and Brainstorming*, Gower, Victoria, Australia

Reich, R (1987) Entrepreneurship reconsidered: the team as hero, Harvard Business Review, May–June, pp 77–83

Roddick, A (1992) *Body and Soul*, Vermilion, London

Rosenberg, M (1969) From Now On: A model for nonviolent persuasion, Community Psychological Consultants, St Louis

Rosenberg, M (1999) *Nonviolent Communication – A language of compassion*, Puddle Dance Press, Del Mar, California

Rosenthal, N (1991) *Winter Blues*, HarperCollins, London

Rotter, J B (1966) Generalised expectancies for internal versus external control of reinforcement, *Psychological Monographs*

Seibert, K B and Kleiner B H (1991) Right brain approach to time management, *Management Decision*, MCB University Press Limited, **29** (4), pp 46–48

Seligman, E P (1992) *Learned Optimism*, Random House, NSW, Australia.

Seligman, M E (1975) *Helplessness*, W H Freeman, Reading, England

Sharp, G (1974) The politics of nonviolent action, in *Methods of Non-violent Action*, ed M Finklestein, Porter-Sargent Publications, Boston MA

Sharp, G (1980) *Social Power and Political Freedom*, Porter-Sargent Publications, Boston MA

Shlain, L (1998) *The Alphabet versus the Goddess*, Allen Lane, The Penguin Press, London

Smith, L and Wagner, P (1983) *The Networking Game*, Network Resources, Denver

Spender, D (1980) *Man Made Language*, Routledge and Kegan Paul, London.

Staples, L H (1990) Powerful ideas about empowerment, *Administration in Social Work*, **14** (2), pp 29–42

Stewart, I and Joines, V (1987) *TA Today: A new introduction to transactional analysis*, Lifespace Publishing, Nottingham, England

Stewart, R (1982) *Choices for the Manager – A guide to managerial work and behaviour*, McGraw-Hill Company, Maidenhead, England

Taylor, D (1999) The hammer that cracked a nuclear lab, *The Guardian*, 25 October, pp 6–7

Toffler, A (1970) *Future Shock*, Random House, New York

Toffler, A (1991) *Powershift – Knowledge, wealth and violence at the edge of the 21st century*, Bantam Books, New York

Torbert, W R (1991) *The Power of Balance – Transforming self, society and scientific inquiry*, Sage Publications, California

Trist, E (1981) The Evolution of Sociotechnical Systems, in *Perspectives on Organization Design and Behaviour*, ed A H van de Ven and W F Joyce, Wiley Interscience, New York

Tyler, T and McGraw, K (1986) Ideology and the interpretation of personal experience: procedural justice and political quiescence, *Journal of Social Issues*, **42** (2), pp 115–28

Tyson, T (1997) *Working with Groups*, 2nd edn, MacMillan, Melbourne, Australia

Vecchio, R P, Hearn, G and Southey, G (1988) *Organisational Behaviour – Life at work in Australia*, Harcourt Brace Jovanovich, Sydney, Australia

Vogler, C (1992) *The Writer's Journey: Mythic structure for storytellers and screen writers*, Michael Wiese Productions, Studio City, USA

Vogt, J F and Murrell, K L (1990) *Empowerment in Organizations*, University Associates Inc., California

Waley, A (1934) *The Way and the Power – A study of the Tao Te Ching and its place in Chinese Thought*, Allen and Unwin, London

Wilson, K (1987) Participatory planning, unpublished paper

Further reading

Antonovsky, A (1987) *Unraveling the Mystery of Health: How people manage stress and stay well*, Jossey-Bass, San Francisco

Apsey, L S *et al* (1981) *Transforming Power for Peace*, Religious Education Committee Friends Education Committee, Friends General Conference, Pennsylvania

Beer, J E and Stief, E (1999) *The Mediator's Handbook*, New Society Publishers, Gabriola Island, Canada

Bem, S L (1974) The Measurement of Psychological Androgyny, *Journal Consult. Clinical Psychology*, **42** (2), pp 155–62

Bendix, R (1962) *Max Weber: An intellectual portrait*, Doubleday, Anchor, New York

Brislin, R W and Yoshida, T (1994) *Improving Intercultural Interactions: Modules for cross-cultural training programmes*, Sage, California

Brown, M and May, J (1989) *The Greenpeace Story*, Child and Associates, NSW, Australia

Cousins, N (1979) *Anatomy of an Illness as Perceived by the Patient*, W W Norton, New York

Covey, S R, Merrill, A R and Merrill, R R (1994). *First Things First: To live, to love, to learn, to leave a legacy*, Simon and Schuster, New York

Cunningham, W G (1991) *Empowerment – Vitalising personal energy*, Humanics New Age, Georgia

Dewsbury, D (1981) Effects of novelty on copulatory behavior – the Coolidge Effect and related phenomenon, *Psychological Bulletin*, (89), pp 464–82

Dick, B (1987) *Helping Groups to be Effective: Skills, processes and concepts for group facilitation*, Interchange, Queensland, Australia

Downs, S (1981) *How Do I Learn?*, Further Education and Curriculum Review and Development Unit, London

Downs, S *et al* (1982) *Research Report: How Do I Learn?*, Occupational Research Unit, Department of Applied Psychology, University of Wales Institute of Science and Technology

Downs, S *et al* (1986) *Developing Skilled Learners – Helping trainees to learn for themselves*, Occupational Research Unit, Applied Psychology Department, University of Wales Institute of Science and Technology

Freire, P (1997) *Pedagogy of Hope: Reliving the pedagogy of the oppressed*, Continuum, New York

Goleman, D (1998) *Working with Emotional Intelligence*, Bloomsbury, London

Goleman, D and Thurman, A F (eds) (1991) *Mind Science an East–West Dialogue*, Wisdom Publications, Boston MA

Heron, J (1987) *Confessions of a Janus-Brain – A personal account of living in two worlds*, Endymion Press, London

Hodges, P (1990) The application decade begins, *Datamation*, **36** (2), pp 22–30

Hogan, C F (1995) Creative and reflective journal writing processes, *The Learning Organization*, **2** (2), pp 4–17

Hogan, C F (1996a) Cross-cultural communication workshop, *Training and Management Development Methods*, **10** (2), pp 8.01–8.16

Hogan, C F (1996b) Water buffaloes get bewitched – observations of a participatory rural appraisal training workshop, *Empowerment in Organisations*, **4** (1), pp 34–46

Hogan, C F (1996c) Going Home: Transition skills and processes to enable you to make effective transitions back to your home country, Curtin University, Perth, Western Australia

Houston, J (1992) *The Hero and the Goddess: The odyssey as mystery and initiation*, Ballantine Books, New York

Illich, I (1973) *Celebration of Awareness*, Penguin, Harmondsworth, England

Illich, I *et al* (1977) *The Disabling Professions*, Marion Boyars, London

Inglesby, T (1990) Microcomputers in manufacturing: Part 2, *Manufacturing Systems*, **8** (11), pp 52–68

James, M and Jongeward, D (1983) *Born to Win – Transactional analysis with gestalt experiments*, Addison-Wesley Company Inc, *where

James, M and Klein, D (1988) *The Practical Guide to Crystal Healing*, Mercury Press Ltd, Perth, Western Australia

Janis, I L (1971) Groupthink, *Psychology Today*, American Psychological Association

Kanter, R M (1979) Power failure in management circuits, *Harvard Business Review*, **24**, pp 65–75

Kanter, R M (1983) *The Change Masters: Innovation for productivity in the American corporation*, Simon and Schuster, New York

Kets De Vries, M F R (1991) Whatever happened to the philosopher-king? The leader's addiction to power, *Journal of Management Studies*, **28**, 4 July, pp 339–51

Kipnis, D (1976) *The Powerholders*, University of Chicago Press, Chicago

Lindholm, C (1990) *Charisma*, Basil Blackwell, Massachusetts

London, P (1969) Behaviour Control, in *Lifeskills Teaching*, B Hopson and M Scally (1981), McGraw-Hill Company, Maidenhead, England

Mumford, A (1981) *Making experience pay – Management success through effective learning*, McGraw-Hill Company, Maidenhead, England

Osborn, A F (1957) *Applied Imagination*, revised edition, Charles Scribner, New York

Pedler, M and Boydell, T (1985) *Managing Yourself*, Fontana, *where England

Pedler, M *et al* (1986) *A Manager's Guide to Self-development*, 2nd edn, McGraw-Hill, Maidenhead, England

Pfeffer, J and Salancik, G R (1978) *The External Control of Organisations: A resource dependence perspective*, Harper and Row, New York

Progoff, I (1975) *At a Journal Workshop*, Dialogue House Library, New York

Quick, T L (1985) *Power Plays*, Franklin Watts, New York

Quick, T L (1988) *Power, Influence and Your Effectiveness in Human Resources*, Addison- Wesley Publishing Co Inc., New York, USA

Quinn, R E *et al* (1990) *Becoming a Master Manager – A competency framework*, John Wiley and Sons, New York

Rainer, T (1985) *The New Diary*, Angus and Robertson, *where England

Reason, P (1988) (ed) *Human Inquiry in Action – Developments in new paradigm research*, Sage, London

Robbins, A (1986) *Unlimited Power*, Fawcett Columbine, New York

Robertson N (1988) *Getting Better Inside Alcoholics Anonymous*, William Morrow and Co Inc., New York

Rogers, C A (1967) *On Becoming a Person: A therapist's view of psychotherapy*, Constable, London

Rogers, C A (1978) *Carl Rogers on Personal Power*, Constable, London

Semler, R (1993) *Maverick! The success story behind the world's most unusual workplace*, Arrow Business Books, London

Sher, B (1979) *Wishcraft – How to get what you really want*, Ballantine, New York.

Smiles, S (1859) *Self Help*, Murray, London

Tichy, N M and Sherman, S S (1994) *Control Your Destiny or Someone Else Will: Lessons in mastering change*, Harper Business Books, New York

Toffler, A (1984) *The Third Wave*, William Collins, London

Valiente, D (1975) *Natural Magic*, Phoenix Publishing, Washington US

Wilson, J and Wilson, K (1991–95) Personal communication and discussions

Wolf, J F (1988–89) The legacy of Mary Parker Follett, *The Bureaucrat*, Winter, pp 53–57

Index